A New Commentary On
Paul's Letter To
The Saints
At Rome

By Robertson L. Whiteside
1945

Ninth Edition, 2004

ISBN 1-58427-069-1

Guardian of Truth Foundation
P.O. Box 9670
Bowling Green, Kentucky 42102

INTRODUCTION

A noted scholar once remarked that the book of Romans was the profoundest production in all literature. Shallow minds and superficial treatment certainly cannot do justice to such an amazing and enduring discussion of redemption from sin as Paul has written in this famous epistle.

R. L. Whiteside is superbly qualified to write a commentary on the book of Romans. He has a rich background of age and experience. He was born in Tennessee, December 27th, 1869, where he attended the public schools, West Tennessee Christian College and the Nashville Bible School. He developed an ambition early in life to know and to teach the word of God. By nature he is modest and rather retiring, but his thirst for knowledge made him a close student, and his loyalty to truth made him an independent thinker.

From the beginning of his study of the Bible he has respected the conclusions of godly and experienced students of the Bible, though he early realized that no man is infallible. He had to be sure of his own ground before he took issue with such men, he greatly admired the intellectual powers, the faith, and stalwart character, and humble bearing of that great man, David Lipscomb. To him David Lipscomb was the ideal teacher, the ideal Christian, and yet on more than one occasion in Bible classes in the Nashville Bible School, he took issue with the expressed views of Brother Lipscomb. On more than one occasion Brother Lipscomb accepted the views of Brother Whiteside.

Brother Whiteside has been a close student of the Bible all of his life. His critical mind and power of reasoning have afforded him an insight into the teaching of the Bible as a whole that few men have. His implicit faith in God has led him to seek to know only what the will of God is, that he might comply with it and teach it without faltering. The degree of his success has left him a store of knowledge covering a wide field and eminently fitted him for producing an outstanding commentary on the book of Romans.

He successfully served as president of Abilene Christian College for two years. He has ministered to some of the strongest congregations as a preacher, spending five successive years with the church in Denton, Texas, where he has lived for many years. He has engaged in a number of oral and written debates, was always confident and at ease and the cause of Christ prospered as a result of each discussion. His deportment has always been that of a gentleman in debate as on all occasions. For a number of years he wrote the Annual Commentary on the Bible School lessons published by the Gospel Advocate. For some ten years he served as Query Editor of the Gospel Advocate and was otherwise a regular contributor to that paper. He is a veteran writer and widely recognized as a very able one.

The commentary on the book of Romans is decidedly not just another book. It is not a plagiaristic rehash of other books that have been written. It is not the green product of a big hurry to write a book or dictate it to a stenographer. The book is a natural. It is a maturity that has been in the process of growth for a long, long time. The author's years of study of, and inspiring essays on the apostolic masterpiece have created a widespread demand for the book, a book that in a way just had to be. It is here. It is a distinct contribution to Christian literature which will be recognized, not only by the church of which he is a member, but by others also. It will find its place into the libraries of Bible students and teachers throughout the land. In some remarkable instances the author has broken new ground which will bring much satisfaction to the student and open up a field of new thoughts. The literary style of the work is highly gratifying. The reader does not have to dig through a lot of superfluous verbiage to get at the thought. It is pointed right at your heart in a straight line. Here is a book you will want, get, and cherish.

C. R. Nichol
Cled E. Wallace
Foy E. Wallace, Jr.

COMMENTARY ON ROMANS

Chapter 1

1 Paul, a servant of Jesus Christ, called *to be* an apostle, separated unto the gospel of God. 2 which he promised afore through his prophets in the holy scriptures. 3 concerning his Son, who was born of the seed of David according to the flesh 4 who was declared *to be* the Son of God with power, according to the spirit of holiness, by the resurrection from the dead; *even* Jesus Christ our Lord, 5 through whom we received grace and apostleship, unto obedience of faith among all the nations, for his name's sake; 6 among whom are ye also, called *to be* Jesus Christ's: 7 to all that are in Rome, beloved of God, called *to be* saints; Grace to you and peace from God our Father and the Lord Jesus Christ.

8 First, I thank my God through Jesus Christ for you all, that your faith is proclaimed throughout the whole world. 9 For God is my witness, whom I serve in my spirit in the gospel of his Son, how unceasingly I make mention of you, always in my prayers 10 making request, if by any means now at length I may be prospered by the will of God to come unto you. 11 For I long to see you, that I may impart unto you some spiritual gift, to the end ye may be established; 12 that is, that I with you may be comforted in you, each of us by the other's faith, both yours and mine. 13 And I would not have you ignorant, brethren, that oftentimes I purposed to come unto you (and was hindered hitherto), that I might have some fruit in you also, even as in the rest of the Gentiles. 14 I am debtor both to Greeks and to Barbarians, both to the wise and to the foolish. 15 So, as much as in me is, I am ready to preach the gospel to you also that are in Rome.

16 For I am not ashamed of the gospel: for it is the power of God unto salvation to every one that believeth; to the Jew first, and also to the Greek. 17 For therein is revealed a righteousness of God from faith unto faith: as it is written. But the righteous shall live by faith.

18 For the wrath of God is revealed from heaven against all ungodliness and unrighteousness of men, who hinder the truth in unrighteousness; 19 because that which is known of God is manifest in them: for God manifested it unto them. 20 For the invisible things of him since the creation of the world are clearly seen, being perceived through the things that are made, *even* his everlasting power and divinity; that they may be without excuse: 21 because that, knowing God, they glorified him not as God, neither gave thanks; but became vain in their reasonings, and their senseless heart was darkened. 22 Professing themselves to be wise, they became fools 23 and changed the glory of the incorruptible God for the likeness of an image of corruptible man, and of birds, and four-footed beasts, and creeping things.

24 Wherefore God gave them up in the lusts of their hearts unto uncleanness, that their bodies should be dishonored among themselves: 25 for that they exchanged the truth of God for a lie, and worshipped and served the creature rather than the Creator, who is blessed for ever. Amen.

26 For this cause God gave them up unto vile passions: for their women changed the natural use into that which is against nature: 27 and likewise also the men, leaving the natural use of the woman, burned in their lust one toward another, men with men working unseemliness, and receiving in themselves that recompense of their error which was due.

28 And even as they refused to have God in *their* knowledge, God gave them up unto a reprobate mind, to do those things which are not fitting; 29 being filled with all unrighteousness, wickedness, covetousness, maliciousness; full of envy, murder, strife, deceit, malignity: whisperers, 30 backbiters, hateful to God, insolent,

haughty, boastful, inventors of evil things, disobedient to parents, 31 without understanding, covenant-breakers, without natural affection, unmerciful: 32 who, knowing the ordinance of God, that they that practise such things are worthy of death, not only do the same, but also consent with them that practise them.

Verse 1: *Paul, a servant of Jesus Christ, called to be an apostle, separated unto the gospel of God.* On the phrase, "Paul, a servant of Jesus Christ," James Macknight remarks: "The original word 'doulos' properly signifies a slave. Here it is a name of honor: for in the East the chief ministers of kings were called 'douloi,' slaves .... This honorable name, therefore, denotes the high authority which Paul possessed in the kingdom of Christ, as one of his chief ministers."

In the phrase, "called to be an apostle," the words "to be" were supplied by the translators. They frequently supplied words with the intention of making the meaning clearer to the English reader. These supplied words are printed in italics. But in this place the supplied words hinder rather than help. The word translated "called" is not a verb nor a participle, but a verbal adjective. It partakes of the nature of a verb and an adjective. The sense is complete and clear, if you read it, "a called apostle." Paul was not telling what he was called to be, but what he was. Some Judaizing teachers charged that he was not a regularly constituted apostle, but that he had merely assumed that office, or had been appointed to that office by the church at Antioch. To meet that charge, Paul asserts that he was "a called apostle"—an apostle that had been called into that office by Jesus Christ. He was separated from Judaism and from all other lines of activity, and dedicated to the one business of preaching the gospel. His own motto was in harmony with his calling—"This one thing I do." It was God's gospel, because it originated with him and came from him. It was in no sense a product of man's theorizing or philosophizing. It was not a mere addition to the law of Moses, as some Judaizers sought to make it. Paul did not preach his conception of Christianity, but he preached the gospel as the Holy Spirit moved him. He preached "a new and living way."

Verse 2: *Which he promised afore through his prophets in the holy scriptures.* Why was Paul so particular to affirm that the gospel to which he had been separated and which he preached had been promised in the Old Testament Scriptures? He would have the Jews know that the very scriptures on which they relied promised the gospel which he preached. In this letter, as well as in much of his other writings, Paul combated the professed Christians among the Jews who taught that the Gentile converts had to be circumcised and had to keep the law of Moses, else they could not be saved. They were willing enough for Paul to make converts among the Gentiles, if he would have them circumcised and require them to keep the law; but because he would not do so, these Judaizing teachers opposed him with all their might. They had drawn the idea that Gentiles could be saved only in subservience to all things Jewish. But Paul taught that Jew and Gentile stood on an equal footing before God, and that the prophets had so foretold.

Verses 3, 4: *Concerning his Son, who was born of the seed of David according to the flesh, who was declared to be the Son of God with power, according to the spirit of holiness, by the resurrection from the dead; even Jesus Christ our Lord.* This connects back with the end of verse 1. It was the gospel of God, but it was concerning his Son. It is the gospel of God, because it originated with him; and it is also the gospel of Christ, because it centers in him. Without Christ, there would be no gospel. It is this gospel to which Paul had been separated and which had been promised through the prophets in the holy Scriptures. Yet some tell us that the prophets said nothing of the gospel as we have it revealed through the apostles. Such teachers occupy a position similar to that occupied by the Judaizing teachers who so zealously opposed Paul.

The contrast in verses 3 and 4 is between the human nature and the divine nature of Jesus. As to his human nature, he was the son of David; as to his divine nature, he was the Son of God. By his genealogy he was proved to be of the seed of David; but the final proof that he was the Son of God was his resurrection from the dead. He had claimed to be the Son of God and that he would arise from the dead the third day after his death. The fact that he was raised as he said he would be, established the truth that he was the Son of God. It is argued by some that the resurrection of the dead here referred to is the resurrection of all the dead, and that this universal resurrection was guaranteed by his own resurrection. But that seems to miss the point. Whatever resurrection is here referred to is used by Paul as proof to declare beyond doubt the truth that Jesus is the Son of God. The resurrection of all the dead is yet future. How can a fact not yet accomplished be proof of anything? But the fact that Jesus did arise from the dead was the only, thing that brought absolute conviction to the hearts of even his disciples

that he was the Son of God. His resurrection from the
dead left in their minds no trace of doubt.

Verse 5. *Through whom we received grace and
apostleship, unto obedience of faith among all the nations, for his name's sake.* In the first verse Paul declares that he was a called apostle; now he gives the
source of that call. He had not forced himself into that
high office, neither had he been called to it by men,
but had received his apostleship direct from the Lord
Jesus Christ. In that respect he was the equal of
any other apostle of the Lord. In another place he
says of himself: "For I reckon that I am not a whit behind the very chiefest apostles" (2 Cor. 11:5) : "For in
nothing was I behind the very chiefest apostles" (2 Cor.
12:11). "Obedience of faith" is the obedience to which
faith leads, and which perfects faith. Paul had been
made an apostle for the obedience of faith among all
nations—an agent of God to bring men to an obedient
faith. Jesus said to him on the way to Damascus, "I
am Jesus whom thou persecutest. But arise, and
stand upon thy feet: for to this end have I appeared
unto thee, to appoint thee a minister and a witness
both of the things wherein thou hast seen me, and of
the things wherein I will appear unto thee; delivering
thee from the people, and from the Gentiles, unto whom
I send thee, to open their eyes, that they may turn from
darkness to light and from the power of Satan unto
God, that they may receive remission of sins and an inheritance among them that are sanctified by faith in
me" (Acts 26:15-18). Paul preached much to Jews,
but he was especially an apostle of the Gentiles. It is
God's plan that Jew and Gentile have equal rights to
the blessings of the gospel.

Verses 6, 7 : *Among whom are ye also, called to be Jesus Christ's: to all that are in Rome, beloved of God, called to be saints: Grace to you and peace from God our Father and the Lord Jesus Christ.* This letter was not addressed to all the people of Rome, but to the called saints in Rome—those who had been called by the gospel into the service of Christ.

Verse 8 : *First, I thank my God through Jesus Christ for you all, that your faith is proclaimed throughout the whole world.* After the introductory remarks in verses 1-7, and before entering into the discussion of the problems of the letter, Paul seeks in verses 8-13 to establish a sort of personal relationship with the Roman brethren. This gives the letter more of a personal touch. He wanted them to know that he thanked God through Jesus Christ for them; he was thankful to God that their faith was so active that it was known and proclaimed throughout the whole Roman Empire. A good church was a thing for which Paul was profoundly thankful to God, especially was he thankful for such a church in the capital city of the Roman Empire. Souls are as needy and as valuable and a church might be as good, in an obscure locality, as in a central city; but a church in a central city would be in a position to exert an influence over a wider territory. A glance at Paul's labors shows that he sought to establish churches in central places. These churches then became radiating centers for spreading the gospel. As Rome was the capital city, and therefore the most important city in the Empire, Paul was especially interested in having a strong and active church there.

Verses 9, 10 : *For God is my witness, whom I serve*

*in my spirit in the gospel of his Son, how unceasingly
I make mention of you, always in my prayers making
request, if by any means now at length I may be prospered by the will of God to come unto you.* "For God
is my witness" was a solemn declaration; he was not
making the statement lightly. Perhaps some Judaizing teacher was at Rome and was trying to discredit
Paul by telling the brethren that Paul's oft-repeated
promises to come were never intended to be fulfilled.
So Paul declares that God was witness to the fact that
always in his prayers for them he had requested that
he might be permitted by the will of God to come to
them. He would have them know that, though he could
make plans to come, his movements were subject to
God's will; and this should remind us that we should
not leave God out of our plans and purposes. On this
point James says: "Come now, ye that say, Today or
tomorrow we will go into this city, and spend a year
there, and trade, and get gain: whereas ye know not
what shall be on the morrow. What is your life? For
ye are a vapor that appeareth for a little time, and then
vanisheth away. For that ye ought to say, If the
Lord will, we shall both live, and do this or that"
(James 4:13-15).

"Whom I serve in my spirit in the gospel of his
Son." The spirit, the inner man, frequently called "the
heart," is the source of our deeds of acceptable service; and this service of the spirit, to be acceptable, must
be in the gospel—that is, in the things the gospel requires. In John 4:24, Jesus says: "God is Spirit:
and they that worship him must worship in spirit and
truth." The spirit, the heart, must be in the worship,
and the worship must be in the way truth marks out.

Verses 11, 12: *For I long to see you, that I may im-*
part unto you some spiritual gift, to the end ye may be
established: that is, that I with you may be comforted
in you, each of us by the other's faith, both yours and
mine. What was this "spiritual gift" which Paul desired to impart to them? Commentators differ. Some
tell us that it was the benefit Paul wished to impart
to them by his teaching; but it can hardly be that, for
Paul was teaching them in this letter. It seems more
likely that he referred to spiritual gifts, though it is
singular that he said "gift" instead of "gifts." Perhaps there were not as many people in that church endowed with miraculous powers as Paul thought there
should be. It is likely that some of the active workers
among Paul's friends had received these powers before they went to Rome. One thing is sure; and that
is, that some people at Rome had been endowed with
these spiritual gifts, for Paul gave instructions about
the proper use of them. (See Rom. 12:6-8). Paul
wanted to impart this spiritual gift, "to the end ye
may be established." He wanted both himself and them
to be comforted in each other's faith. To confer upon
them some spiritual gift would certainly be a comfort
to them, and to see their increase of faith and useful-
ness would be a comfort to him.

Verse 13: *And I would not have you ignorant,*
brethren, that oftentimes I purposed to come unto you
(and was hindered hitherto), that I might have some
fruit in you also, even as in the rest of the Gentiles.
He had been hindered from carrying out his plans to
visit them. This shows that he was not guided by inspiration in forming his plans, for the Holy Spirit
would not guide him in forming plans and then allow

him to be hindered from carrying out his plans. Paul did sometimes form his own plans, or purposes, which the Holy Spirit did not allow him to carry out. When the Lord was directing Paul toward European fields of labor, he wanted to turn aside and preach in Asia, but was forbidden of the Holy Spirit to do so. Then he wanted to go into Bithynia, and the Spirit suffered him not to do so (Acts 16:6-8).

Verses 14, 15: *I am debtor both to Greeks and to Barbarians, both to the wise and to the foolish. So, as much as in me is, I am ready to preach the gospel to you also that are in Rome.* It was not anything these Greeks and Barbarians had done for Paul that put him in debt to them. Jesus had redeemed him, saved him, and made him an heir of heaven, and thus had brought him under obligation to do all he could to carry the same blessings to others. He had thus been brought under obligation to all men. He was ready to do what he could to discharge that obligation to the Romans.

A practical question arises here: Was Paul under any obligation that the rest of us are not under? Are we not in debt the same as he? Are not all Christians under the same obligations? Every one is responsible up to the limit of his possibilities.

Verse 16: *For I am not ashamed of the gospel: for it is the power of God unto salvation to every one that believeth; to the Jew first, and also to the Greek.* For preaching the gospel Paul had been subjected to many indignities and had endured much suffering. His own nation had cast him off. He had been cast out of Antioch of Pisidia, stoned at Lystra, beaten and imprisoned at Philippi and had fled from Thessalonica to avoid his enemies; he had been mocked by the philo-

sophers at Athens, persecuted at Corinth, and a great
mob at Ephesus had sought to do him harm. He had
suffered all this, and much more; and yet he was not
ashamed to preach the gospel "even at Rome; where
riches, pomp, and glory are alone held in admiration,
where the heights of genius and learning are united
with the greatest profligacy of manners; and where,
consequently, the humbling doctrines of a religion
which demands severe self-denial would be likely to
attract derision, and might make the preacher and
professor of it as it were ashamed."

But why should anyone be ashamed of the gospel?
It has God as its source, Jesus Christ and his plan of
salvation its subject matter, the Holy Spirit as its
Revelator, the highest ideals as its philosophy of life,
and heaven as its ultimate goal. To be ashamed of the
gospel is to be ashamed of God, of Christ, and of the
Holy Spirit. Should a person be ashamed to be a child
of the ruler of the universe, ashamed of being a citizen
of the glorious kingdom of Christ, ashamed to be striving for heaven and immortal glory? Yet some people
are ashamed of the gospel; but not so Paul. No sane
person, when he considers, will be ashamed of that
which brings the greatest possible good to his fellows.
He may have many reasons for being ashamed of himself, but not one reason for being ashamed of God.

Paul tells why he was not ashamed of the gospel; and,
in giving the reason for his not being ashamed of the
gospel, he announces the theme of his letter. He does
not abruptly announce his theme, but leads up to it in
an informal way. He spoke of his long-cherished desire to preach the gospel in Rome, that he was a debtor
to all, and that to the extent of his ability he was

ready to preach the gospel in Rome, for he was not ashamed of the gospel; and then he announced the real theme of his letter: "For it is the power of God unto salvation to every one that believeth." But what is the force of that expression?

Bloomfield says: "The sense is, 'For it is the powerful means appointed by God for the salvation of all who believe and embrace it.' Thus the sentence comprehends two assertions: (1) of the complete efficacy of the gospel to salvation; (2) that the extent of this efficacy shall reach unto all who believe and obey it, without distinction of Jew or Gentile; i.e., as far as concerns the gracious design of God, it shall be universal." A note in the Cambridge Greek Testament: "Tr. 'God's power for salvation' closely together— equals God's effective means for saving men. The insertion of the article in A. V. and R. V. only weakens the force of the expression."

Preachers have lessened the force of the expression by emphasizing "the"; as a matter of fact, "the" is not in the original. The gospel is God's power for saving men. God's power has been, and is, manifested in many ways for many purposes. In creating the world, he used his creative power; in saving men he uses his saving power. The power by which God saves men is his gospel. If men are saved, they will be saved by God's power. Paul was not ashamed of the gospel for it is God's power for salvation.

But many religious people do not believe that the gospel is God's power for saving men. Their whole theory of conversion is built on the theory that man is so depraved by nature that he cannot so much as believe the gospel until he is first regenerated, or made alive, by a direct work of the Spirit. That doctrine is set forth in their creeds. With all such religionists, the direct work of the Spirit is the power which saves. Many have been the prayers for God to "send the converting power down and save these sinners now." The mourners'-bench system was the way that theory was carried into practice a few years ago. They have dropped that practice, but still hold to the theory on which it was based. It seems, therefore, that it used to take more praying, singing, and shouting to induce God to send down converting power than it does now! It would be useless to ask any of these fellows to explain why this is so, for they cannot explain it. Neither can they make their theory harmonize with Paul's plain declaration that the gospel is God's power for salvation.

The gospel was made to meet the sinner's needs as he is, and it was preached to him by inspired men as a being responsible for the way he treated their message. In the great commission Jesus gave not one hint that sinners could not obey the gospel, and not one time did any inspired man tell his auditors that they must have a direct work of the Spirit to enable them to do what they were commanded to do. That was Christianity in practice. And the practice of inspired men is worth more than all the theories of all the creeds. It is both interesting and instructive to follow the inspired preachers and see how they proceeded.

When Peter preached to the multitudes on the day of Pentecost, he expected them to hear and understand what he said. He sought to drive conviction to their hearts, depending alone upon his arguments. He succeeded in doing so, for the record says: "Now when they had heard this, they were pricked in their heart, and said unto Peter and the rest of the apostles, Brethren, what shall we do?" They were not so dead but they could hear and understand; not so depraved but that they could feel the force of Peter's arguments, and desire to get rid of their guilt. The Holy Spirit, knowing that they did not need that direct enabling power from above, told them plainly what to do: "Repent ye, and be baptized every one of you in the name of Jesus Christ unto the remission of your sins; and ye shall receive the gift of the Holy Spirit." "And with many other words he testified, and exhorted them saying, save yourselves from this crooked generation." Of course, the only way they could save themselves was to turn from their sins in obeying the gospel. It is certain that they had not been saved up to the time Peter exhorted them to save themselves. And it is just as evident that they could do what they were commanded and exhorted to do. Not one word is said about their being so depraved that they could not do anything; nothing was said as to their need of a direct power to enable them to appropriate the benefits of the gospel. The gospel was adapted to them as they were. No; God did not make a plan to save folks, and then have to save the folks before the plan would operate on them!

Verse 17: *For therein is revealed a righteousness of God from faith unto faith: as it is written 'But the righteous shall live by faith.'* The seventeenth verse has given a good deal of trouble to commentators. They have not so much trouble in determining the meaning of the words as in determining the proper place of the two prepositional phrases namely, "from faith" and

"unto faith." Translators and commentators differ
as to the proper placing of these phrases. Some would
have the phrase "from faith" to modify the word "revealed." But to say that the gospel was revealed from
faith is, to me, meaningless. I can see how the revealed gospel might produce faith, but cannot see how
faith could produce the gospel. And to say, as some
would have it, that the gospel was revealed from one
degree of faith to another is equally meaningless. The
gospel was not revealed by faith, but by inspiration.
If we take into consideration Paul's reason for making
the statement, together with a correct conception of
the plan of salvation, we should not have much difficulty in arriving at a proper understanding of the
verse. Notice carefully this clear statement by James
Macknight: " 'The righteousness of God revealed from
faith to faith' is an assembly of words to which no distinct meaning can be attached. But the original, rightly construed, gives the following clear literal sense:
'The righteousness of God by faith is revealed in it, in
order to faith.' The apostle was not ashamed of the
gospel, because a righteousness of God's appointment,
to be obtained by faith, is revealed in it, in order to
produce faith in them to whom it is preached. The latter clause, 'as it is written, The just shall live by faith,'
were better translated, 'The just by faith shall live.' "
I. B. Grubbs, in his commentary, says: "We follow
the translation given in the English Revised Version—
deviating only as to the rendering of the clause in question, a deviation which, as we think, can be abundantly
justified. The sentence with its separately indicated
parts will read as follows: (1) 'Therein is revealed
(2) a righteousness of God by faith (3) in order to

faith'." Other authorities can be cited to the same
effect.

But what is the meaning of "righteousness of God?"
Paul does not mean to say that the truth that God is
a righteous Being is revealed in the gospel—that truth
had been fully revealed in the Old Testament. Of the
Jews, Paul said: "For being ignorant of God's righteousness, and seeking to establish their own, they did
not subject themselves to the righteousness of God"
(Rom. 10:3). The Jews were not ignorant that God
was a righteous Being, but they were ignorant of this
gospel plan of righteousness, and therefore did not
submit to it. In Phil. 3:9, Paul refers to it as a righteousness "which is through faith in Christ, the righteousness which is from God by faith." In the gospel is
revealed a plan by which God makes men righteous.

To be righteous is to be free from guilt. If a man
never sinned, he would be righteous by his own works.
But all have sinned and are under condemnation. If no
plan had been devised by which guilty sinners might be
made righteous, the whole world would be lost without
remedy. Some power had to be brought to bear on the
sin-polluted sons and daughters of men that would
make them clean and holy, or all were lost. Paul affirms that the power which accomplishes that very
thing is the gospel. "But thanks be to God, that,
whereas ye were servants of sin, ye became obedient
from the heart to that form of teaching whereunto ye
were delivered; and being made free from sin, ye became servants of righteousness" (Rom. 6:17, 18).
When a sinner obeys the gospel, he is made free from
sin; he is then in God's sight as free from sin as if he
had never sinned; he is justified; he is righteous; he

is clean. If the gospel did not accomplish this for the sinner, it would not be God's power to save. Such a person is not righteous because he has always lived right, but because he has obtained righteousness by becoming obedient to the gospel.

But what of the phrase "in order to faith"? Is it in harmony with the rest of the Bible to say that a plan of righteousness, or justification, is revealed in the gospel as an inducement for men to believe? Notice the following: "Yet knowing that a man is not justified by the works of the law but through faith in Jesus Christ, even we believed on Christ Jesus, that we might be justified by faith in Christ, and not by the works of the law" (Gal. 2:16). To get out from under condemnation, to be released from the penalty of sin, to be justified in God's sight—is that not enough to make any sin-burdened person want to become a Christian?

The gospel, then, is God's power for saving men, because in it is revealed God's plan of righteousness by faith. The gospel makes those who accept it righteous, and that great benefit to be found in the gospel induces men to believe it.

Verse 18: *For the wrath of God is revealed from heaven against all ungodliness and unrighteousness of men, who hinder the truth in unrighteousness.* God's wrath is legal wrath rather than emotional. His law has been violated, and the wrath of the law must be visited upon the transgressor, unless some means can be devised whereby God can be just while justifying the sinner. The "for" at the beginning of this verse is significant, and establishes close connection between this verse and what had just been said. A plan of righteousness has been made known, because God's

wrath is revealed against all sin. It is singular that
God would devise a plan by which he could save the
sinner from his own wrath. Had his wrath been of
that furious type manifest by men, he would not have
wanted to save any one from it. He would have taken
delight in giving it full sway. But while man was resting under God's judicial wrath, God's love went out to
him, and prompted him to devise a plan by which man
could be delivered from the legal consequences of his
sin.

To sum up: The gospel is God's power for salvation
to those who believe it, for a way for sinners to become
righteous is revealed in it, as an inducement for men
to believe it so as to escape the penalty of a violated
law.

If the gospel was to be a real benefit to man, a real
power to save him, there must first be a need for it. If
the world was not lost, there was no need for anything
to save it; or if the world was lost and there was already at hand a means of saving it, there was no need
for the gospel. From chapter 1:18 to chapter 3:20
Paul shows that both Jew and Gentile were lost without the gospel. The reasonings—the professed wisdom
—of the Gentiles had plunged them into the depths
of moral pollution instead of saving them, and the law
had condemned the Jew instead of saving him. All
were sinners, and all were under condemnation.

This gives us a better insight into the real purpose
of the gospel. It is God's way of meeting man's needs;
it was designed as a means of saving the lost. Jesus
came to seek and to save the lost; he came not to condemn, but to save. Without the gospel, the whole world
was lost. "The whole world lieth in sin." The

question is frequently asked: "What will become of the heathen who never heard the gospel?" If a person understood the real purpose and philosophy of the gospel, he would never ask that question. To set such questioners to thinking, we ask: What would have become of the same heathen, if there had never been any gospel? The gospel was designed to save a world already condemned. It is only in a relative sense that people are lost because they do not obey the gospel. Primarily people are lost because they are sinners. To illustrate: a boat is rushed out to rescue a drowning man. He refuses to be rescued, and is drowned. Now, why did he drown? "O," some one replies, "he drowned because he would not get in the boat." Wrong. The boat had nothing to with his drowning; he drowned because he was in the water, and he would have drowned just the same had there never been a boat. Of course, his refusing to be rescued made his drowning a case of suicide. Just so with the sinner. The gospel is sent out to rescue the perishing. When the sinner refuses to be rescued, it intensifies his guilt and shows it to be a case of spiritual suicide. But the gospel had nothing to do with his perishing; he would have perished had there never been a gospel. The boat was a means of rescue, and so is the gospel.

God's wrath is revealed against all ungodliness and unrighteousness of men. Occasionally a Bible reader wonders about these words, both as to their meaning and as to the parties to whom they apply.

We will get a better grasp on the meaning of ungodliness by first considering the meaning of godliness. The meaning of this word has been obscured by trying to make it mean godlikeness. It has no such meaning

in the Bible; the Greek word from which it is translated has no such meaning. Godliness is piety, reverence.
A godly person is one who has respect for God and
sacred things. Ungodliness is impiety, irreverence, a
lack of respect for God and sacred things. Godliness
is a right attitude toward God; ungodliness is a wrong
attitude toward God. Righteousness refers more particularly to our right attitude toward our fellow men.
It is treating our fellow men right. Unrighteousness
is the failure to do right toward our fellow men.

Ungodliness is worse than unrighteousness, though
not generally so regarded. Our first and primary duty
is to God. If we revere God as we should, we will respect his word, his church, and his worship. Those
who blaspheme the name of God, or speak lightly of any
of God's commands, are ungodly. Through sudden
passion or some great weakness a person might do
wrong to his fellow man, and then be filled with great
penitence toward God for the wrong he had done. Such
a one still retained his reverence for God. David did
that. He did unrighteous things; but his reverence
for God was unfailing, and always brought him to repentance. But the ungodly are not so; they do not
take God into account in anything they do.

There is ungodliness in the church, and even in the
pulpit. It manifests itself in many ways. Some men
are so careless as to what the Bible says that they put
themselves to no real trouble to find exactly what any
given passage means. A godly man wants to know
exactly what the will of God is. Some are so ungodly
as to destroy a church to carry their own selfish ends.
A godly man loves and respects that which belongs to
God. Many pulpits in this land are radiating centers

for all sorts of infidelity. The masses in this country have never been righteous. There has been, and is yet, too much disregard for the rights of others; too much cheating, defrauding, and robbery; too much lying, deceit, and slander; too much fighting and killing. In addition to our unrighteousness, we are fast becoming an ungodly people. We are eliminating God from our thinking and from our program of life. We deny him a part in creation and do not take him into account in what we do. And as men eliminate God from creation and thus make human beings no more than a group of animals, unrighteousness of all sorts is bound to increase; for, if we are no more than animals, why should I respect a man's rights any more than I would respect the rights of any of the lower animals? As ungodliness increases, crime of all sorts is bound to increase.

The last clause in verse 18 reads as follows in the King James Version: "Who hold the truth in unrighteousness." In the American Standard Version: "Who hinder the truth in unrighteousness." The Greek word means both "to possess" and "to hinder"; but of course, it cannot have both meanings in the same place. The connection in which it is used must determine its meaning. Some people argue that the person who knows the truth, but will not obey it, holds it in unrighteousness. But this could hardly be said of the persons of whom Paul was here speaking; for, though they had once known God, they had "refused to have God in their knowledge" (verse 28) and had "exchanged the truth of God for a lie" (verse 25). Paul was speaking of these people as they were when he wrote. It could not be said of them that they at that time knew the truth, but would not obey it. **They had** known the truth, but had drifted so far away from it that they were worshiping gods of their own making. At that time they were not holding the truth at all; but their awful sinfulness, as depicted by Paul in the rest of the chapter, was a mighty barrier to the advancement of the truth. By their unrighteousness they were hindering the truth.

It is a fearful thing to hinder the truth of God, and God's wrath is revealed against all who hinder his truth. Even church members often hinder the truth by their unrighteousness. We profess to be friends of God, and then hinder him in what he is seeking to do for man. By such conduct we become enemies of God.

Verse 19: *Because that which is known of God is manifest in them; for God manifested it unto them.* The nineteenth verse is a continuation of the things affirmed in the eighteenth verse. It was not unjust for God to punish these ungodly and unrighteous men, "because that which is known of God is manifest in them," or among them. Of course, finite minds cannot fully comprehend the Infinite Being, but the knowable things of God had been manifest among them; "for God manifested it to them." As the pronoun "it" is not in the Greek, it seems that it would be more in harmony with Paul's argument to translate the last clause thus: "For God manifested himself to them." In various ways along down the ages God had manifested himself to the peoples of the earth. He had made an extensive revelation of himself to the Jews; that is easily seen. But what of his manifestations to the other peoples of the earth? In selecting the children of Israel for a special purpose, did God deliberately reject the other peoples? Did he leave them without any light, and that, too, because he did not want them to have any light? Could any one have such thoughts concerning Jehovah? Is that the idea we have of the One whom we worship as our heavenly father?

The people of every nation find a common ancestor in Noah. Noah stood in great favor with Jehovah. Both before and after the flood God talked to Noah. By means of the flood God revealed to Noah and his family in a very striking way his hatred of sin, his justice, his power, and his providence. Those descendants of Noah who went into idolatry had first to reject what they knew of God. Later God manifested himself to Abraham, to Isaac, to Jacob, and to Joseph. Many people would learn of the one God through these great men. Then God manifested himself to the Egyptians and to the children of Israel in a wonderful way when he brought Israel out of bondage. God intended that these wonderful miracles wrought in the deliverance of Israel should teach all nations, as is clearly shown by what he said to Pharaoh; "But in very deed for this cause have I made thee to stand, to show thee my power, and that my name may be declared throughout all the earth" (Ex. 9:16). That these miracles were told among the nations is indicated by what Rahab of Jericho told the spies. (See Josh. 2:10-14). Jonah carried the knowledge of Jehovah to the capital city of the Assyrians, and brought the king and the whole city of Nineveh to repentance and to a confession of Jehovah. When the kingdom of Israel was carried into captivity by the Assyrians, they were scattered about through that vast kingdom. Among them would be found some who were faithful to Jehovah and who would carry the knowledge of Jehovah where they were placed.   Then, after Babylon gained the mastery of that whole country, they carried the kingdom of Judah into captivity.   Among these were many faithful men and women who carried the knowledge of Jehovah to all the provinces of that vast empire. Daniel and his companions were such active servants of Jehovah as to cause Nebuchadnezzar to make a decree concerning Jehovah, and publish it throughout his kingdom.   Later Darius made a similar proclamation When the time came for the Jews to return from this captivity, Cyrus made a proclamation in which he announced that Jehovah had given him his great dominion and had charged him to build Jehovah a house in Jerusalem.   Much later the Jews and their synagogues were to be found in all parts of the Roman Empire.   The Jew stood squarely against idolatry and for the one God.   In their synagogues the Scriptures were read and the doctrine of Jehovah was propagated. Also, along down the ages there had been such men as Melchizedek, Jethro, Job, and Balaam before his fall.   Many of the Grecians of prominence, such as Solon and Plato, believed in the one Supreme Being. This is only a brief outline of one of the ways the nations had of knowing God, if they had wanted to know him.   But Paul mentions another way which God had manifested himself to all.

Verse 20: *For the invisible things of him since the creation of the world are clearly seen, being perceived through the things that are made, even his everlasting power and divinity; that they may be without excuse.* Invisible things are things which we cannot see with the natural eye; but things invisible to the natural eye are sometimes clearly seen with the mind's eye. To see is often used in the sense of to understand, to comprehend. Paul so uses it here. The invisible things of God are clearly seen, being perceived, or understood, by the things that are made. These invisible things of God are explained as "his everlasting power and divinity." We know that power is necessary to change, or to make, or to create, anything; but how do the things which God made enable us to see clearly "his everlasting power"? The things we see about us were either made or they are themselves everlasting; but no one argues that the universe as we see it is everlasting. It was, then, made by everlasting power, or else by created power. But no created power could have made this universe; but even if it could, there is yet back of it a Creator. Nothing less than divinity could have made and put into motion so vast a machine as the universe. In the created things we see the power and glory of their Maker. Read the following translation by Leeser: "The heavens relate the glory of God and the expanse telleth of the works of his hands. Day unto day uttereth speech, and night unto night showeth knowledge. There is no speech, there are no words, their voice is not heard. But their melody extendeth through all the earth, and to the end of the world their words" (Ps. 19:1-4). The stars in the heavens speak no words and we hear not their voice, yet they speak wonderful things to the thoughtful mind. All created things are God's witnesses—silent, but none the less convincing. On this point Paul said to the men of Lystra: "And yet he left not himself without witness, in that he did good and gave you from

heaven rains and fruitful seasons, filling your hearts
with food and gladness" (Acts 14:17). There was no
reason why any nation should have forgotten God.
Every star proved his existence, and every raindrop
and growing plant demonstrates his presence in the
operations of nature. As inspiration viewed the matter, all nations were without excuse for their idolatry
and their corrupt morals.

Verse 21: *Because that, knowing God, they glorified him not as God, neither gave thanks; but became
vain in their reasonings, and their senseless heart was
darkened.* These heathen nations had known God;
their knowledge of him had been sufficient to rob them
of any excuse for their gross sins. But though they
knew him, they did not glorify him as God. Their
knowing him had been of no benefit to them; they had
sinned against the light they had.

To glorify God as God is to recognize him as the
Creator, Preserver, and rightful Ruler of all things,
and to seek earnestly to comply with his will—to do
the work he intended us to do. In his prayer on the
night of his betrayal, Jesus said: "I glorified thee on
the earth, having accomplished the work which thou
hast given me to do" (John 17:4). Only in this way
may we glorify him. If a machine fails to do the work
which it was made to do, it certainly reflects no glory
on the one who made it; but if it does perfectly the
work it was designed to do, it glorifies its maker. If
any of our inventions, plans, or purposes succeed, we
thereby bring worldly glory upon ourselves. In the
very nature of the case it cannot be otherwise. It is
therefore impossible to glorify God by our own plans
and purposes, no matter how successful they may seem

to be. Only by doing the things he designed we should do can we glorify him. Herein the nations had miserably failed. And having put God out of their philosophy of things, there was no longer any gratitude in their hearts to the Giver of all good things. When people deny God, they are, of course, not thankful.

They became vain in their reasonings—that is, their speculations were foolish and without value. How else could they be? There can be no solid process of reasoning without a starting point, and no process of reasoning that eliminates God has any starting point. It must begin with a guess, an assumption, and proceed in the dark. If God did not create the universe, then any theory as to its origin is a blind guess. If God did not create us, then any theory as to the origin of life and as to how we became human beings is founded on a series of baseless guesses. Hence, when nations eliminated God from his universe, they became vain, empty, foolish, in their reasonings. Having shut themselves off from the only Source of light, "their senseless heart was darkened."

Verse 22: *Professing themselves to be wise, they became fools.* To claim superior wisdom is characteristic of those who deny God his place in his own creation. In their estimation the man who believes the Bible is a back number, an ignoramus. They never seem to realize that the man who professes himself to be wise is a fool, and they have not learned enough to know that no man is richly endowed with any virtue or accomplishment of which he boasts.

If a man thinks and acts contrary to common sense, he is a fool, no matter how much he may know about some things. Common sense is the knowledge the human family has accumulated by experience and observation. We have learned that fire burns. If a man should deny that and act according to his theory, he would act foolishly. Only a fool would say that it would not hurt to run full tilt against a stone wall. And only a fool will say that a thing can be made without a maker, for experience and observation teach us that every made thing has a maker. Recently I read that a rayon factory was being built with such complete machinery that one man could sit at a switch-board and operate the whole plant. After that factory is finished and in operation what would you think of a man who, while watching it operate, would argue that no one built it, and that it ran without any force applied to it, and that no one directed, or controlled, its operations? Well, that is exactly what I think about the man who argues that no one made this great machine we call the universe, that it operates by its own power, and that no one controls, or directs, that power. "The fool hath said in his heart, There is no God." If there is no God, then the universe was made without a maker, and now runs by perpetual motion—nothing made it, nothing started it in motion, and nothing keeps it going! If these fellows are right then those who tried to invent machines that would run without any power were not such cranks, after all. If there is no God, then perpetual motion is a reality! If a man is a fool who thinks a watch might just happen to be he is much more so who thinks this universe just happened to be. And so the nations who thought themselves too wise to believe in God had in reality become fools.

But people cannot remain in a state of negation;

they will believe in something. When a people deny God, they are but one step from idolatry. The nations of whom Paul speaks denied God, "and changed the glory of the incorruptible God for the likeness of an image of corruptible man, and of birds, and four-footed beasts, and creeping things" (verse 23). Men will worship something; if not God, then they will worship some sort of an idol. And they will recognize infallibility somewhere. Segregate our "wise men" of today so that they will not be restrained by any outside influence, and they will drift into some form of idolatry. There is but a step between denying God and the worshiping of any sort of a god.

Because these nations denied God and turned to the worship of idols, God gave them up to follow their own lusts. He did not give them up till they first gave him up. He let them go because they were set on going. From their rationalism they soon plunged into the basest of sins and the most degrading sort of superstition.

God gave us reasoning powers, and intends for us to use them; but there is a limit to reason. It cannot fully fathom God, nor correctly blaze out a way which it has never trod. "It is not in man that walketh to direct his steps." But since God has revealed his will to us, it is our duty to use our best reasoning powers to search out that will. But to reject revelation and depend upon reason as the true source of light is rationalism; and to do so is to make reason our god, and that is a form of idolatry. It is easy to drift from one form of idolatry to another.

Reason without reverence for a Higher Power is a dangerous thing. Superstition is not so dangerous. In

fact, superstition and reverence are closely related. As
a matter of fact, superstition is ignorant reverence.
The superstitious can be taught; but even God himself
gave the rationalist up to follow his own ways.

Verse 23: *And changed the glory of the incorruptible God for the likeness of an image of corruptible man,
and of birds, and four-footed beasts, and creeping
things.* The glory of God is here used in contrast with
the shame of idolatry, and God is described as incorruptible in contrast with corruptible man.   These nations had known God, but had turned from that knowledge to their own speculations.   When men come to
rely on their own speculations instead of on the sure
knowledge of God, they will, sooner or later, repudiate
him altogether. Men naturally want to deny the existence of a God whom they will not honor.   They will
change him off for something else.   The nations
changed the glorious God for the various images common to idolaters. They rejected the One from whom all
blessings come, and worshiped everything else that
seemed to be of any benefit to them, and also the things
which they feared.

Verse 24: *Wherefore God gave them up in the lust
of their hearts unto uncleanness, that their bodies
should be dishonored among themselves.* When people are determined to reject God for their own way,
God allows them unhindered to follow their chosen
course so that they may the sooner see the degradation
that comes to those who follow their own wisdom. When
men are not held in restraint by a feeling of personal
responsibility to God nor by associating with those who
do honor God, their passions become the controlling
force in their lives; they plunge into all sorts of im-

moralities, and they dishonor their bodies among themselves. When a whole nation forsakes God for idols, there is not then so much as the conventions of society to hold them in check. It takes a power outside itself to keep anything from going downward, both in physics and in morals.

Verse 25: *For that they exchanged the truth of God for a lie, and worshipped and served the creature rather than the Creator, who is blessed forever. Amen!* Their whole system of speculations and their doctrines pertaining to the worship of idols is here called a "lie." It is strange that men will deliberately turn from the truth to a lie, but that is what any one does who turns from God to human wisdom. And the mind of man must become densely ignorant before it can consent to worship man and beasts rather than the Creator. But such conduct detracts nothing from God's glory. Whether we worship or not, he "is blessed forever." The "Amen" is added as a strong affirmation—so let it be.

Verses 26, 27: *For this cause God gave them unto vile passions: for their women changed the natural use into that which is against nature: and likewise also the men, leaving the natural use of the woman, burned in their lust one toward another, men with men working unseemliness, and receiving in themselves that recompense of their error which was due.* Paul is not indulging in a lot of fanciful speculations nor presenting baseless theories. He is showing how the heathen nations had reached the lowest degree of moral degradation. When a people cease to respect God, they will not long respect their own bodies. They give themselves up to passions of dishonor. Their women become abusers of their own bodies. The men indulged in the debasing practice of sodomy. We are told that this was a common practice among the prominent men of Greece, and also the Romans. When the greatest men of a nation descend to the lowest conceivable form of immorality, it shows how powerless education and philosophy are to save men from the deepest depths of moral pollution.

Verse 28: *And even as they refused to have God in their knowledge, God gave them up unto a reprobate mind, to do those things which are not befitting.* Again Paul states the reason for their corruption. For the word *refused* the marginal reading has "Greek, *did not approve.*" "They tested or proved God and decided not to keep him" (R. St. John Parry). The God of heaven was not the God they wanted, and they rejected him from their system of knowledge, or philosophy. The rationalists of today occupy the same grounds. God is entirely ruled out. Because the nations then ruled God out of their affairs, "God gave them up unto a reprobate mind." "A reprobate mind" is a mind that did not stand the test, and hence was rejected. They rejected God, and God in turn rejected them. They had so degenerated in their thinking that God could no longer tolerate them.

Paul had shown that when they so dishonored God they began to worship idols, they also began to dishonor their own bodies. In verses 29-31 he speaks mostly of the crimes that men commit toward one another. If a man does not regard God nor the honor of his own body, it is not likely that he will have much regard for his fellow man. Such people are ready for any sin that their passions or their self-interests dictate.

NOTE:—What Paul says about the sins of these idolatrous nations throws light on a question that occasionally comes up—that is, whether or not a person that is not in covenant relations with the Lord is held accountable for his deeds. That question was first brought to my attention when a good brother said concerning some non-Christian young people, "It does not make any difference what they do, for the Lord does not take any notice of them, anyway. Not being in covenant relations with the Lord, they are not under any law of God: they therefore violate no law of God, no matter what they do." I could not believe that doctrine then, and I believe it less now. If that doctrine is true, an alien sinner is not a sinner at all! He could not be, if God holds nothing against him; and if the doctrine be true, there is no such thing as baptism for the remission of sins. But the language of Paul shows the doctrine to be false. Certainly these heathen nations were not in covenant relations with God; yet they were great sinners. Notice the long list of sins they were continuously indulging in. The whole plan of salvation is based on the fact that men are sinners and need to be saved. Jesus came to call sinners to repentance. God now commands all men everywhere to repent. If the nations had not been sinners, they would not have needed the gospel. To prove the universal need of the gospel, Paul starts in to prove that all men are sinners.

Verses 29-31: *Being filled with all unrighteousness, wickedness, covetousness, maliciousness; full of envy, murder, strife, deceit, malignity; whisperers, back-*

biters, hateful to God, insolent, haughty, boastful, inventors of evil things, disobedient to parents, without understanding, covenant-breakers, without natural affection, unmerciful. The sins which Paul here enumerates are sins which people commit against one another. Paul had already showed how they had dishonored and rejected God and had abused and dishonored their own bodies, and now he proceeds to list the sins they commit against one another. It makes a dark picture, but history tells us that the heathen nations were guilty of everything Paul charges against them.

They were "filled with all unrighteousness." It is not that they sometimes did unrighteous things, but they were full of all unrighteous deeds. "Unrighteousness" does not here include all sinful deeds, for it is mentioned as one kind of a long list of sins. It here means *injustice*. The Greek conveys that idea. Injustice is unfair and dishonest dealings and grows out of a lack of regard for others. An unjust man cheats and defrauds and has no interest in the welfare of the man with whom he deals. Paul does not mean that injustice is found only among the heathen nations; but these nations, having denied God and adopted idol worship, had nothing to hold them in the paths of just dealing. Where God and his word are revered, men are not full of injustice. To the Hebrews God said: "Ye shall do no unrighteousness in judgment, in measures of length, of weight, or of quantity. Just balances, just weights, a just ephah, and a just hin, shall ye have" (Lev. 19:35, 36). But Christianity teaches a higher code than justice. Instead of giving a just measure, we are taught to give a measure shaken down, heaped up, and running over. We are taught to be generous, forbearing, and merciful. The genuine Christian deals justly, with generosity added. It is a shame that some professed Christians are really idolators in that they worship gain, and are therefore, as tricky as any other heathen.

Wickedness, maliciousness, malignity—these words all occur in verse 29. Disregarding for the present the words that come between them, I have put them together in this paragraph, because they are kindred in meaning. In fact, the Greek words from which these are translated sometimes have practically the same meaning. It is evident that they do not mean the same thing here. If they had everywhere meant the same thing, Paul would have used but one of them in the same verse. The Greek words in order of occurrence in this verse are *poneria, kakia,* and *kakoetheia.* Of the first two words Thayer says: *"Kakia* denotes rather the vicious disposition, *poneria* the active exercise of the same." In his "Synonyms of the New Testament," Section 11, Trench says: "We shall not err in saying *kakia* is more the evil habit of mind, *poneria* the outcropping of the same." *Poneria,* translated "wickedness" in the American Standard Version, refers to the wickedness of the deeds; it is *malice* of the heart, *ill will, a desire to injure,* carried in action. It is the outcropping of *kakia, ill will, a desire to injure.* The other word (*kakoetheia,* translated *malignity*) Jeremy Taylor calls "a baseness of nature by which we take things by the wrong handle, and expound things always in the worst sense." Trench says of this word: "The position which it occupies in St. Paul's list of sins entirely justifies us in regarding it as the peculiar form of evil which manifests itself in the malignant interpretation of the actions of others, an attributing of them all to the worst motive."

Here, then, is a group of words describing some very pernicious sins, so common among the heathen nations as to enable Paul to say these nations were full of them. A man might in a passion injure his fellow man, but that is quite different from practicing injurious things because of a deep-seated desire to injure some one. When a person reaches that stage of depravity of mind, there is little, if any, good in him. Such a person can see no good in another. No matter what another does, such a person feels sure he had an evil motive in doing it. He could hardly think otherwise, for he knows of no motives except those that are evil. His own character is his standard of judgment.

It is a pity that such sins are found even in this country. It could not be truthfully said that this country is full of such sins, but they are too common. If a man is really a Christian, if he loves his neighbor as himself, he will not want to do anything to injure his neighbor. A Christian does not want to hurt; he wants to help.

Covetousness is avarice, a greedy desire for possessions. The heathen nations were full of a desire to get the things of others. If the laws of the land or a desire to appear decent did not restrain the covetous man, he would take what belonged to another any way he could get it. Paul tells us that covetousness is idolatry. This is one form of idolatry that is practiced even in this country. A man who wants property more than he wants to serve God makes property his god. He might as well worship an idol of gold on his mantel as a sack of gold in his bank.

Envy is defined as "chagrin or discontent at another's excellence or good fortune; malicious grudging." It is certainly a perverted nature that is full of such feelings. While it could not be said that the people of this land are full of envy, it certainly is true that there is too much envy even in this land. Perhaps few people are entirely free of it. "A tranquil heart is the life of the flesh; but envy is the rottenness of the bones" (Prov. 14:30). Envy crucified the Son of God. Pilate protested the crucifixion of the Son of God, "for he perceived that for envy the chief priests had delivered him up" (Mark 15:10). Envy corrodes and corrupts the character, and sometimes leads to murder. It may not be an accident that Paul places murder immediately after envy.

Murder is included in the list of sins laid to the charge of the nations that had turned away from God to follow their own wisdom. Having denied God and plunged into a sinful course of life, they had come to have little regard for human life. The word Paul used was not confined to the taking of human life with premeditated malice by a person of sound mind. It would include any killing that grew out of disregard for human life. "It is scarcely necessary to show that this was common among the Gentiles. It has prevailed in all communities, but particularly prevalent in Rome. It is necessary only to refer the reader to the common events in the Roman history of assassinations, deaths by poison, and the destruction of slaves. But in a special manner the charge was properly alleged against them, on account of the inhuman contests of the gladiators in the amphitheaters. These were common at Rome, and constituted a favorite amusement

of the people. Originally, captives, slaves, and criminals were trained for combat; but it afterwards became common for even Roman citizens to engage in
these bloody combats, and Nero at one show exhibited
no less than four hundred senators and six hundred
knights as gladiators." (Barnes). But what concerns us most is the increase of murders in this country; and it is practically useless to bewail the murder-
ous habits of our countrymen so long as the causes
that produce murders are ignored and even taught. As
it now is, criminals go unpunished; our children are
taught that human beings are a sort of high grade animals with no souls, and God's word is ignored and even
jeered at by some of our educators. Justice has been
mocked and is now only a name, man has been de-
graded to the status of an improved ape, and God has
been dethroned and laughed out of his own world. It
is foolish to expect anything but an increase of murders so long as these conditions prevail. Three things
will decrease murders:—namely, (1) quick and sure
punishment of the killer, (2) impress upon the growing
generation higher regard for human life, and (3) teach
them a deeper reverence of God and his word by im-
pressing upon them that God is the rightful ruler and
that we must give account to him. And it would do a
lot of good for people to be reminded that a lot of
foolish speculation does not abolish hell. The pure and
unadulterated gospel is the remedy for this sin, as well
as for the others Paul mentions.

For "strife" the King James Version has "debate."
But the word "debate" does not now mean a personal
wrangle, quarrel, or fight, as it did three hundred years
ago, and as did the word Paul used. A debate now is

a discussion to elicit or to propagate truth. It was not so three hundred years ago. The word Paul used meant a quarrel, a wrangle, or fight. No one should try to make it appear that Paul taught that a discussion is wrong.

The Greek word, here translated deceit, is defined by Liddell and Scott as, "strictly *a bait*, for fish; hence, any *snare, cunning contrivance for deceiving* or *catching;* in general, *any trick* or *crafty attempt;* and so in the abstract, *wile, craft, cunning, treachery.*" Hence deceit is an attempt to get the advantage of another without letting him know your intentions; it is to profit at his expense by keeping him in the dark. The man who does such things is without principle. It is a pity that even in this country there are men who will deceive others for advantage. Selfishness and a disregard for the rights of others are at the bottom of deceit. A deceitful person is altogether unreliable.

Whisperers are cowardly sneaks who have not the courage to come out in the open and say damaging things about others, but secretly peddle their slanderous statements and insinuations against the object or objects of their campaign of spite. They usually add: "Be sure not to use my name in connection with the matter, for I do not want to get mixed up in the mess." Such characters have been aptly termed "snakes in the grass." They would destroy a good name, and then gloat over what they had been able to accomplish. Only the Lord can properly award such characters.

Backbiters, slanderers, defamers, who delight in destroying the good name of others. Such characters are not particular as to the truth of what they tell. Whisperers and backbiters are of the same breed, ex-

cepting that the backbiters are more open and bold.
Neither of them has the courage to face the accused
with their slanders.   Neither is worthy of a place
among decent people.   It is a pity that the slimy trails
of both are found in this good land of ours.

Haters of God—I have here adopted the marginal
reading as the one more in harmony with the context; for Paul is here listing the sins of the nations,
and puts this down as one of the sins.   It would seem
that a person had reached the depth of depravity when
he becomes a God hater.   But the man that continues
to defy God and his laws will eventually become a
hater of God.

Insolent is defined by Webster as, "haughty and
contemptuous or brutal in behavior or language; over-
bearing; grossly disrespectful."   In its milder manifestations, insolence is uppishness.   The insolent person has a feeling of superiority over others; at least,
he assumes to be superior.   The feeling makes one
brutal or insulting to others.   He is bolder than the
backbiter; he likes to crush and humiliate one who is
present, and delights to have others witness his triumph.

There is but a shade of difference between "haughty" and "insolent."   Webster's first definition: "Dis-
dainfully or contemptuously proud; arrogant; super-
cilious."   Such a person is proud of himself; he likes
to strut and swagger.   He is embodied egotism.   If
such a person could ever realize that every time he is
trying to show off he is acting a fool, it would help
his manners.   He needs the sobering influence of the
gospel.

Boastful—An empty pretender: he boasts of things

he does not possess or of things he has never done. He wants people to think of him as rich and a great doer of things. He likes to talk about himself; he is a little man swelled up. Such fellows are shoddy goods marked up. When a man boasts, he is generally lacking in the things of which he boasts.

Inventor of Evil things—People who indulge in worldly and sinful pursuits are constantly seeking new thrills. Old forms of pleasure and sin grow stale, and new forms of indulgence are constantly being sought out. There are now more ways to sin than ever before in the world's history, and the end is not yet.

Disobedient to parents—Not many things break down the morals of a country more quickly and cause more lawlessness than disrespect for parents. If children disrespect parental authority, they will disrespect all authority. If they have no regard for their parents, they are not likely to have regard for anything. But when such conditions prevail, parents are not blameless. Obedience and respect are matters that have to be learned. "Though he was a Son, yet learned obedience by the things which he suffered." Parents that do not try to train their children in right principles and good habits care very little for them. But it is hard for you to train up your children as they should be trained when everybody else lets theirs run loose and do as they please. However, nothing but a decay of morals can be expected where children are not taught obedience and respect to parents. Children who properly love and esteem their parents will care for them when they become too old or too helpless to care for themselves.

Without understanding—It is no crime for a mentally defective person to be unable to understand. These people had a mind, but they had not filled it with truth and right principles. They did not have an understanding of the real philosophy of correct living. So many people are without understanding because they will not understand. They have closed their eyes and stopped their ears to keep from learning the right. They prefer darkness. There is such a thing as willful ignorance. God has never withheld light from any one who wanted the light.

A covenant breaker is one who will not stand to his agreements, whether these agreements be written or oral. Sometimes you hear some one say of another, "His word is as good as his bond." It is a fine thing for a man to have that sort of reputation, but it is a bad state of affairs when that can be mentioned as a point of distinction. Keeping one's word should be so common among men that it would not be a point of distinction for any man. A man who will not keep his word, whether written or oral, is a sorry specimen of humanity.

Without natural affection—These nations were without the affections that should exist on account of the ties of nature; there was no proper affection between parents and children. Paul's charge against them is abundantly proved by the heathen writers of those days.

Unmerciful—They were harsh and unfeeling. There can be no mercy when the heart has no sympathy, for mercy is sympathy in action; it is the tender and kind feeling bearing the fruit of helpfulness. The wicked may become so hard of heart as to be devoid of mercy.

And even the Christian needs to watch himself. A person who has high ideals and a high sense of honor may become rather harsh toward those who make no special effort to do right. "Blessed are the merciful: for they shall obtain mercy." Let us watch ourselves; mercy is a grace worth cultivating. "For judgment is without mercy to him that hath showed no mercy." "With what judgment ye judge, ye shall be judged."

Verse 32: *Who, knowing the ordinance of God, that they that practice such things are worthy of death, not only do the same, but also consent with them that practice them.* They had no revelation. How, then, did they know the ordinance of God and the penalty for its infraction? But Paul does not say that they knew the entire law of God. So far as his language shows, they knew only that those who practice such sins as he enumerates are worthy of death. But how did they know that these sins and that those who practiced them were worthy of death?

There is embedded in man's nature a consciousness of right and wrong. If he never had a revelation from God, he knows that it is wrong to abuse his body and to mistreat his fellows. The fact that the heathen nations then had and now have laws for the punishment of crime shows that they recognize that there was such a thing as crime and that certain crimes should be punished by death.

Let us be fair with God's word. A revelation from God was never intended to create any new faculties in man. It does not plant in the human heart a consciousness of right and wrong, but it does guide and refine that consciousness, and places motives before man to induce him to do right. If a man were to reach the point where he had no consciousness of right and wrong, his case would be hopeless. The goodness that is in the gospel has no appeal to the person who has no idea of goodness. But the heathen nations had an idea of right and wrong and knew that certain crimes were worthy of death. Yet they indulged in the things they knew to be wrong. Not only so, "but consent with them that practice them."

Chapter 2

2:1 Wherefore thou art without excuse, O man, whosoever thou art that judg-est: for wherein thou judgest another, thou condemnest thyself: for thou that judgest dost practise the same things.   2 And we know that the judgment of God is according to truth against them that practise such things.   3 And reckonest thou this, O man, who judgest them that practise such things, and doest the same, that thou shalt escape the judgment of God?   4 Or despisest thou the riches of his goodness and forbearance and longsuffering, not knowing that the goodness of God leadeth thee to repentance?   5 but after thy hardness and impenitent heart treasurest up for thyself wrath in the day of wrath and revelation of the righteous judgment of God;   6 who will render to every man according to his works: 7 to them that by patience in well-doing seek for glory and honor and incorruption, eternal life: 8 but unto them that are factious, and obey not the truth, but obey unrighteousness, *shall be* wrath and indignation,   9 tribulation and anguish, upon every soul of man that worketh evil, of the Jew first, and also of the Greek;   10 but glory and honor and peace to every man that worketh good, to the Jew first, and also to the Greek: 11 for there is no respect of persons with God.   12 For as many as have sinned without the law shall also perish without the law: and as many as have sinned under the law shall be judged by the law;   13 for not the hearers of the law are just before God, but the doers of the law shall be justified: 14 (for when Gentiles that have not the law do by nature the things of the law, these, not having the law, are the law unto themselves;   15 in that they show the work of the law written in their hearts, their conscience bearing witness therewith, and their thoughts one with an-other accusing or else excusing *them*);   16 in the day when God shall judge the secrets of men, according to my gospel, by Jesus Christ.

17 But if thou bearest the name of a Jew, and restest upon the law, and gloriest in God,   18 and knowest his will, and approvest the things that are excellent, being instructed out of the law,   19 and art confident that thou thyself art a guide of the blind, a light of them that are in darkness,   20 a corrector of the foolish, a teacher of babes, having in the law the form of knowledge and of the truth: 21 thou therefore that teachest another, teachest thou not thyself?   thou that preach-est a man should not steal, dost thou steal?   22 thou that sayest a man should not commit adultery, dost thou commit adultery?   thou that abhorrest idols, dost thou rob temples?   23 thou who gloriest in the law, through thy transgression of the law dishonorest thou God?   24 For the name of God is blasphemed among the Gentiles because of you, even as it is written.   25 For circumcision indeed profiteth, if thou be a doer of the law: but if thou be a transgressor of the law, thy cir-cumcision is become uncircumcision.   26 If therefore the uncircumcision keep the ordinances of the law, shall not his uncircumcision be reckoned for circumcision?   27 and shall not the uncircumcision which is by nature, if it fulfil the law, judge thee, who with the letter and circumcision art a transgressor of the law?   28 For he is not a Jew who is one outwardly; neither is that circumcision which is outward in the flesh: 29 but he is a Jew who is one inwardly; and circumcision is that of the heart, in the spirit not in the letter; whose praise is not of men, but of God.

Verse 1: *Wherefore thou art without excuse, O man, whosoever thou art that judgest: for wherein thou judgest another, thou condemnest thyself; for thou that judgest dost practice the same things.* This verse has been so twisted as to make it teach nonsense and also to condemn its writer. It has been twisted into meaning that, if you judge another to be guilty of a crime, you thereby become guilty of the same thing. Paul had just charged many crimes against the Gentiles. It is foolish to put a meaning into his words that makes him guilty of the same things. What does the language mean?

Paul had charged that the Gentiles were guilty of many crimes and were, therefore, worthy of death. The Jew charged the same things against the Gentiles, therefore, Paul, in effect, said: "You are as sinful as the Gentiles; you practice the same things they do. Hence, in judging them to be such criminals as to be worthy of death, you condemn yourself." The Jew was, therefore, himself under condemnation, for Verse 2 says, *We know that the judgment of God is according to truth against them that practice such things.* There was no use for the Jew to think he would escape the judgment visited upon the Gentiles so long as he was as guilty as they.

God had been rich in goodness and forbearance and longsuffering toward the Jews. Instead of being led to repentance by this goodness, as God had intended, they had despised it and had grown more sinful. They were treasuring up for themselves "wrath in the day of wrath and revelation of the righteous judgment of God; who will render to every man according to his works." In that day the Jew will not escape any more than will the Gentile.

Verses 3-5: *And reckonest thou this, O man, who judgest them that practice such things, and doest the same, that thou shalt escape the judgment of God? Or*

*despisest thou the riches of his goodness and forbear-
ance and longsuffering, not knowing that the goodness of God leadeth thee to repentance? But after
thy hardness and impenitent heart treasurest up for
thyself wrath in the day of wrath and revelation of
the righteous judgment of God.* It was an easy matter to get the Jew to agree that the Gentiles were
sinners; but, for his own good, it was necessary for
the Jew to see himself as a condemned sinner, else he
would not see his need of the gospel. But to convince
the Jew that he was a sinner and needed salvation was
a task that demanded a good deal of skill. Paul's first
point was that the Jew had no right to condemn the
Gentile, for he was also guilty of the same sins. The
Jew boasted that he was the object of God's special
favor. Because of this Paul asked: "Or despisest
thou the riches of his goodness and forbearance and
longsuffering, not knowing that the goodness of God
leadeth thee to repentance?" That is, the goodness of
God was intended to lead them to repentance, but
they despised it and were treasuring up, or heaping
up, wrath for themselves.

Verses 6-11: *Who will render to every man according to his works: to them that by patience in well-
doing seek for glory and honor and incorruption, eternal life: but unto them that are factious, and obey
not the truth, but obey unrighteousness, shall be
wrath and indignation, tribulation and anguish, upon
every soul of man that worketh evil, of the Jew first,
and also of the Greek; but glory and honor and peace
to every man that worketh good, to the Jew first, and
also to the Greek: For there is no respect of persons
with God.*

God "will render to every man according to his works." God will judge without favoritism and will render to each man according to his works. It is not that God will sum up all you have done, whether good or bad, and pay you wages in proportion to the amount you have done. He will not count the hours you have worked and measure out your wages on the basis of so much pay for so many hours. But the kind of works you do shows what sort of person you are; they are the index to character. God rewards according to the nature, and not the amount, of our works. Some people whose heart is as far from God as it can well be never commit as many crimes as some others who are no worse. Some lack the energy and the courage to be great criminals, and others lack physical ability or are hindered by their environments. Some people whose heart is as true to God as the heart of any are lacking in ability or are hindered by physical defects. Such people do what good they can. God will render, or give back to you, according to the nature of your works.

A Caution.—We must not put a construction on the teaching of salvation by works that will contradict the doctrine of salvation by grace. Ponder this: On God's side our salvation is wholly a matter of grace, for he receives no pay for saving us; on our side our salvation is wholly a matter of works, for we can furnish no grace.

Eternal life is to be rendered "to them that by patience in well doing seek for glory and honor and incorruption." Verse 7 connects closely with verse 6. "Eternal life" is the object of "render"—God will render eternal life to those who "by patience in well-doing seek for glory and honor and incorruption." Of course, the glory and honor that we are to seek is the glory and honor that we shall have with God in the world to come. We are forbidden to seek the glory and honor that comes from men in this life. We shall attain to glory and honor and incorruption in the world to come by patience in well-doing.

But what is eternal life? The materialist holds to the idea that eternal life is mere eternal existence. He might not avow that in so many words, but he does say it in other words just as plain and emphatic. If you have ever heard one in a discussion on eternal punishment, you have heard him try to make the doctrine absurd by referring to eternal punishment as eternal life in hell! But Paul's language, as well as other scriptures, shows eternal life to be much more than eternal existence. God renders eternal life to those who seek glory and honor and incorruption. Does Paul mean to say that if we will seek one thing, God will give us another? Will he not give us what we seek? Can you not see that Paul here really defines eternal life? Hence, so far as this text shows, eternal life consists of glory, honor, and incorruption—a happy existence in the heavenly kingdom.

If you are still in doubt, consider the matter recorded in the following parallel passages: Matt. 19:16-29; Mark 10:17-30; Luke 18:18-30. A rich young ruler asked Jesus: "What good thing shall I do, that I may have eternal life?" Jesus told him certain things to do, and added, "And thou shalt have treasure in heaven." As Jesus was giving him the information he sought, we know that having eternal life and enjoying treasure in heaven are the same. When the young man refused the offer, Jesus said: "It is hard for a rich man to enter into the kingdom of heaven." Here we have another term describing the same thing. To have eternal life, to enjoy treasure in heaven, and to be in the heavenly kingdom are the same. But this statement about the rich man startled the disciples, and they asked: "Who then can be saved?" Certainly they were asking a question about the matter under discussion—namely, eternal life. They referred to salvation in the world to come, or everlasting salvation. To have eternal life, to be enjoying treasure in heaven, to be in the heavenly kingdom, and to have eternal salvation are the same. And to show that eternal life was still the matter under consideration, Jesus tells his disciples that those who had left all worldly things for his sake and the gospel's would have a hundredfold in this life, "and in the world to come eternal life." So, then, mere eternal existence and eternal life are as wide apart as hell and heaven.

Eternal life is conditional for eternal life must be sought by patience in well-doing. In the eighth and ninth verses Paul affirms that tribulation and anguish will be visited upon those who do evil. Any person who can think at all should be able to see that, if damnation is conditional, salvation must also be conditional. One cannot be conditional and the other unconditional. If doing wrong causes a person to be lost, then, to be saved he must leave off the wrong and do right. If being lost is conditional, so is being saved. There is no way to escape that conclusion. When the rich young ruler asked Jesus what he must do to inherit eternal life, Jesus said: "If thou wouldest enter into life, keep the commandments." Of Jesus Paul said:

"Having been made perfect, he became unto all them that obey him the author of eternal salvation" (Heb. 5:9). And we have already seen that God will render eternal life to those who by patience in well-doing seek it. "Marvel not at this: for the hour cometh, in which all that are in the tombs shall hear his voice, and shall come forth; they that have done good, unto the resurrection of life; and they that have done evil, unto the resurrection of judgment" (John 5:28, 29). If eternal life is not conditional, no one can give a reason why one person is saved and another lost, "for there is no respect of persons with God." "Of a truth I perceive that God is no respecter of persons: but in every nation he that feareth him, and worketh righteousness, is acceptable to him." It would be well if all preachers could come to see as clearly as did Peter.

Verse 12: *For as many as have sinned without the law shall also perish without the law: and as many as have sinned under the law shall be judged by the law.* In Paul's language, "the law" referred to the law of Moses. The law of Moses did not extend to the Gentiles. The grievous sins charged against them in the preceding chapter had not been committed under the law of Moses, nor against the law. We are sure of two things with reference to them—namely, (1) they had sinned, and (2) they had not sinned under the law of Moses. This being true, they would not be judged by the law of Moses, but would perish without the law. From Mount Sinai to the cross of Christ the children of Israel were under the law of Moses. The sins they committed were committed under the law and against the law, and by the law they will be judged. But Paul's language clearly shows that only those who were under the law will be judged by the law. As this law did not extend to the Gentiles, they will not be judged by it.

Verse 13: *For not the hearers of the law are just before God, but the doers of the law shall be justified.* The Jews trusted too much in the fact that God had made them custodians of the law, and that it was always with them. They could read it when they so desired, and they heard it read in the synagogues every sabbath. They put too much stress on their hearing the law and on their knowledge of the law. As a result, they neglected the doing of the law. That was a fatal mistake; for not hearers, but doers of the law were justified.

The law condemns the guilty and justifies the innocent. Paul does not affirm that any Jew had so kept the law that he would be justified by it. He merely lays down the principle that the doer of the law shall be justified. Absolute justification by the law could be had only by perfect obedience to the law. But no one kept the law perfectly, and for that reason the law justified no one. "Because by the works of the law shall no flesh be justified in his sight; for through the law cometh the knowledge of sin" (Rom. 3:20). "Yet knowing that a man is not justified by the works of the law but through faith in Jesus Christ, even we believed on Christ Jesus, that we might be justified by faith in Christ, and not by the works of the law: because by the works of the law shall no flesh be justified" (Gal. 2:16). It is plain, therefore, that no Jew kept the law so perfectly as to be justified by it. The law convicted the violator instead of justifying him.

Verse 14: *For when Gentiles that have not the law do by nature the things of the law, these, not having the law, are the law unto themselves.* Macknight gives a more exact translation of Paul's language: "When therefore the Gentiles, who have not a law, do by nature the things of the law, these persons, though they have not a law, are a law to themselves." You will notice that he puts "the" before "law" only once. In that respect he exactly represents Paul. The Gentiles had no revealed law, and so they were a law unto themselves. The Gentiles never had the law of Moses, but there are certain fundamental principles that inhere in the nature of our existence and in our relations to one another. Some things are right, and some things are wrong, within themselves. If a man never had a revelation from God, he would know that it was wrong to murder his fellow man, or to rob him of his possessions, or in any way to infringe on his rights. Cain sinned in killing his brother and felt his guilt, though we have no record that God had told him not to kill. God's moral law is the same to all nations. The moral requirements of the law of Moses are the things which the Gentiles might do by nature. The Jews did these things by revelation; the Gentiles, by nature; that is, in so far as they did them at all. But let us remember that the law under which any person lives condemns him, if he does not keep it perfectly. Paul does not say that the Gentiles lived up to their natural law any more than the Jews lived up to the revealed law. On the contrary, he was seeking to show that all were sinners and needed the gospel of Christ to save them. But they did have an idea of right and wrong.

Verse 15: *In that they show the work of the law written in their hearts, their conscience bearing witness therewith, and their thoughts one with another accusing or else excusing them.* The construction of the Greek shows plainly that it was the work of the law, and not the law itself, that was written on the hearts of the Gentiles. This, of course, referred to the moral requirements of the law. The moral requirements of the law are just such things as any decent set of people would recognize as proper and right, even if they never had a revelation. Their conscience, like the conscience of those who had a revealed law, would accuse them when they failed to live up to their standard of right, and approve them when they did right as they saw it. That is the office of conscience.

But what is conscience? It is frequently referred to as a guide. But conscience is not a guide at all; that is not its office. Also, it is said that conscience is a creature of education; but I see not how any one would go about educating his conscience. It is also defined as the moral judgment, but that definition does not fit. Your moral judgment may tell you that a certain person did very wrong, but his act does not affect your conscience in any way, unless you feel responsible for his action. Liddell and Scott define the Greek word that is translated "conscience" thus: "(1) A knowing with one's self, consciousness; (2) conscience." Where we have two words—"consciousness" and "conscience"—the Greeks had one word, and the connection determined its meaning, or, perhaps speaking more accurately, the connection determined its application. "Consciousness" has a broader application than "conscience." A person is conscious of his own bodily sensations, whether pleasurable or painful; he is also conscious of his own thoughts and emotions. We are getting at conscience when we think of it as that feeling of pleasure when we do what we think is right, and of pain when we do what we think is wrong. It is that which backs up our moral judgment. Saul of Tarsus always did what he thought was right, and therefore always had a good conscience. But his information was wrong, and therefore his moral judgment was wrong. Our judgment may be wrong because the ideas upon which we base our judgment may be wrong. But no matter how we have been taught, we can expect our conscience to urge us to do what we have judged to be right, unless it has been deadened by long indulgence in things we know to be wrong. It seems to me that a live, tender conscience is infallible. But as to moral judgment, no man can safely say that he is right on everything. Gain all the information you can so that you can form correct judgments, and give heed to the urge of conscience.

Verses 17-20: *But if thou bearest the name of Jew, and restest upon the law, and gloriest in God, and knowest his will, and approvest the things that are excellent, being instructed out of the law, and art confident that thou thyself art a guide of the blind, a light of them that are in darkness, a corrector of the foolish, a teacher of babes, having in the law the form of knowledge and of the truth.* It is not known when the name "Jew" was first used. After the ten tribes followed Jeroboam in the revolt against Rehoboam, the two remaining tribes—Judah and Benjamin—became known as the kingdom of Judah, because Judah was so much more powerful than the tribe of Benjamin.

Later they became known as "Jews," the name being derived from "Judah." When the kingdom of Judah was about to be carried into captivity, the name was used a few times in the book of Jeremiah. During the captivity and thereafter "Jew" became the common name of all the people. They were proud of the name "Jew" and of what, in their estimation, the name stood for. And they gloried in God and not in idols. They were confident that they were able to teach all who foolishly worshiped idols. Their privileges, their belief in the one God, and their knowledge of his will, should have made them humble and ashamed that they had made such poor use of their privileges and blessings; but, instead of that, they were boastful, and they maintained an air of superiority over all other people. And so every blessing has its corresponding danger. Is there not danger that we fall into a similar state of mind? We have the Bible, abhor creeds, glory in the name we wear, and feel able to teach the whole world. Are we not inclined to be proud and arrogant? Should we not rather feel humble and ashamed that we have not made better use of what we have?

Verses 21-23: *Thou therefore that teachest another, teachest thou not thyself? thou that preachest a man should not steal, dost thou steal? thou that sayest a man should not commit adultery, dost thou commit adultery? thou that abhorrest idols, dost thou rob temples? thou who gloriest in the law, through thy transgression of the law dishonorest thou God?* These are searching questions. Any man is a poor teacher if he does not teach himself while he is teaching others. He is a poor preacher that cannot preach better than he can practice, but he is a poorer preacher if he does not try hard to live up to his preaching. The Jews had reached the point where they taught much and practiced little. We are reminded of what Jesus said of the Jewish leaders: "They say, and do not." No one should be guilty of adultery, and certainly the man who preaches against it should not be guilty of it. The American Standard Version's rendering of the question about abhorring idols and robbing temples is not easily understood. But the word translated "rob temples" means either *to rob temples or to commit sacrilege.* The meanings are closely related; for, if a person robbed a temple, he would, in the estimation of the worshipers at that temple, commit sacrilege. To commit sacrilege is to abuse sacred things, or to make common use of them. The Jews were very much given to profaning God's holy things. Ezekiel 22:26 makes this charge: "Her priests have done violence to my law, and have profaned my holy things." He immediately explains how they had done this: "They have made no distinction between the holy and the common, neither have they caused men to discern between the clean and the unclean." They had profaned God's holy things by putting the common and the unclean—things of their own devising— into the worship and service of God. The Jews in Paul's day had profaned God's holy things by their traditions and in converting the temple into a place of merchandise and fraud. In many ways they committed sacrilege, but it is not so manifest that they robbed temples. Hence, on this point the rendering of the King James Version seems better: "Thou that abhorrest idols, dost thou commit sacrilege?" What avails it, if a person abhors idols and yet is so disrespectful to God as to commit sacrilege against God's holy things? It would be difficult to tell whether the idolater or the professed believer who commits sacrilege dishonors God the more. The Jews gloried in the law—gloried in the fact that the law had been given to them; yet in their transgressions of the law they dishonored God's law.

Verse 24: *For the name of God is blasphemed among the Gentiles because of you, even as it is written.* The Jews sought to make proselytes. Jesus said they would compass sea and land to make one proselyte. They might have had great success, if they had lived up to their preaching. It is hard to make any one believe there is any good in your doctrine, if it has not done you any good. The Jews had so lived as to cause the Gentiles to blaspheme their preaching instead of believing it. The Jews had become a hiss and a byword. Read Isaiah 52:5.

The greatest hindrance to the spread of the gospel today is the conduct of many of its professed believers. Immorality, worldly-mindedness, dishonest dealing, and divisions hinder Christianity. Opposition from without is not what hurts the most. The right kind of living on the part of professed Christians gives them a favorable hearing when they present the gospel. Do not try to sell the gospel by mere talk; show them a sample of what the gospel will do for the people who really believe it. You will then likely make a believer instead of a blasphemer. "Even so let your light shine before men; that they may see your good works, and glorify your Father who is in heaven" (Mt. 5:16).

Verse 25: *For circumcision indeed profiteth, if thou be a doer of the law: but if thou be a transgressor of the law, thy circumcision is become uncircumcision.* Of circumcision God said to Abraham: "It shall be a token of a covenant betwixt me and you." Descendants of Abraham and Jacob were not brought into the covenant by circumcision; they were born into that covenant, and were circumcised as a sign of their membership in the covenant. If one was not circumcised, he was cut off from his covenant relationship. "And the uncircumcised male who is not circumcised in the flesh of his foreskin, that soul shall be cut off from his people; he hath broken my covenant" (Gen. 17:14). Hence, to the Jew circumcision was indispensable to continued membership in the covenant; and it was profitable to him, if he lived in obedience to God. But if he did not obey God's commands, his circumcision was worthless to him; he was the same as if he had not been circumcised. It was a sign, or token, of the covenant. Paul was seeking to show the Jews that this sign of covenant relationship was worthless to the one who did not live up to the covenant requirements. What avails it for me to show a written covenant between me and another man, if he can show that I have broken every covenant requirement? If he can do so, it is the same as if I had no written contract. And that fairly represents the condition of the Jew. Why boast of being circumcised and of having the law, if he had broken the covenant? The Jew put stress upon the sign and not the substance. He boasted of the covenant, and broke it every day.

Verse 26: *If therefore the uncircumcision keep the ordinances of the law, shall not his uncircumcision be reckoned for circumcision?* Paul had just stated the doctrine that circumcision was of no value to the person who did not live right. But what of the Gentile who lived in harmony with the moral requirements of the law, though he had not been circumcised? In not being circumcised the Gentile violated no law, for the law did not require the Gentile to be circumcised. Hence, the Gentile could neglect circumcision without sin; and if he lived a moral upright life, he would be considered as if he had been circumcised. But Paul's reasoning on this point does not warrant any one to neglect anything God has commanded him to do. It is singular that, in their anxiety to get rid of the necessity of baptism, some have argued that Paul's reasoning on circumcision could be applied to baptism. They ask: "If an unbaptized person lives right, shall he not be considered as if he had been baptized?" But their effort at running that sort of parallel fails. Gentiles had not been commanded to be circumcised, and therefore violated no law, committed no sin, in not being circumcised; whereas gospel obedience, including baptism, is required of all people. And here is another point their theory fails to consider. Every one to whom the command to be circumcised extended had to be circumcised or be cut off from his people; he had broken the covenant, and was no longer considered one of God's people. If, therefore, these theologians could establish a parallel between circumcision and baptism, they would thereby prove that every one to whom the command to be baptized extended would have to be baptized or be cut off.

But Paul does not affirm that any Gentile had so kept the ordinances of the law as to be sinless. In fact, his purpose was to make all men see themselves as condemned sinners and to cause them to realize their need of salvation through Christ.

Verse 27: *And shall not the uncircumcision which is by nature, if it fulfill the law, judge thee, who with the letter and circumcision art a transgressor of the law?* Some commentators regard this as a direct affirmation instead of a question. But it matters little whether it is a question or an affirmation; in either form the meaning is the same. "The uncircumcised by nature" are the Gentiles. "Judge" is here used in the sense of condemn. "The letter" refers to the law of Moses. The Jews had the law and were circumcised. Paul, therefore, affirms that the Gentile, if he fulfilled the law, would condemn the Jew. This does not mean that the right-living Gentile would sit in final judgment on the disobedient Jew, but that his conduct by contrast condemns the Jewish transgressor, just as Noah by his obedience, condemned the world (Heb. 11:7).

Verses 28, 29: *For he is not a Jew who is one outwardly; neither is that circumcision which is outward in the flesh: but he is a Jew who is one inwardly; and circumcision is that of the heart, in the spirit not in the letter; whose praise is not of men, but of God.* So far as the flesh was concerned, a Jew was a Jew, no matter how he lived; but he was not God's Jew, not such a one as God would recognize, unless he was at heart true to God. Outward circumcision was necessary to a Jew, but outward circumcision was worthless unless it was accompanied by the circumcision of the heart. Circumcision of the heart is the cutting off of the stubbornness and sinful desires of the heart. So many of the Jews depended on outward appearance, but were inwardly full of corruption. In God's sight an honest-hearted Gentile was better than a corrupt Jew. Man looks on the outward appearance, and praises show and display; God looks on the heart, and praises honesty and virtue.

Chapter 3

3:1 What advantage then hath the Jew? or what is the profit of circumcision?
2 Much every way: first of all, that they were intrusted with the oracles of God.
3 For what if some were without faith? shall their want of faith make of none
effect the faithfulness of God? 4 God forbid: yea, let God be found true, but
every man a liar; as it is written,

That thou mightest be justified in thy words,
And mightest prevail when thou comest into judgment.

5 But if our unrighteousness commendeth the righteousness of God, what shall
we say? Is God unrighteous who visiteth with wrath? (I speak after the manner
of men.) 6 God forbid: for then how shall God judge the world? 7 But if the
truth of God through my lie abounded unto his glory, why am I also still judged
as a sinner? 8 and why not (as we are slanderously reported, and as some affirm
that we say), Let us do evil, that good may come? whose condemnation is just.

9 What then? are we better than they? No, in no wise: for we before laid
to the charge both of Jews and Greeks, that they are all under sin; 10 as it is
written,

There is none righteous, no, not one:
11 There is none that understandeth,
There is none that seeketh after God;
12 They have all turned aside, they are together become unprofitable;
There is none that doeth good, no, not so much as one:
13 Their throat is an open sepulchre;
With their tongues they have used deceit:
The poison of asps is under their lips:
14 Whose mouth is full of cursing and bitterness:
15 Their feet are swift to shed blood;
16 Destruction and misery are in their ways:
17 And the way of peace have they not known:
18 There is no fear of God before their eyes.

19 Now we know that what things soever the law saith, it speaketh to them
that are under the law; that every mouth may be stopped, and all the world may
be brought under the judgment of God: 20 because by the works of the law shall
no flesh be justified in his sight: for through the law cometh the knowledge of sin.

21 But now apart from the law a righteousness of God hath been manifested,
being witnessed by the law and the prophets; 22 even the righteousness of God
through faith in Jesus Christ unto all them that believe: for there is no distinction;
23 for all have sinned, and fall short of the glory of God; 24 being justified freely
by his grace through the redemption that is in Christ Jesus: 25 whom God set
forth to be a propitiation, through faith, in his blood, to show his righteousness
because of the passing over of the sins done aforetime, in the forbearance of God:
26 for the showing, I say, of his righteousness at this present season: that he might
himself be just, and the justifier of him that hath faith in Jesus. 27 Where then
is the glorying? It is excluded. By what manner of law? of works? Nay: but
by a law of faith. 28 We reckon therefore that a man is justified by faith apart
from the works of the law. 29 Or is God the God of Jews only? is he not the God
of Gentiles also? Yea, of Gentiles also: 30 if so be that God is one, and he shall
justify the circumcision by faith, and the uncircumcision through faith.

31 Do we then make the law of none effect through faith? God forbid: nay,
we establish the law.

Verse 1: *What advantage then hath the Jew? or what is the profit of circumcision?* The proud hearted Jew resented any idea that put him on a level with the people of other nations. To the Jew who prided himself on being a Jew and who put stress on outward show it would seem that Paul was seeking to make it appear that there was no advantage in being a Jew and no profit in circumcision. Paul was here anticipating an objection of the Jew. Paul did not give a full answer to such an objection.

Verse 2: *Much every way: first of all, that they were intrusted with the oracles of God.* The Jews had enjoyed many blessings and advantages, including a land of their own; but their chief profit or advantage was, that they had been intrusted with the oracles of God. "The oracles of God" included all that we find in what we now know as the Old Testament— having that intrusted to them was the Jews' chief advantage, their greatest profit. How much greater is our advantage in having also the New Testament. The Jews "received the law as it was ordained by angels, and kept it not" (Acts 7:53).

Verses 3, 4: *For what if some were without faith? shall their want of faith make of none effect the faithfulness of God? God forbid: yea, let God be found true, but every man a liar; as it is written, That thou mightest be justified in thy words, And mightest prevail when thou comest into judgment.* God had promised to bless the Jews. If he failed to bless them, even though they sinned, would he not be false to his promise? Would their lack of faith interfere with God's promise? But God's promises are conditional. No matter what theories people may have, we must let

God be true, even if we must regard all theories as
false and every man a liar. Only in that way can we
be justified in our words and prevail when we come
into judgment.

Verses 5, 6: *But if our unrighteousness commendeth the righteousness of God, what shall we say? Is
God unrighteous who visiteth with wrath?* That this
is another objection that a Jew might make is shown
by the fact that Paul immediately adds, "*(I speak
after the manner of men.)*" The possible objection
is stated in a very cautious way. If man's sin is the
occasion of God's displaying his plan of righteousness
through the gospel, then what shall we conclude? Shall
we conclude that God is unrighteous in punishing us
for living so as to cause him to make such a display
of his righteousness? *God forbid,* or May it not be
so. If it were so, *then how shall God judge the world?*

Verses 7, 8: *But if the truth of God through my
lie abounded unto his glory, why am I also still judged
as a sinner?* The Jew regarded Christianity as a lie
and that Paul's preaching it made it his lie, and that
in forsaking Judaism for Christianity he committed
about the greatest sin that a Jew could commit. Paul
is here adopting the objector's method of reasoning.
If you justify your sins on the grounds that your sins
brought out and displayed God's righteousness, why
condemn me for what you consider my great sin? On
that theory, *"why not (as we are slanderously reported, and as some affirm that we say), let us do evil,
that good may come?"* If the theory stated in the objection were correct, then the more we sin, the better
it would be for us. But Paul adds that the condemnation of such slanderers is just.

Verse 9: *What then? are we better than they?*
Are we Jews better than the Gentiles? *No, in no wise:
for we before laid to the charge both of Jews and
Greeks, that they are all under sin.* To prove that all
were under sin had been the object of all that he had
said from the eighteenth verse of chapter one. This
he had done to prove that all were under condemnation and needed the gospel as God's power to save
them. To further establish the sinfulness of man, he
quotes extensively from the prophets.

"What then? are we better than they?" These
are questions a Jew would ask after hearing Paul's
reasoning in the preceding verses. The Jew had so
many advantages he would naturally think himself
better than others. But he had made such poor use
of these advantages that Paul unhesitatingly answers:
"No, in no wise: for we before laid to the charge both
of Jews and Greeks, that they are all under sin." The
Jew had not lived up to the law, and therefore was not
justified; the Gentile had also failed of justification,
for he had not lived up to the light he had. So far
as meriting justification was concerned, neither was
superior to the other, for they were all sinners.

Verses 10, 11: *As it is written, There is none righteous, no not one; There is none that understandeth,
There is none that seeketh after God.* Paul gives a
number of quotations from the Old Testament Scriptures to prove from their own prophets the sinfulness
of the Jews. After making the general statement that
none of them were righteous, Paul shows wherein they
were sinful.

The Jews were great students of their Scriptures,
and yet they did not understand. Wherein they had

an accurate understanding of the requirements of the law, they failed to understand the significance of the things required. They did not understand that their whole system was temporary and typical. In their estimation the whole system of Judaism was God's permanent order of things, and they were always to be God's special people. But Jesus used language about them more pointed than the language Paul quotes —"blind guides," "fools and blind." To those who were supposed to be especially skilled in the law Jesus said: "Woe unto you lawyers! for ye took away the key of knowledge." Even the key to a correct understanding of their Scriptures had been hidden in the rubbish of their notions or traditions. Let those who think the Jews had such an accurate understanding of kingdom matters consider what Jesus and his inspired apostle said about them.

There is none that seeketh after God. Perhaps no people ever studied the Scriptures more than did the Jews; yet they were not seeking after God. To seek after God is to seek to know and to do his will—to make his thoughts our thoughts and his ways our ways. Pharisees, lawyers, and scribes studied that they might be informed and formally correct, so that they might stand well with their fellow Jews. Instead of seeking to be justified in the sight of God, they sought to justify themselves in the sight of men. Jesus said to them: "Ye are they that justify yourselves in the sight of men; but God knoweth your hearts: for that which is exalted among men is an abomination in the sight of God" (Luke 16:15). They loved the praise of men more than the praise of God (John 12:43). Such a frame of mind utterly unfitted them for heart-seeking after God. "How can ye believe, who receive glory one of another, and the glory that cometh from the only God ye seek not?" (John 5:44). When a person studies the Scriptures for any other purpose than to know God and to be able to do his will, there is no telling what sort of absurd conclusions he may arrive at. "And let us know, let us follow on to know Jehovah" (Hos. 6:3).

Verse 12: *They have all turned aside, they are together become unprofitable; There is none that doeth good, no, not so much as one.* This, because they did not understand and would not seek after God. To Jehovah they were not profitable—he could not use them in his plans. But they were not born in that condition, but had turned aside and become unprofitable. None were absolutely good—all had sinned.

Verse 13: *Their throat is an open sepulchre; With their tongues they have used deceit: The poison of asps is under their lips.* That is a strong figure of speech. From their throats would come words as offensive as the odors from an open sepulchre. How expressive of the filthiness of their speech! Deceit was one of the sins charged against the Gentiles. Now the Jews are also charged with the same sin. No dependence can be put in what a deceitful person says. Paul also charges that their words were poison like the poison of asps, that their mouth was full of bitterness and cursing. A deceitful person is a liar for gain of some sort, but he expects every one to believe him; and if you find out that he is a liar, he becomes bitter toward you.

Verse 15: *Their feet are swift to shed blood.* This expresses their readiness to murder. From the trial of Jesus we learn that even their high court sometimes was eager to murder an innocent victim.

Verse 16: *Destruction and misery are in their ways.* They had come to be a turbulent race. Read what Josephus says took place inside Jerusalem while the Roman army laid siege to that unfortunate city.

Verses 17, 18: *And the ways of peace have they not known: There is no fear of God before their eyes.* Had they loved peace, they could have found it. They did not know how to be peaceable. On this point Jesus testified against them. "And when he drew nigh, he saw the city, and wept over it, saying, If thou hadst known in this day, even thou, the things which belong unto peace! but now they are hid from thine eyes." That Jesus here referred to their social and political peace is clear from what he immediately adds: "For the days shall come upon thee, when thine enemies shall cast up a bank about thee" (Luke 19:41-44). They did not know how to be at peace with God nor man. And here is the reason: "There is no fear of God before their eyes." They had no reverence for God, and therefore no regard for their fellow man.

Verse 19: *Now we know that what things soever the law saith, it speaketh to them that are under the law: that every mouth may be stopped, and all the world may be brought under the judgment of God.* Here the entire Old Testament is referred to as the law, for Paul had been quoting from various parts of the Old Testament. What he had quoted were, therefore, words directed to the Jews—they were guilty of the crimes mentioned in the quotations. "That every mouth may be stopped." That all might so feel their guilt as to be unable to answer back or make any defense. The Jews could not deny what their own inspired prophets had said. "And all the world may be brought under the judgment of God." The Jew readily granted that the Gentile was under the judgment of God, and now Paul proves from the Jewish Scriptures that the Jew was likewise under the judgment of God.

Verse 20: *Because by the works of the law shall no flesh be justified in his sight; for through the law cometh the knowledge of sin.* Had they kept the law perfectly, they would have been justified by the law; but Paul had proved by their own Scriptures that they had not so kept the law. He had shown them to be guilty of many and grievous sins; "for through the law cometh the knowledge of sin." That which might have been the means of their justification had, on account of their sins, become the means of their conviction. This conviction, this feeling of sinfulness, did not come to them through some direct operation of the Holy Spirit, but through the plain statements of inspired men.

One Point Established.—In the portion of the letter that we have considered, Paul showed that the Gentile, while relying upon natural law as his human wisdom interpreted it, had plunged into all sorts of sin. He had not even lived up to the law of nature. Paul also showed that the Jew, instead of living up to the demands of the law of Moses so as to be justified by it, had so transgressed the law as to be condemned by it. All, both Jews and Gentiles, were condemned sinners, and were lost, unless some plan could be presented that would make righteous men out of sinners. The law would justify a man, if he kept it perfectly;

but it could not justify one after he had transgressed the law.

Verse 21: *But now apart from law, a righteousness of God hath been manifested, being witnessed by the law and the prophets.* (American Bible Union Version.) In Paul's language, the term "the law" refers to the law of Moses. The American Standard Version has "apart from the law," but there is no "the" in this phrase in the Greek. This righteousness was "apart from law," any law, whether the law of Moses or the law under which Gentiles lived.

The "now" is emphatic—now, in the present case, or in the present dispensation, a plan of righteousness has been manifested, made known, or brought to light. This plan is distinct from law. And yet the Jew should not have been astonished at the inauguration of this new plan of righteousness, for both the law and the prophets had borne witness concerning this plan of righteousness—"being witnessed by the law and the prophets."

"Being borne witness to. It was not a *new doctrine;* it was found in the Old Testament. The apostle makes this observation with special reference to the Jews. He does not declare any new thing, but that which was fully declared in their own sacred writings." (Barnes' "Notes on the Epistle to the Romans.") Barnes was a Presbyterian, and usually fairly clear-headed; but it is impossible for a person who does not comprehend God's plan of human redemption to see clearly some points. Paul does not say that this plan of righteousness was taught and developed by the law and the prophets, but that they bore witness, gave their testimony, concerning this plan of righteousness which was now, apart from the law, brought to light.

But how witnessed by the law and the prophets? The tabernacle, with its various services and offerings, was a type of the better things to come. In speaking of these things, Paul adds this explanatory clause, "Which is a figure for the time present," or for the present time (Heb. 9:9). In this way, and also in God's promise to Abraham, the law testified, or gave witness, concerning this plan of righteousness. And the prophets also gave their testimony concerning this plan of salvation through Christ, this plan that has now been manifested, or brought into view.

Dislocating or Perverting Prophecy—A future-kingdom advocate makes this bold statement: *"But the Old Testament knows nothing whatever of Christianity!"* That is, there is not a prophecy in the Old Testament concerning the gospel plan of salvation! Can you believe it? Yet that expresses boldly what is generally believed by the future-kingdom folks. But, in saying that the prophets gave witness concerning this plan of righteousness now made known, Paul flatly contradicts such assertions. In such teaching, these folks are not speculating about unfulfilled prophecies, so much as they are dislocating prophecies. They are taking prophecies that have been fulfilled, and prophecies that are now in the process of fulfillment, and setting them forward as prophecies that are yet unfulfilled. If they did no more than speculate about unfulfilled prophecies, their talk would not be worth considering. I deplore the fact that brethren have given them a decided advantage by referring to their theories as "speculation about unfulfilled prophecy." When they say that the land of promise to Abraham

has not been fulfilled; that the prophecies concerning
the restoration of the Jews have not been fulfilled;
that the prophecy of Dan. 2:44 is not fulfilled in the
church; that the prophecy that Christ would sit on
David's throne has not been fulfilled; and then you
say, "Oh, yes; more speculation about unfulfilled
prophecy," have you not conceded every point they
claim? They say that these prophecies have not been
fulfilled, and you agree with them by referring to their
perversions as "speculations about unfulfilled prophecy." And when they say that none of the prophecies
of the Old Testament refer to this gospel plan of salvation through Christ, why yield that point to them
by calling such talk "speculation about unfulfilled
prophecy?" I know of no greater perversion of Scripture than to say that none of the prophecies of the
Old Testament refer to this present dispensation!

Paul said the gospel to which he had been separated
had been promised afore through the prophets in the
Holy Scriptures (Rom. 1:1). Jesus said that it had
been written in the prophets that repentance and remission of sins should be preached in his name among
all nations beginning at Jerusalem (Luke 24:45-48).
But why multiply Scriptures? The idea that the prophets said nothing of this "church age" was never heard
of till some became wiser in their own minds than the
apostles and Jesus Christ! And I have been astound-
ed beyond expression to hear brethren continually
refer to such perversions of Scripture as "speculation
about unfulfilled prophecy"!

Verses 22-24: *Even the righteousness of God
through faith in Jesus Christ unto all them that believe; for there is no distinction; for all have sinned,*

and fall short of the glory of God; being justified freely by his grace through the redemption that is in Christ Jesus. Verses 21-24 connects closely with chapter 1, verses 16 and 17. This righteousness which is apart from the law is attained through faith in Jesus Christ; and it is for all who believe, for there is no distinction between Jew and Gentile. All, both Jew and Gentile, need this gospel salvation; for all have sinned—all have come short of the glory of God. This salvation for all was according to God's plan and purpose.

No Distinction.—God had chosen Abraham and his seed for a special purpose. The Jews had failed to grasp God's purpose; they thought of Jehovah as their God, and no one else's. In their thinking he was a tribal, or national, God. It took a special miracle to convince Peter that Jehovah was the God of any but the Jews. To correct this deep-seated idea among the Jews, Paul frequently reminded the Jewish Christians that now there was no distinction between Jews and Gentiles. Some of the Jewish Christians never did get over that tribal idea, and drifted into a sect known as Ebionites. It is a pity that some brethren of late years have revived, slightly modified, perhaps, the Jewish idea that Jehovah is the Jew's national God.

Let us read Rom. 3:21-24, leaving out an apparent parenthetical expression: "But now apart from the law a righteousness of God hath been manifested, being witnessed by the law and the prophets; even the righteousness of God through faith in Jesus Christ unto all them that believe; . . . being justified freely by his grace through the redemption that is in Christ Jesus." To justify a person is to declare him free from guilt. Law cannot declare a person just, or free from guilt, if he had violated it in only one point. Justification by law was impossible, for all sinned. But apart from the law, a plan of righteousness had been revealed. The apostle tells us that this justification is free; and he further emphasizes the fact that it is free by adding that it is by grace. It is bestowed gratuitously. It is not arrived at by merit, but comes by grace. And it is by faith. By the term "faith" Paul means all that is implied in accepting Jesus Christ as our Savior, Prophet, Priest, and King. This will later be discussed more fully. The justification that is offered apart from the law is also through the redemption that is in Christ Jesus, or by Christ Jesus. It is by what he did that we have redemption.

SOME TERMS DEFINED

Just here it might be well to study some words Paul uses. It stands to reason that no one can understand a passage of Scripture unless he understands the words of the passage. In studying these words we shall consider only those meanings that relate to the salvation of sinners.

Justify—To justify a person is to pronounce him just, or righteous; to declare him not guilty. Of course, if a person kept the law perfectly, he would be justified; he would be declared not guilty. If God forgives a sinner, there is then nothing against him. He is free from guilt—he is as righteous as if he had never sinned.

Grace—Grace is favor. It is a benefit bestowed without pay—the gratuitous bestowal of a thing that a person needs. The sinner needs forgiveness—needs to be righteous. Only through God's grace is it possible for a sinner to be forgiven, or to be justified. No matter how many things he may be required to do as conditions of forgiveness, it does not destroy the fact that, on God's part, his forgiveness and justification are wholly of grace. No amount of works will destroy the fact that forgiveness is by grace.

Redeemer—A redeemer is one who rescues another from bondage, or liberates another from any condition wherein he is held. Jesus redeems us from the bondage of sin and from the power of the devil. He is our only Redeemer.

Ransom—Ransom is the price for redeeming. Jesus came "to give his life a ransom for many" (Matt. 20:28; Mark 10:45). Hence, he became that which is given in exchange for another as the price of his redemption (1 Tim. 2:6). "Christ died for the ungodly" (Rom. 5:6). "Who gave himself for us, that he might redeem us from all iniquity, and purify unto himself a people for his own possession, zealous of good works" (Tit. 2:14).

Redemption—Redemption is the act of redeeming. Christ is called "redemption," because the whole process of redemption is centered in him (1 Cor. 1:30).

Jesus is our Redeemer—no one else can rescue us from the bondage of sin. He is also our Ransom, for he was the price paid for our redemption. And in him God graciously provided a means by which sinners can be justified.

Verses 25, 26: *Whom God set forth to be a propitiation, through faith, in his blood, to show his righteousness because of the passing over of the sins done aforetime, in the forbearance of God; for the showing, I say, of his righteousness at this present season:*

*that he might himself be just and the justifier of him
that hath faith in Jesus.* "Whom God set forth"—
that is, publicly exhibited him. To propitiate is to
appease, to render favorable. When Jacob was to meet
Esau, he sent gifts to Esau to appease his wrath, to
cause him to have a more favorable feeling toward
Jacob. It is not meant that God was angry toward
the sinner in the sense that men become angry. On
the contrary, the whole plan of redemption grew out
of God's pity and compassion for sinful men. But
God's law had been violated, his authority had been
disregarded, and man was under condemnation. There
is, so to speak, such a thing as legal or judicial wrath.
A judge and a jury may find that a man is guilty as
charged in the indictment; and yet the man's sorrow
and repentance may be so manifest that both judge
and jury would earnestly wish that there might be
some way to clear him, and at the same time uphold
the majesty of the law; but there is no way that they
can show that they are right in freeing him. To maintain the law they must condemn him. Let that serve
as a faint illustration. God's law had been violated
again and again; and yet in this present dispensation
he was justifying sinners; and he had passed over the
sins done aforetime—that is, sins committed under
the former dispensation. How could he show that he
was just in so doing? To ignore sins, or to treat
them with indifference, would wreck his moral government. He must be just and the majesty of his law
upheld. Justice demands that the guilty be punished,
and the majesty of the law requires that the penalties
of the law be inflicted on the guilty. How, then, could
God be just in passing over the sins of the former

dispensation and in justifying sinners in the present time? Only because Jesus died for us. He suffered the penalties of the violated law. Even though he paid the penalty for our redemption from sin and death, he forces no one to accept the freedom he purchased. The plan arranges only that those who now believe in Jesus may be justified. In the light of the foregoing comments re-read verses 25, 26. The death of Christ made it possible for God to be righteous in passing over the sins committed before the coming of Christ, for the sacrifices they offered pointed to Christ; the death of Christ made it possible also for God to be just while justifying sinners now, who believe in Christ.

Verse 27: *Where then is the glorying? It is excluded. By what manner of law? of works? Nay: but by a law of faith.* If a man were to live a perfect life, he would have grounds for boasting that he had always done the right thing, that no taint of sin ever soiled his spotless life, and that he stood justified on his own record. But none so lived, for all have sinned. In recognizing one's self as a condemned sinner, there is a cause for humility, but no grounds for boasting. And the greatest ground for humility is the knowledge that an innocent Person died to save me from my own folly. Instead of being the proud possessor of a spotless character, I have to rely on another to cleanse me from my own defilement. And this depending on the innocent to justify the guilty is what Paul calls the "law of faith." This law of faith is the plan, or arrangement, in which is required faith in Jesus, who died for us.

Verse 28: *We reckon therefore that a man is justified by faith apart from the works of the law.* Here we may draw hurtful conclusions, if we do not keep in mind Paul's line of argument. Paul is not contrasting faith and the obedience of faith, but he is contrasting justification by works of law and justification by faith. In chapter 1:5 he speaks of "the obedience of faith" —that is, obedience of which faith is the source or foundation—an obedient faith. Works of law is an entirely different thing from obedience of faith. When Paul talks about faith, he means an obedient faith. Many have stumbled through Romans without ever recognizing the fact that Paul makes that plain in the very beginning of his letter. To make works of law refer to the obedience of faith is to enshroud ourselves in a fog of confusion from which we will not be able to emerge with any clear ideas of the gospel plan of salvation. To be justified by works of law requires that works, as measured by law, be perfect. A sinner can never be justified by works of law, for no amount of works will change the fact that he has sinned. But the death of Christ made it possible for those who believe in him to be justified. But just here another hurtful error has been made—namely, the limiting of faith to an acceptance of him as a sacrifice for our sins. Faith is decidedly too limited in scope, if it does not include also submission to Jesus as our King; for Jesus will save no one in whose heart he is not allowed to reign as King. But the death of Jesus for all made it possible for all to be saved.

Verses 29, 30: *Or is God the God of Jews only? is he not the God of Gentiles also? Yes, of Gentiles also: if so be that God is one, and he shall justify the circumcision by faith, and the uncircumcision through faith.* The Jews did not think that God would recognize a Gentile, unless he became a part of the Jewish nation. In their estimation he was the God of the Jews only—a tribal, or national, God. Many of the early Christians of Jerusalem taught that Gentile Christians had to be circumcised and keep the law, or they could not be saved. They could see no salvation for any but Jews; hence, they demanded that Gentile Christians become Jews. It is a pity that this tribal idea of God is now being advocated, with slight modifications, by Christians among Gentiles. Paul had much contention with those who had that conception of God. This one verse, properly considered, will destroy any such false conceptions of God. He is the God of both Jews and Gentiles—the God of all nations. He is equally related to all and all are equally related to him, for he is one. He is not one kind of God to the Jews and another to the Gentiles.

It would seem that Paul meant to make a distinction between the phrases "by faith" and "through faith," else why use the two phrases? But the distinction, if any, is too subtle for me to discover.

Verse 31: *Do we then make the law of none effect through faith? God forbid: nay, we establish the law.* With the Seventh-Day adventists "the law" means the Ten Commandments. They use this passage in an effort to prove that "the law" is not abolished in Christ, but established. But, unfortunately for their argument, the article "the" is not before law in the Greek in this verse. The marginal reading of the American Standard Version shows that to be true. "Do we then make law of none effect through faith? God forbid: nay, we establish law." In claiming that "the law" is the Ten Commandments they lose their argument in this passage, for Paul does not use "the" before law in this verse. We do not make any law of none effect through faith. Law here evidently is that universal rule of right and wrong that is binding on all nations and peoples of all time. That law is established by faith.

But how do we establish law by faith? Certainly not in the sense that we set it up or make it binding. But if we come to the Lord Jesus Christ that we may be forgiven of sins committed against the universal moral law, do we not thereby show that we recognize its binding force?

Chapter 4

4:1 What then shall we say that Abraham, our forefather, hath found according to the flesh? 2 For if Abraham was justified by works, he hath whereof to glory; but not toward God. 3 For what saith the scripture? And Abraham believed God, and it was reckoned unto him for righteousness. 4 Now to him that worketh, the reward is not reckoned as of grace, but as of debt. 5 But to him that worketh not, but believeth on him' that justifieth the ungodly, his faith is reckoned for righteousness. 6 Even as David also pronounceth blessing upon the man, unto whom God reckoneth righteousness apart from works, 7 saying,

Blessed are they whose iniquities are forgiven,
And whose sins are covered.

8 Blessed is the man to whom the Lord will not reckon sin.
9 Is this blessing then pronounced upon the circumcision, or upon the uncircumcision also? for we say, To Abraham his faith was reckoned for righteousness. 10 How then was it reckoned? when he was in circumcision, or in uncircumcision? Not in circumcision, but in uncircumcision: 11 and he received the sign of circumcision, a seal of the righteousness of the faith which he had while he was in uncircumcision: that he might be the father of all them that believe, though they be in uncircumcision, that righteousness might be reckoned unto them: 12 and the father of circumcision to them who not only are of the circumcision, but who also walk in the steps of that faith of our father Abraham which he had in uncircumcision. 13 For not through the law was the promise to Abraham or to his seed that he should be heir of the world, but through the righteousness of faith. 14 For if they that are of the law are heirs, faith is made void, and the promise is made of none effect: 15 for the law worketh wrath; but where there is no law, neither is there transgression. 16 For this cause it is of faith, that it may be according to grace: to the end that the promise may be sure to all the seed; not to that only which is of the law, but to that also which is of the faith of Abraham, who is the father of us all 17 (as it is written, A father of many nations have I made thee) before him whom he believed, even God, who giveth life to the dead, and calleth the things that are not, as though they were. 18 Who in hope believed against hope, to the end that he might become a father of many nations, according to that which had been spoken. So shall thy seed be. 19 And without being weakened in faith he considered his own body now as good as dead (he being about a hundred years old), and the deadness of Sarah's womb; 20 yet, looking unto the promise of God, he wavered not through unbelief, but waxed strong through faith, giving glory to God, 21 and being fully assured that what he had promised, he was able also to perform. 22 Wherefore also it was reckoned unto him for righteousness. 23 Now it was not written for his sake alone, that it was reckoned unto him: 24 but for our sake also, unto whom it shall be reckoned, who believe on him that raised Jesus our Lord from the dead, 25 who was delivered up for our trespasses, and was raised for our justification.

Verses 1, 2: *What then shall we say that Abraham, our forefather, hath found according to the flesh? For if Abraham was justified by works, he hath whereof to glory; but not toward God.* To see clearly the meaning of an author it is necessary that we get his background, and be able to grasp the purpose of his writing. Why did Paul labor so earnestly to set forth the distinction between the law and the gospel and to prove that men are justified by faith, and not by works of law? In much of what he said in Romans, Galatians, and Hebrews, he set forth plainly that the gospel was a thing apart from the law of Moses, that the law ended at the cross, and that the gospel is God's perfected plan for man's redemption. But what was back of all this effort? What special need was there for so much teaching along that line? The reader will also find some very pointed teaching along the same line in Second Corinthians, Ephesians, and Colossians. Why was it so necessary that all the churches be informed along these lines?

The first converts to Christ were Jews. They were so wedded to the law of Moses that they broke away from it slowly. At first they thought the gospel was for Jews only. The conversion of Cornelius convinced them that God had also granted to the Gentiles repentance unto life (Acts 11:18). But they still thought and contended that these Gentile Christians had to keep the law of Moses. After the church was planted at Antioch, "certain men came down from Judea and taught the brethren, saying, Except ye be circumcised after the custom of Moses, ye cannot be saved" (Acts 15:1). When appeal was made to the apostles and elders in Jerusalem, the Holy Spirit through them decreed that the Gentiles should not be required to keep the law. But this decree did not stop the mouths of some of these extreme Judaizing Christians. These went about among the churches, making much trouble in the churches where there were Gentile members. They sought to make the church a mere sect of the Jews and the gospel a sort of adjunct to the law of Moses. Judging from a human standpoint, they would have succeeded had it not been for Paul. Because he fought them on every point of their contentions, they were his bitter enemies.

A little thought will enable one to see that Paul's whole line of reasoning along these lines was directed against the contention of these Judaizing Christians, and not toward the unbelieving Jews. When he dealt with the unbelieving Jews, he sought to convince them that Jesus was the Christ of whom the prophets spoke. It would have been useless to argue to one who did not believe in Jesus as the Christ that the law ended at the cross and that the Jew had become dead to the law that he might be married to Christ Jesus; but it was eminently fitting to so argue to one who believed in Christ and yet held that the law was still binding. It was necessary also to indoctrinate the churches on this point so as to limit the pernicious influence of these Judaizers.

These Judaizers put stress on their fleshly relation to Abraham and on the fleshly mark of circumcision. In effect Paul said to them: "You put so much stress on the flesh, now tell us what Abraham obtained according to the flesh. He came out of heathenism, and therefore had no fleshly connections of which he could boast, and he was also justified before he was circumcised. He was not justified by works, and therefore could not boast toward God." Then he quotes the Scriptures to remind them that Abraham was justified on a plan contrary to their contention.

Verse 3: *For what saith the scripture? And Abra-*

ham believed God, and it was reckoned unto him for righteousness. This is a quotation from Gen. 15:6. Jehovah had just promised Abraham a son and a posterity as numberless as the stars, though he was old and Sarah was past the age of childbearing. "And Abraham believed God, and it was reckoned unto him for righteousness." One of the strangest things in all the field of Bible exegesis is the contention so generally made that this language refers to the justification of Abraham as an alien sinner. It seems to be taken for granted that up to the time spoken of in this verse he was an unforgiven, condemned sinner. It has been argued that Paul here spoke of Abraham's justification as a sinner and that James (2:21-24) spoke of his justification as a righteous man. It is surprising that any person at all familiar with the history of Abraham would so contend, for the facts are all against such a supposition. But what are the facts? For a number of years previous to the promise to Abraham of a son and numerous posterity Abraham had been a faithful servant of God. Consider carefully the following facts:

1. God had appeared to Abraham in Ur of the Chaldees and commanded him to go into a land which would be shown him, and promised to bless him, and to make a great nation of him, and to bless all families through his seed (Gen. 12:1-3; Acts 7:2, 3).

2. "By faith Abraham, when he was called, obeyed to go out unto a place which he was to receive for an inheritance; and he went out, not knowing whither he went" (Heb. 11:8). By faith he obeyed, and trustingly did as commanded, not knowing where he was

going. Strange conduct for an unforgiven, condemned sinner!

3. When he reached the place of Shechem, in the land of Canaan, "Jehovah appeared unto Abram, and said, Unto thy seed will I give this land: and there builded he an altar unto Jehovah, who appeared unto him" (Gen. 12:6, 7). Why this promise, and why this worship, if Abraham was then an unforgiven sinner?

4. Abraham moved on to a mountain between Bethel and Ai; "and there he builded an altar unto Jehovah, and called upon the name of Jehovah" (Gen. 12:8).

5. After his unfortunate visit to Egypt, he returned to the altar between Bethel and Ai; "and there Abram called on the name of Jehovah" (Gen. 13:3, 4). Can any one believe that an unforgiven sinner was thus worshiping Jehovah and calling on his name?

6. When he returned from the slaughter of the kings who had taken Lot captive, Melchizedek, priest of God Most High, "blessed him, and said, Blessed be Abram of God Most High." As Abram was blessed, or happy, and as he was described as "Abram of God Most High," it is certain that he was not a condemned alien sinner.

7. After these things and before the promise of a son, the Lord said to him: "Fear not, Abram: I am thy shield, and thy exceeding great reward" (Gen. 15:1). That settles it. God would not tell an unforgiven sinner not to fear; neither is he the shield and exceeding great reward of such a sinner.

Why have not all these things been taken into consideration by our super-exegetes? It is certain therefore that the language in Gen. 15:6 and Rom. 4:3 does

not refer to the justification of an alien sinner, and
they greatly err who so apply it. It is true that Paul
was trying to convince the Jews that this justification happened before the giving of the law, but he was
using this well known fact to offset their claim that
a person had to be circumcised after the manner of
Moses, or he could not be saved. Their own father
Abraham, of whom they boasted, would be cut off by
their arguments for the law.

An author whom I have been reading quotes verses
3-6 and makes this remark: "Just as Abraham was
reckoned righteous, not because of his works, but because of his faith in God, so the sinner is reckoned
righteous because of his faith in Christ." If the author
will look a little more closely, he will see that Paul does
not say that Abraham was reckoned righteous because
of his faith in God. God reckons to a man only that
which he has or should have. Abraham believed God,
and his belief was reckoned to him, or put down to his
account, or considered. Neither does the record say
that faith was counted, or reckoned, as if it were righteousness, nor was it counted as a substitute for righteousness. But the record does say that Abraham's
faith was reckoned, or counted, to him for (*eis*, into,
or in order to, or unto) righteousness. On the grounds
of his faith God forgave him of whatever sins he might
have been guilty, and so declared him to be righteous.
If no guilt attaches to a man, if there is no sin charged
against him, he is a righteous man. If a man never
sinned, he would be righteous by works; if he sins and
God forgives him, removes sin entirely from him, he
is then righteous by grace, or favor. But the man who
attains righteousness through forgiveness has no
grounds for boasting. For that reason Abraham had

no grounds for boasting; for the same reason none
now have grounds for boasting.

Verses 1-3 connect back with the twenty-seventh
verse of the third chapter, which says: "Where then
is the glorying? It is excluded. By what manner of
law? of works? Nay: but by a law of faith." Moffatt's
rendering of this verse, as quoted by K. C. Moser, in
"The Way of Salvation," cannot justly be considered a
translation at all: "Then what becomes of our boasting? It is ruled out absolutely. On what principle?
On the principle of doing deeds? No, on the principle
of faith." Much is said about the "principle of faith."
Now, faith is an act of the mind, or heart; and a person might as well talk about the principle of thinking
or the principle of joy, as to talk about the principle of
belief. Such an expression as "the principle of faith"
conveys no idea to the mind. If a man's life were as
perfect as the Pharisee imagined his to be, he could
boast; but if a man sins and is forgiven, there is
ground for humility, but not for boasting.

Verse 4: *Now to him that worketh, the reward is
not reckoned as of grace, but as of debt.* The word
reckon is met with so often in this fourth chapter that
it is well for us to notice carefully its significance. The
reward is reckoned to the person that works, because
it is his due. Paul is not condemning salvation by
works in this verse; he is merely stating a truth. We
can rest assured that if we could so work as to bring
God in debt to us to the extent of our salvation, he
would pay that debt. But for that to be true, a person's work would have to be perfect—he would have to
so live as to never sin, never incur any guilt. But if
a man sins once, salvation can never come to him as a

debt. Such a man can never be justified by works of law. He needs forgiveness, and the law does not forgive; it condemns. No perfection of works will blot out, or forgive, a sin already committed, nor make void grace in the forgiveness of that sin.

Much random talk has been indulged in on this verse (verse 4), and much of it is very hurtful. It has been made to do service in an effort to prove that a sinner could do nothing in order to be saved. Paul had no such point in view. If we keep in mind his argument, we will have no trouble in seeing his point; but if we switch his language from his line of argument and make his language refer to the conditions on which pardon is offered to an alien sinner, we misrepresent him and lose ourselves in the confusion of our own notions. To me it seems inexcusable that a person should so misunderstand Paul as to draw the following conclusion: "Indeed, it seems to be difficult even at the present time for many to grasp the idea of righteousness that does not depend on human effort." Surely the author did not properly consider the import of his words. If a Universalist or an Ultra-Calvinist had penned such words, we would not be surprised. Not only am I not able to grasp the idea of a righteousness that does not depend on human effort, but I do not believe there is such righteousness in any human being. If a human being is made righteous without any human effort, then why are not all righteous? It is certain that the most of them are not making any effort to attain to righteousness.

Verse 5: *But to him that worketh not, but believeth on him that justifieth the ungodly, his faith is reckoned for righteousness.* The reader will notice

that Paul says nothing about "the one who depends on
works," nor "the one who depends not on works." He
speaks of the one who *works* and the one who *does not
work*. *Works* must have the same significance in both
cases (verses 4 and 5), for Paul had not changed his
subject. Only perfect works, works without any guilt
of sin, can bring salvation as a debt. The one "who
worketh" is, therefore, the one whose works are so
perfect that he has no guilt of sin. But no one has so
lived. Hence, to the one whose work is not perfect,
but who believes in Jesus Christ, God reckons, or counts
his faith for (*eis*, in order to) his righteousness—that
is, in order that, on the basis of his faith, he may forgive his sins and thus constitute him a righteous person. Let us not be so unjust with Paul as to switch
his language from his line of reasoning and make it
apply to the acts of obedience required in the gospel.
Certainly Paul did not mean to say that God makes the
person righteous who will not obey him, the person
who simply does nothing. If so, he puts a premium
on the very thing from which the gospel is intended
to save us, and contradicts other things said by him.

Paul did not have special reference to the salvation
of alien sinners, as will be seen by observing his quotation from David. The connection in Ps. 32, from which
Paul quotes, shows that David had special reference
to his own forgiveness. He did not have in mind the
forgiveness of alien sinners, but the forgiveness of a
servant of God. God counts the man righteous, whose
sins are forgiven. To such a man the Lord does not
reckon sin, because his sins have been forgiven, and
he is no longer guilty. Such a one is righteous.

Paul and James. Paul says: "But to him that

worketh not, but believeth on him that justifieth the ungodly, his faith is reckoned for righteousness" (Rom. 4:5). James says: "Ye see that by works a man is justified, and not only by faith" (2:24). Paul says: "For if Abraham was justified by works, he hath whereof to glory" (Rom. 4:2). James says: "Was not Abraham our father justified by works, in that he offered up Isaac his son upon the altar?" (2:21). Some have thought that there is a conflict between Paul and James, but rightly considered there is not even a seeming discrepancy between them. However, James does flatly contradict the explanation sometimes given to Paul's language. Trouble comes from misunderstanding Paul or misapplying James, or both.

Paul was talking about works of law; James was talking about works of faith. Paul was showing the Judaizing Christians that no one could be righteous, or justified, by works of law, for no one kept the law perfectly, and that to be justified, or made righteous, a person must believe in Christ. To the one who does not fulfill the works of the law, but believes in God, faith is reckoned for righteousness. Paul was arguing that works without faith would not justify, and James was arguing that faith without works would not justify. To exclude either is to fail of justification. Both referred to Abraham to illustrate their points. Abraham was justified without works of law, but he was justified by works of faith. James laid down the principle that faith without works is dead, and will not justify. He used Abraham as an illustration, and then drew the broad conclusion that a man —any man—is justified by works, and not by faith only.

An effort is sometimes made to explain Paul and James by saying that Paul was talking of justification of an alien sinner, and James, about the justification of a Christian. It is argued that an alien sinner must be justified by faith only, in order that it may be by grace, and that if the sinner has to perform any conditions, his salvation is of works and not of grace. But what about the Christian? It is strange that these super-exegetes do not see that if works of faith destroy grace, then the works which they say a Christian must perform to be justified destroys all grace from the life of a Christian. Tell us, ye super-exegetes, how according to your judgment, there can be any grace in the justification of a Christian by works.

But the theory that Paul's argument eliminates all conditions from the salvation of a sinner not only contradicts James, but Paul also. If all works are eliminated, faith itself is eliminated, for it is a work. "They said therefore unto him, What must we do, that we may work the works of God? Jesus answered and said unto them, This is the work of God, that ye believe on him whom he hath sent" (John 6:28, 29). And Paul tells us emphatically that eternal life is granted to those who "by patience in well-doing seek for glory and honor and incorruption" (Rom. 2:6, 7). To seek by patience in well-doing requires human effort. Again: "But thanks be to God, that, whereas ye were servants of sin, ye became obedient from the heart to that form of teaching whereunto ye were delivered; and being made free from sin, ye became servants of righteousness" (Rom. 6:17, 18). They obeyed from the heart. That means that their faith expressed itself in obedience to God. By this obedience they were made free from sin. Here again is human effort.

Grace provided the plan by which sinners are saved, or made righteous, and grace tells us how to come into possession of that salvation. If people would quit arraying the *commands of God* against the *grace of God*, they would have a clearer vision of the scheme of redemption. God's grace is in every command he gives. The sinner was lost; God prepared a way by which he could get out of that lost state. That was grace. But that was not enough. He needed to know how to find that way, and how to walk in it. It is as much a matter of grace to tell him how to find that way, and how to walk in it as it is to provide the way. But when the way is fully prepared, and full directions given as to how to find the way, and how to walk in it, the next move is man's. The whole matter is strikingly illustrated by the events of Pentecost. The way had been prepared and revealed to the people; and then, in response to their question, Peter told them how to get in that way. That was all a matter of grace. Then Peter exhorted them to save themselves. Many did what was commanded and were saved. On God's side their salvation was wholly a matter of grace. And the people were as prompt in their obedience as if their salvation were wholly a matter of works. And so far as anything they could do about it was concerned, their salvation was wholly a matter of works.

Verses 6-8: *Even as David also pronounceth blessing upon the man, unto whom God reckoneth righteousness apart from works, saying Blessed are they whose iniquities are forgiven, and whose sins are covered. Blessed is the man to whom the Lord will not reckon sin.* The Lord does not reckon sin, but does reckon

righteousness, to the person whose sins are forgiven.
The Lord reckons, or imputes, sin to the person so long
as he is a sinner, and because he is a sinner. But when
his sins are forgiven, the Lord does not reckon them
against him any more. The forgiven man is righteous, and hence the Lord imputes, or reckons, righteousness to him.

It has been erroneously assumed and falsely argued
that to impute a thing to a person is to put to his account something he does not have, or somewhat more
than he has. The Presbyterian and Baptist Confes-
sions of Faith, and a host of theologians of both schools,
teach that the righteousness of Christ is imputed, or
credited, to the sinner. I was sorry to see it also
taught in "The Way of Salvation." The doctrine is
wholly without scriptural support. If *to impute* means
to consider a person somewhat more than he is, or to
credit him with something which belongs to another,
then to impute sin to a person would be to consider
him worse than he is, or to charge to him the sins of
another! Righteousness belongs to character, and it
is absurd to think that personal righteousness can be
transferred to another. When by the power of the
gospel a man has been made clean and free from sin,
God reckons righteousness to him, because he is righteous. God does not pretend that a man is righteous
when he is not. The denominational doctrine of imputed righteousness reminds one of the children's game
of "play-like." And their doctrine discredits the gospel as God's saving power, and belittles the merits and
efficacy of the blood of Christ, for it teaches that some
corruption remains in the regenerate, but he is counted

righteous because ne is clothed with the righteousness of Christ. That is "play-like" theology.

But the gospel makes men righteous, just as a soiled garment may be made clean, as clean as if it had never been soiled, by carrying it through a process of cleansing. So the gospel takes the sin-defiled person through a process of cleansing that makes him as clean as if he had never sinned. The Lord does not "play-like" he is righteous; he makes him righteous by the gospel.

Verse 9: *Is this blessing then pronounced upon the circumcision, or upon the uncircumcision also? for we say, To Abraham his faith was reckoned for righteousness.* "This blessing" is the blessing mentioned in verses 6-8—the blessing of having the sins forgiven, so as to be counted righteous. "The circumcision" were the Jews; "the uncircumcision" were the Gentiles. Paul's questions are equal to affirming that this blessing may be upon the Gentiles as well as upon Jews. "For we say"—that is, we all say. There is one thing upon which we all agree—namely, "To Abraham his faith was reckoned for righteousness." And what they said was based on Gen. 15:6. It shows clearly that it was his faith that was reckoned, or put to his account, *for* or *in order to,* his righteousness. As Abraham was righteous before he was required to be circumcised, so might the Gentile, of whom circumcision had never been required, be righteous without it.

Verse 10: *How then was it reckoned? when he was in circumcision, or in uncircumcision? Not in circumcision, but in uncircumcision.* Paul had reminded the Judaizer that Abraham was justified without the works of the law. Of course, they knew this, but may not have thought of the bearing it would have on their contention. But now they might reply that he was circumcised. To that possible objection, Paul replies that he was righteous even before he was circumcised. Abraham's case shows that a person who had not been commanded to be circumcised could be righteous without it, and every Jew knew that Gentiles had never been commanded to be circumcised. It was possible, therefore, for them to be righteous without it.

Verse 11: *"And he received the sign of circumcision, a seal of the righteousness of the faith which he had while he was in uncircumcision: that he might be the father of all them that believe, though they be in uncircumcision, that righteousness might be reckoned unto them.* Circumcision was a sign of the covenant made with Abraham; it was to be perpetuated as a sign of membership in that covenant. It did not bring one into the covenant, as some think. Every child of Jewish parentage was a member of that covenant by virtue of his descent from Abraham. "And the uncircumcised male who is not circumcised in the flesh of his foreskin, that soul sha`` be cut off from his people; he hath broken my covenant" (Gen. 17:14). It could not be said that a person broke the covenant by failing to be circumcised, if he were not in the covenant.

But circumcision was more than a sign to Abraham; it was a seal of the righteousness of his faith, a stamp of God's approval of his faith. To the Hebrews it was a sign of the covenant; to Abraham only was it a seal of the righteousness of the faith which he had in uncircumcision.

Something was done that Abraham might be the

father of all who believe, both of Gentiles and Jews. What was it? It does not seem possible that Paul meant that Abraham was circumcised that he might be the father of the uncircumcised believer. Evidently, it was the righteousness of the faith which he had in uncircumcision that constituted him "the father of all them that believe, though they be in uncircumcision, that righteousness might be reckoned unto them"— that is, he is the father of the Gentile believers, though they be not circumcised. And God reckons righteousness to them without circumcision.

Verse 12: *And the father of circumcision to them who not only are of the circumcision, but who also walk in the steps of that faith of our father Abraham which he had in uncircumcision.* Paul does not use the term "father Abraham" as the Jews would use it, but he uses it in its Christian sense. He does not say that Abraham is the father of *the* circumcision. With Paul he is not the father of Jews as such, but only of those Jews who "walk in the steps of that faith of our father Abraham which he had in uncircumcision." He is the father of the believers, whether they be Gentiles or Jews. There is no difference; "for in Christ Jesus neither circumcision availeth anything, nor uncircumcision; but faith working through love" (Gal. 5:6). This accords with what Peter said in reply to the Judaizing teachers in Jerusalem: "And he made no distinction between us and them, cleansing their hearts by faith" (Acts 15:9).

In a national and fleshly sense Abraham was the father of the whole Jewish nation, but that is not the sense in which Paul here uses the term "father Abraham." God promised Abraham: "In thy seed shall

all the nations of the earth be blessed" (Gen. 22:18).
We do not have to guess to whom this promise refers,
for Paul says: "Now to Abraham were the promises
spoken, and to his seed. He saith not, and to seeds,
as of many; but as of one, And to thy seed, which is
Christ" (Gal. 3:16). Abraham's seed, through whom
the world was to be blessed, was Jesus the Christ, and
none other. But there is a sense in which all Christians are Abraham's seed. "And if ye are Christ's,
then are ye Abraham's seed, heirs according to promise" (Gal. 3:29). In the high gospel sense contem-
plated in the promise made to Abraham, he is the father of only those who believe in Christ. A Jew, as
such, has no part in this promise. The spiritual family of Abraham has superseded the fleshly family.
God's order is: the fleshly first, then the spiritual.

Verse 13: *For not through the law was the promise
to Abraham or to his seed that he should be heir of the
world, but through the righteousness of faith.* The
marginal reading has "through law." The Greek has
no "the" before "law" in this verse. Abraham did not
receive the promise through law, evidently meaning
that the promise was not given him on account of his
perfectly keeping any law. That he should be the
heir of the world is not definitely stated in any of the
promises made to Abraham. The promise here referred to cannot be the land promise, for that promise
did not include the world. And Paul's argument in
the remainder of the chapter shows that he did not
have the land promise in mind. When God called
Abraham out of Ur of the Chaldees, he promised to
make of him a great nation, and then added the promise
that refers to Christ: "And in thee shall all the fami-

lies of the earth be blessed" (Gen. 12:1-3). That this promise includes all the nations is plainly declared when God renewed this promise to Abraham: "And in thy seed shall all the nations of the earth be blessed" (Gen. 22:18). When God made the covenant of circumcision with Abraham, he referred to the promise made to Abraham in Ur of the Chaldees, saying: "For the father of a multitude of nations have I made thee" (Gen. 17:5). God had already constituted him a father of a multitude of nations when circumcision was commanded. In a fleshly sense Abraham was not the father of a multitude of nations; in a spiritual sense he was. Jesus was made heir of all things. Heb. 1:1, 2; Ps. 2:7, 8 shows that it was the people to which Christ became heir.

Verse 14: *For if they that are of the law are heirs, faith is made void, and the promise is made of none effect.* The world was not promised to Abraham's natural seed. God promised to make of his natural seed a great nation, and to give them a definite territory, but they were not constituted the heirs of the world. The seed that was to bless the world was Christ. "Now to Abraham were the promises spoken, and to his seed. He saith not, And to seeds, as of many; but as of one, And to thy seed which is Christ" (Gal. 3:16). "Whom he appointed heir of all things" (Heb. 1:2). With this agree the words of David: "I will tell of the decree: Jehovah said unto me, Thou art my son; this day have I begotten thee. Ask of me, and I will give thee the nations for thine inheritance, and the uttermost parts of the earth for thy possession" (Ps. 2:7, 8). Now, this promise of world-wide inheritance was not made to Abraham through the righteousness

of the law, but through the righteousness of faith. Paul
had shown the Judaizing teachers that Abraham was
not righteous by law, but by faith.   Now he shows
briefly that the promise of the Messiah was through
the righteousness of faith, and not through the righteousness of law.

"Through the law" means *through the righteousness
of the law,* for the person who does not keep the law
perfectly receives nothing through the law but punishment. *"They that are of the law"* means *they that are
righteous by law.* If such are heirs, faith as a basis
for righteousness is void. If the promise was made to
those who would keep the law, the promise would have
been of no effect, for no one kept the law; there would
have been no one to whom the promise applied. All
would have been subject to penalty for violating law,
instead of receiving a reward for keeping it.

Verse 15 :   *For the law worketh wrath; but where
there is no law, neither is there transgression.* This
cannot mean that the law stirs up wrath in man toward
him who gave the law. The law brings wrath upon
man, because he violates it. If it were kept perfectly,
it would bring the rewards of righteousness; but it
brings punishment, for no one keeps it perfectly. Because men violate law, it works wrath.

Paul's statement that there is no transgression
where there is no law does not mean that there ever
was a people that had no law, for he had already shown
that both Jews and Gentiles were all under sin. The
moral law is always in force, and applies to all. What,
then, does Paul mean? No one transgresses a law that
has not been given. Abraham did not transgress the
law of Moses, for it had not been given in his day.

Neither did he transgress the law of baptism or the Lord's Supper. There were no such requirements in his day. Even the law of Moses was binding only on those to whom it was given. "Now we know that what things soever the law saith, it speaketh to them that are under the law" (Rom. 3:19). The Gentiles were never under the law, and, therefore, never did transgress it. The Gentile Christians were, therefore, not guilty of any transgression in failing to be circumcised, or in failing to keep the law of Moses. For them there was no such law. Thus, in a few words, Paul refutes the contention of the Judaizing teachers, who demanded that the Gentile Christians be circumcised and keep the law of Moses.

Verse 16: *For this cause it is of faith, that it may be according to grace; to the end that the promise may be sure to all the seed; not to that only which is of the law, but to that also which is of the faith of Abraham, who is the father of us all.* The promised inheritance, in which Christians share, is of faith, instead of through the righteousness of law, that it may be according to grace. If the promise had been made on the condition that people keep the law, it would not have been sure to any one, for no one kept the law. And, had any one kept the law perfectly and thereby come into the inheritance, it would not have been by grace, but by merit. But as it is, the promise extends to all who are of the faith of Abraham, whether they be Jews or Gentiles.

Verse 17: *(As it is written, a father of many nations have I made thee) before whom he believed, even God, who giveth life to the dead, and calleth the things that are not, as though they were.* In the parenthesis is a quotation from Gen. 17:5. To see the force of the past tense of this quotation, it is necessary to go back and consider the events narrated in Gen. 17:1-14. Jehovah appeared to Abraham when Abraham was ninety-nine years old and said to him: "I am God Almighty; walk before me, and be thou perfect. And I will make a covenant between me and thee." Here was a covenant about to be made, and the sequel shows that it was the land covenant, with circumcision as the sign of the covenant. Be it remembered that God had (Gen. 12:1-3) promised Abraham that in his seed all the families of the earth should be blessed, and also that Peter, in Acts 3:25, quotes this promise and calls it a covenant. That was not the covenant that God proposed to make with Abraham in Gen. 17:2. When this covenant was proposed, "Abraham fell on his face: and God talked with him, saying, As for me, behold, my covenant is with thee, and thou shalt be the father of a multitude of nations." "My covenant is with thee"—that is, he had already covenanted with him to make him a father of a multitude of nations. Hence, he says in the next verse: "the father of a multitude of nations have I made thee." He had already constituted him a father of many nations. This shows that the covenant to make him the father of a multitude of nations, which was made in Ur of the Chaldees, was distinct from the land and circumcision covenant. And Paul's use of the statement in Gen. 17:5 shows that it was fulfilled in Christ as the Savior of the world. The law of Moses, which the Judaizing teachers were so zealously seeking to fasten on the Gentile Christians, had nothing to do with the promise, or covenant, to make Abraham the father of a multitude of nations.

This is made still plainer in Gal. 3:16, 17: "Now to Abraham were the promises spoken, and to his seed. He saith not, And to seeds, as of many; but as of one, And to thy seed, which is Christ. Now this I say: A covenant confirmed beforehand by God, the law which came four hundred and thirty years after, doth not disannul, so as to make the promise of none effect." Here, again, the promise to bless the world through Abraham's seed is called a covenant, and its absolute distinction from the law of Moses is emphasized.

God gives life to the dead. He is the source of all life, both physical and spiritual. Dead matter comes to life at his command. At the time God constituted Abraham the father of a multitude of nations, Abraham had no son. Before Isaac was born, God changed his name from "Abram," *exalted father*, to "Abraham," *the father of a multitude*. Thus he "calleth the things that are not, as though they were." Abraham is the father of all who walk in the steps of his faith.

To understand some things Paul says about Abraham's faith and hope, it is necessary to bear in mind some facts and dates in the life of Abraham. Before he was seventy-five years old, "by faith Abraham, when he was called, obeyed to go out unto a place which he was to receive for an inheritance" (Heb. 11:8). On the way to Canaan he tarried at Haran till his father died; "and Abraham was seventy and five years old when he departed out of Haran" (Gen. 12:4). He was eighty-six years old at the birth of Ishmael, and one hundred years old at the birth of Isaac (Gen. 16:16; 21:5).

Verse 18: *Who in hope believed against hope, to the end that he might become a father of many na-*

*tions, according to that which had been spoken, So
shall thy seed be.* The promise—"so shall thy seed be"
—was made to Abraham before Ishmael was born. To
say that Abraham's body was then as good as dead is
to commit one to the theory that Ishmael was miracu-
lously begotten. It is not likely that any one will take
that position. Abraham was then still in possession
of the full powers of his manhood. But Sarah was
barren, and hence there were no natural grounds for
Abraham to hope that she would ever bear a son. Yet,
God had promised to make his seed as numberless as
the stars. "And he believed in Jehovah; and he reckoned it to him for righteousness" (Gen. 15:6). In
hope he believed against hope—believed that he would
become a father in spite of Sarah's barrenness. It
seems that Abraham and Sarah tried to help God out
of the seeming difficulty. "And Sarai said unto
Abram, Behold now, Jehovah hath restrained me from
bearing; go in, I pray thee, into my hand-maid; it may
be that I shall obtain children by her. And Abram
hearkened to the voice of Sarai" (Gen. 16:2). As a
result of this step of unbelief, a son was born to Abraham by Hagar. Evidently Abraham thought that
move settled the difficulty, and that Ishmael was the
one through whom the promise would be fulfilled; for
when God later promised that he should have a son
by Sarah, he said to God: "Oh that Ishmael might live
before thee" (Gen. 17:15-18). But when Jehovah informed him that his covenant would be established
with the son to be born to him by Sarah, he believed
God.

Verses 19-22: *And without being weakened in faith
he considered his own body now as good as dead (he*

being about a hundred years old), and the deadness of Sarah's womb; yet, looking unto the promise of God, he wavered not through unbelief, but waxed strong through faith, giving glory to God, and being fully assured that what he had promised, he was also able to perform. Wherefore also it was reckoned unto him for righteousness. It required strong faith on the part of Abraham to accept God's promise that he would be the father of a son by Sarah when both were incompetent; but he had been a strong believer in God so long that his faith was able to stand the test. "He wavered not through unbelief"—he was not weakened in faith. Concerning this manifestation of faith Paul adds: "Wherefore also it was reckoned unto him for righteousness." Just when Abraham first became a righteous man we do not know.

While Abraham was yet in Ur of the Chaldees, God promised him through the righteousness of faith that he should be the heir of the world (Gen. 12:1-3; Rom. 4:13). How long he had been a believer in God before this promise was made through the righteousness of faith we know not. Some years later, when God promised him that his seed should be as numberless as the stars, it is said that he believed in God, and he counted it to him for righteousness (Gen. 15:5, 6). But it is certain that this was not the beginning of his righteousness by faith. About fifteen years later, when God promised him that Sarah should bear him a son, whom he should call Isaac, his faith did not weaken (Gen. 17:15-21). Concerning his faith at this time Paul says: "Wherefore also it was reckoned unto him for righteousness." Later, perhaps twenty-five years later, God commanded him to offer up Isaac. Again his faith failed not. Of this greatest test of his faith James says: "Was not Abraham our father justified by works, in that he offered up Isaac his son upon the altar? Thou seest that faith wrought with his works, and by works was faith made perfect; and the scripture was fulfilled which saith, And Abraham believed God, and it was reckoned unto him for righteousness; and he was called the friend of God" (James 2:21-23). Hence, that Abraham was righteous by faith is affirmed of him on four separate occasions, covering a period of perhaps fifty years. It is astonishing that so many Bible students have overlooked these plain and important facts. To me it seems inexcusable that any Bible student should take Gen. 15:6 as an example of the justification of an alien sinner. And it seems doubly inexcusable for the same writer to so mix events as to make Gen. 15:6 and Rom. 4:22 refer to the same event, and then, though the statements refer to events fifteen years apart, use both as examples of the justification of an alien! These things were not written to show how alien sinners are justified. Paul was meeting the demands of the Judaizers, who claimed that Gentile Christians had to keep the law. The justification of an alien sinner was not the point at issue, but whether a Gentile Christian had to keep the law to be justified as a Christian. It does not appear that the Judaizers denied that the Gentile believers were saved, but their contention was that Gentile Christians must, as servants of God, keep the law to be eternally saved, or to remain in a state of salvation. To offset their contention, Paul shows that all down through Abraham's life of service to God he was righteous by faith. Note Paul's next statement.

Verses 23-25: *Now it was not written for his sake alone, that it was reckoned unto him; but for our sakes also, unto whom it shall be reckoned, who believe on him that raised Jesus our Lord from the dead, who was delivered up for our trespasses, and was raised for our justification.* That Abraham's faith was reckoned unto him for righteousness was written for the sake of those who now believe. It is a guaranty that the believer's faith will now be reckoned unto him for righteousness. We must believe in the resurrection of Christ as well as his death, for without his resurrection his death would have availed nothing. But there must be a union of faith and works. Paul shows that works without faith cannot save, and James shows that faith without works is dead, and, therefore, worthless.

A Summary.—The gospel is God's power to save man, for in it is revealed a plan by which sinners may be made righteous. It is man's only hope, for God's wrath is revealed against all ungodliness and unrighteousness of men. Gentile and Jew were alike sinners, and could not be justified by law. But this gospel plan of righteousness was a thing apart from the law, though it was witnessed by the law and the prophets. This gospel righteousness is a state to which we attain by the forgiveness of our sins. It is, therefore, of grace and not of merit. If a man's works were perfect, his reward would be as of debt. But if a man sins, his forgiveness and consequent righteousness cannot be otherwise than a matter of grace. No amount of works that a person may do will make his forgiveness any less a matter of grace. Salvation by grace through faith is open to all, for Christ died for all. Both Jew and Gentile believers are heirs of the promise made to

Abraham. They are wrong who claim that Christians must keep the law of Moses to be justified, for Abraham was justified by faith without the law.

Chapter 5

5:1 Being therefore justified by faith, we have peace with God through our Lord Jesus Christ; 2 through whom also we have had our access by faith into this grace wherein we stand; and we rejoice in hope of the glory of God. 3 And not only so, but we also rejoice in our tribulations: knowing that tribulation worketh stedfastness; 4 and stedfastness, approvedness; and approvedness, hope; 5 and hope putteth not to shame; because the love of God hath been shed abroad in our hearts through the Holy Spirit which was given unto us. 6 For while we were yet weak, in due season Christ died for the ungodly. 7 For scarcely for a righteous man will one die: for peradventure for the good man some one would even dare to die. 8 But God commendeth his own love toward us, in that, while we were yet sinners, Christ died for us. 9 Much more then, being now justified by his blood, shall we be saved from the wrath of God through him. 10 For if, while we were enemies, we were reconciled to God through the death of his Son, much more, being reconciled, shall we be saved by his life; 11 and not only so, but we also rejoice in God through our Lord Jesus Christ, through whom we have now received the reconciliation.

12 Therefore, as through one man sin entered into the world, and death through sin; and so death passed unto all men, for that all sinned:—13 for until the law sin was in the world; but sin is not imputed when there is no law. 14 Nevertheless death reigned from Adam until Moses, even over them that had not sinned after the likeness of Adam's transgression, who is a figure of him that was to come. 15 But not as the trespass, so also is the free gift. For if by the trespass of the one the many died, much more did the grace of God, and the gift by the grace of the one man, Jesus Christ, abound unto the many. 16 And not as through one that sinned, so is the gift: for the judgment came of one unto condemnation, but the free gift came of many trespasses unto justification. 17 For if, by the trespass of the one, death reigned through the one; much more shall they that receive the abundance of grace and of the gift of righteousness reign in life through the one, even Jesus Christ. 18 So then as through one trespass the judgment came unto all men to condemnation; even so through one act of righteousness the free gift came unto all men to justification of life. 19 For as through the one man's disobedience the many were made sinners, even so through the obedience of the one shall the many be made righteous. 20 And the law came in besides, that the trespass might abound; but where sin abounded, grace did abound more exceedingly: 21 that, as sin reigned in death, even so might grace reign through righteousness unto eternal life through Jesus Christ our Lord.

Verse 1: *Being therefore justified by faith, we have peace with God through our Lord Jesus Christ.* Or, literally, "Having been justified by faith, we have peace with God." Greek writers were more exact in the use of participles than we are. We would say, "Mounting a horse, he rode away;" but the Greeks would say, "Having mounted a horse, he rode away." The mounting preceded the riding. And in Paul's language the *justification* precedes *peace with God.*

To justify a person is to pronounce him free from any guilt or blame. When a man through faith puts sin out of his heart and life, and submits to the will of God, he is forgiven of his sins. He is then declared to be righteous. As no guilt or blame then attaches to him, he is justified. It is evident that in Paul's language, to be righteous and to be justified is the same thing; for he had been arguing that we are made righteous by faith, and then adds: "Having therefore been justified by faith, we have peace with God."

Paul had been arguing that we are made righteous by faith in Christ, instead of by works of the law. It was equivalent to saying that we become righteous by obedience to the gospel instead of by obedience to the law. With Paul, faith in Christ means full acceptance of Christ as he is revealed to us and the faithful ordering of our lives according to his will. They greatly err who seek to prove by Paul that we are justified by faith only, without obedience to the gospel. The phrase "justified by faith," does not warrant the conclusion that we are justified by faith only.

It is a sound principle of exegesis to find out the use a writer makes of a word or phrase, and then to interpret his language in the light of that discovery. It is not difficult to find out the use Paul makes of the phrase in question, for he uses it more than do all the other writers of the New Testament. A few of the many examples found in the eleventh chapter of Hebrews will illustrate Paul's use of the phrase "by faith." "By faith Abel offered unto God a more excellent sacrifice than Cain." (verse 4). Every step that Abel took and every lick that he struck in preparing the altar, the wood, and the sacrifice were included in the phrase "by faith." "By faith Noah, being warned of God concerning things not seen as yet, moved with godly fear, prepared an ark to the saving of his house" (Verse 7). That was a huge task, requiring many days of hard labor; but it was all done by faith. All the labor and toil expended in building that ark are included in the phrase "by faith." It was a working faith that built that ark. Justified by faith—ark built by faith. Unless a person is willing to affirm that the ark stood completed the moment Noah believed, he should not contend that a person is justified the moment he believes. "By faith the walls of Jericho fell down" (Verse 30). Here the phrase "by faith" includes thirteen trips around the walls of the city of Jericho. The walls did not fall down by faith only. "By faith they passed through the Red Sea as by dry land" (Verse 29). Here the phrase "by faith" spans the channel of the Red Sea from shore to shore, and includes all that was done in the crossing. It therefore includes their baptism unto Moses, for in crossing they were baptized unto Moses in the cloud and in the sea (1 Cor. 10:1, 2). So also in our deliverance from sin the phrase "by faith" includes our baptism into Christ. Proof: "For ye are all sons of God, through faith, in Jesus Christ. For as many of you as were baptized into Christ did put on Christ" (Gal. 3:26, 27). They were children of God by faith in Christ because their faith had led them to be baptized into Christ. These illustrations, with many more that could be given, show us that faith is taking God at his word and doing what he commands. By taking God at his word and doing what he said, Noah built an ark; and by taking God at his word and doing what he said, we are justified. A faith that will not do whatever God commands will not justify any one. There is more rebellion than faith in the heart of one who will not do what God commands.

Verses 1-5: *Being therefore justified by faith, we have peace with God through our Lord Jesus Christ; through whom also we have had our access by faith into this grace wherein we stand; and we rejoice in our tribulations: knowing that tribulation worketh stedfastness; and stedfastness, approvedness; and approvedness, hope: and hope putteth not to shame; because the love of God hath been shed abroad in our hearts through the Holy Spirit which was given unto us.* In this chapter Paul sets forth the blessings of gospel righteousness, or justification. Those who are justified by faith have peace with God. All rebellion having been put out of our hearts, we are fully submissive to God; and as all sins have been forgiven, God holds nothing against us. We are at peace with God through our Lord Jesus Christ. It is through Christ that we have had access by faith into his grace, or favor, wherein we stand. Not only are we now at peace with God and stand in his favor, but we rejoice in the glory yet to come. On account of our exalted state we even rejoice in the tribulations which we suffer as Christians; for we know that tribulations endured work steadfastness of character. God approves steadfastness, and that gives us hope; and hope toward God does not put to shame, or disappoint us. The love of God here mentioned is the love that God has for us. The Holy Spirit, by revelation, by miracles, and by spiritual gifts, filled their hearts with the knowledge of God's love. These are some of the blessings that come to the children of God.

Some of the blessings of gospel justification were considered in the preceding paragraphs, among which was hope. "And hope putteth not to shame; because the love of God hath been shed abroad in our hearts through the Holy Spirit which was given unto us" (Verse 5). This fact is assigned as a reason as to why this hope will not put to shame, or be disappointing. God has promised great things for the faithful Christian, and has given him the Holy Spirit as a pledge that every promise will be fulfilled. "Now he that establisheth us with you in Christ, and anointed us, is God; who also sealed us, and gave us the earnest of the Spirit in our hearts" (2 Cor. 1:21, 22). "Now he that wrought us for this very thing is God, who gave unto us the earnest of the Spirit" (2 Cor. 5:5). Webster defines *earnest:* "Something of value given by a buyer to a seller to bind a bargain."

Verse 6: *For while we were yet weak, in due season Christ died for the ungodly.* We were weak when Christ died for us, or rather we were weak up to the time Christ died for us. The language does not mean that we are now unable to believe God nor do what he commands. It refers to man's helplessness without the death of Christ. Men were condemned sinners, with no means of escape from sin and condemnation. They were helpless. But the death of Christ opened up the way of escape, and removed the weakness spoken of in this verse. Christ died in due time—at the time which God in his wisdom had selected. "But when the fullness of the time came, God sent forth his

Son" (Gal. 4:4). At the proper time Christ died for
the ungodly—for those without God.

Verse 7: *"For scarcely for a righteous man will
one die: for peradventure for the good man some one
would even dare to die."* In the strict sense of *righteous*, as Paul here uses the term, a righteous man is
one who acts on the cold principle of justice. Such a
man neither gives nor takes. He gives neither short
measure nor over measure. He is the proverbial man
that splits a grain of wheat that he and the man with
whom he deals may each have his exact portion, regardless of the needs of the person with whom he deals.
We may admire the strict honesty of such a man but
we do not feel so devoted to him as to die for him.
We cannot feel any deep affection for him. But the
good man is more than just; he is kind, amiable, and
generous. He is devoted to the welfare and happiness
of others. He stirs our emotions, and gets hold of the
deep affections of our heart. For such a man some
might dare to die, but that would be unusual.

Verse 8: *"But God commendeth his own love toward us, in that, while we were yet sinners, Christ
died for us."* Here Paul shows the greatness of God's
love by contrasting it with man's love. To die for a
good man is great love. But Jesus died for sinners—
for those who were his enemies. To die for those who
hate and abuse us is love supreme. Jesus did that.
He died even for those who mocked, scourged, and
crucified him. He died that those who shed his blood
might live. Never other love like that.

Verse 9: *"Much more then, being now justified by
his blood, shall we be saved from the wrath of God*

through him." As he died for us while we were enemies, thus bringing about our justification through
his blood, much more shall we as his friends be saved
from future wrath.

Verse 10: *"For if, while we were enemies, we were
reconciled to God through the death of his Son, much
more, being reconciled, shall we be saved by his life."*
This is really a restatement of what was said in verses
8 and 9. We were enemies, but were reconciled to
God by the death of Jesus. His death for us opened
up a way through which we could be reconciled to God,
and his suffering for us so touched our hearts that we
wanted to be reconciled. If he accomplished so much
for us when he seemed to be so weak that his enemies
put him to death, much more, that he now lives to in-
tercede for us and to rule our hearts and our lives, shall
we be eternally saved. But it is left to us as to whether
we avail ourselves of the benefits of either his death
or his life.

Verse 11: *"And not only so, but we also rejoice in
God through our Lord Jesus Christ, through whom
we have received the reconciliation."* We rejoice in
God—rejoice in the glory of his being and the perfection of his attributes, and we rejoice in what he is
to us and what he has done for us. These great benefits and blessings come to us through our Lord Jesus
Christ, "through whom we have now received the reconciliation." That is, it was through the Lord Jesus
Christ that we were reconciled to God.

The remaining portion of this chapter is considered
very hard to understand. It is easy to see that Paul
was still setting forth the blessings of gospel justifica-

tion, but it is not so easy to understand some of his reasoning.

Verse 12: *"Therefore, as through one man sin entered into the world, and death through sin; and so death passed unto all men, for that all sinned.* Though Eve first ate of the forbidden fruit, Adam's eating it completed the transgression and made it unanimous. Paul follows the usual custom of speaking of the man instead of the woman. He indulges in no reasoning as to why they sinned; he merely states the fact that they did sin. He speaks of it merely to draw a contrast between the effects of what Adam did and the effects of what Christ did; and he did this to show how the gospel of Christ more than overcomes the effects of Adam's sin. Christianity is not concerned with the origin of sin so much as with the fact of sin. The gospel did not bring sin into the world, but it was brought into the world as the panacea for sin and all its ills. Death resulted from sin. But what death is here meant? It is true that physical death came as a result of sin, but so also does spiritual death. The context and the nature of Paul's argument must determine which death is here meant. In this Roman letter Paul frequently uses the word *death*, without saying which death he means, leaving the reader to determine from the context which death he means. The context favors the idea that *death* in verse 12 is spiritual death. The moral and spiritual condition of man and the gospel plan of justification had been the matter under discussion. Besides, the death here mentioned passed upon all men on account of their own sins. Physical death came upon all on account of Adam's sin, but the death here mentioned came only

upon those who sinned. Facts are against the idea that
all men suffer physical death on account of their own
sins; but spiritual death does come in that way, and in
no other way. The condition of infants and idiots is
not taken into consideration in the discussion of sin
and spiritual death. They die a physical death, even
though they have not sinned.

It is generally agreed that verses 13-17 (chapter 5)
are parenthetical, and that the thought started in verse
12 is resumed in verse 18. Such parentheses are fre-
quent in Paul's writing.

Verse 13: *"For until the law sin was in the world;
but sin is not imputed when there is no law."* In the
Greek text there is no *the* before *law* in this verse.
When Paul referred to the law of Moses, he generally,
if not always, put *the* before *law*. But what does "until law" mean? R. St. John Parry, in his explanatory
notes to the Cambridge Greek Testament for Schools
and Colleges, says that the phrase in question "equals
just so far as there was law, there was sin. It has
been shown (2:14, 15) that there was law, in a certain
and true sense, before the law given to Moses. . . .
So I take it *achri nomou* equals, up to the degree
of law, just to the extent to which law was present."
There has never been a people who were not under
the moral law. From Adam on down the ages people
have been under that law, have violated that law, and
were, therefore, sinners. The fact that sin was in the
world proves that there was law, for people are not
counted sinners when there is no law. Paul's statement that sin is not imputed when there is no law is
equal to his statement that where there is no law
there is no transgression. People who were not cir-

cumcised before the law of circumcision was given were not counted sinners for their failure to be circumcised, and so with any other positive command, or law. Nothing is plainer than that there was law before the law of Moses was given, and that people were sinners during that time, but they were sinners only to the extent of the law which they had.

Verse 14: *Nevertheless death reigned from Adam until Moses, even over them that had not sinned after the likeness of Adam's transgression, who is a figure of him that was to come."* This does not mean that the people from Adam to Moses did not sin at all, for that would contradict other things that Paul had said, but it means that they did not sin after the likeness of Adam's sin. They were not guilty of a sin like Adam's sin. To say that they did not sin after the likeness of Adam's sin is equal to affirming that they were guilty of a different kind of sin. Adam violated a positive law; these people violated the moral law. And that was not like Adam's sin. But if the statement in verse 12, that all sinned, means that all sinned in Adam, then all did sin after the likeness of Adam's sin. Thus, in an unexpected place, we have positive proof that we are not all guilty of Adam's sin. Death reigned over those who were guilty of sin, but were not guilty of a sin like Adam's sin.

Verse 15: *"But not as the trespass so also is the free gift. For if by the trespass of the one the many died, much more did the grace of God, and the gift by the grace of the one man, Jesus Christ, abound unto the many.* The gift through Christ was not merely, as some one has said, "coextensive in application with the ruin wrought through Adam," but abounded much more, or much beyond the evil effects of Adam's trespass. To meet the needs of humanity it had to be more extensive in application than the ruin wrought through Adam. In addition to the evils resulting from Adam's sin, there are the ruinous effects of our own sins that must be overcome, or else we are hopelessly lost. But Paul assures us that the blessings through Christ abound much more than the curse through the trespass of Adam; they include deliverance from our own sins.

Verse 16: *"And not as through one that sinned, so is the gift: for the judgment came of one unto condemnation, but the free gift came of many trespasses unto justification.* Here the personal guilt of Adam is emphasized, but the free gift of God was not simply coextensive with the sin of Adam. The judgment came of one trespass, unto condemnation. The one trespass was the eating of the forbidden fruit, and the condemnation here mentioned is the condemnation pronounced upon Adam and Eve in the garden. (See Gen. 3). The condemnation came of one trespass, but the free gift came of many trespasses—that is, Jesus came to save us from our many trespasses as well as from the evil consequences of Adam's sin. It is another proof that God's grace through Christ covers a greater range of evils than the one trespass of Adam. The free gift came to save us from our many trespasses and to bring us into a state of justification.

Verse 17: *"For if, by the trespass of the one, death reigned through the one; much more shall they that receive the abundance of grace and of the gift of righteousness reign in life through the one, even Jesus Christ."* The act of one brought death into the world.

"Death reigned." *Reigned* is ingressive—that is, death began to reign. But what death? Were it not for the contrast Paul draws, we would readily conclude that he referred to physical death; but he contrasts *death* with the *gift of righteousness,* which is the spiritual life. The death that reigns through the one man Adam is overcome, or destroyed, by the gift of righteousness through Christ. It is a fact that spiritual death, as well as physical death, entered the world through the sin of Adam; and it is a fact that spiritual life entered the world through Jesus Christ. But are we all dead spiritually because Adam brought spiritual death into the world? No more than that we are all alive spiritually because Christ brought spiritual life into the world. As we do not partake of the spiritual life unconditionally, so neither do we partake of the spiritual death unconditionally. If Adam had introduced measles into the world, that would not prove that all his descendants are born with the measles! But people live in a sin-infested country, and sin is more contagious than measles. To say that people are born subject to sin is far from saying that people are born sinners. Adam was created subject to sin, and he sinned; but that does not prove that he was created a sinner, nor even with a depraved nature.

Paul speaks of the gift of righteousness; but if a person is not free to accept or reject a thing, it cannot be properly called a gift. If we merited it by the perfection of our works, it would not be a gift. It is a righteousness to which we attain through the forgiveness of our sins. We are made righteous by the cleansing power of the gospel of Christ. To that plan of righteousness we must submit. Spiritual life and spiritual death are both the results of our own choice. It is surprising that any one ever thought that the personal righteousness of Christ is given to the believer.

Verse 18: *"So then as through one trespass the judgment came unto all men to condemnation; even so through one act of righteousness the free gift came unto all men to justification of life.* This verse connects back with verse 12. From the condemnation that came upon all men through one trespass we are released by the justification of life through the one act of righteousness of Jesus Christ. It seems certain that this one act of righteousness was the death of Christ. Hence, the justification to life frees us from the condemnation that came through the trespass of Adam. The matters of this verse are more fully stated in the next verse.

Verse 19: *"For as through the one man's disobedience the many were made sinners, even so through the obedience of the one shall the many be made righteous."* "The many" here includes all that arrive at the years of responsibility. Paul does not say how these were made sinners by the disobedience of Adam, nor how they are to be made righteous by the obedience of Christ. It is pure assumption to argue that the disobedience of Adam is imputed to his offspring, or that the obedience of Christ is imputed to anybody. Neither guilt nor personal righteousness can be transferred from one person to another, but the consequences of either may, to some extent, fall upon others. By his sin Adam brought about conditions that make every person subject to temptation. In this way he made sinners. Tom Paine made infidels; but that does not mean that his infidelity was imputed to others, or that they did not become infidels by their own free choice. Christ became obedient unto death (Phil. 2:8), and that act of obedience makes many people righteous. As Adam's disobedience did not make the many sinners without their choice, so neither does the obedience of Christ make the many righteous without their choice.

Verse 20: *"And the law came in besides, that the trespass might abound; but where sin abounded, grace did abound more exceedingly."* Here again there is no *the* before *law* in the Greek text. "Law came in." This would include all divine law given before Christ—the law of Moses as well as whatever law was given before Moses. Some laws were revealed to man before the law of Moses was given. *Law* in this verse must refer to revealed law, instead of the moral law that is inherent in the very nature of the relations that exist among men. Law came in "that the trespass might abound." One thing is certain, and that is that God did not give laws for the purpose of making people any worse sinners. Law was given to restrain people from wrong and guide them in the right way. There is this, however: the more things law prohibits and the more things it requires, the more points there are where we may violate law. In that way law may increase the number of sins. A man might observe the moral law out of regard for himself and his fellow man, without any regard for God; but a positive law determines his attitude toward God. If a man has rebellion in his heart, positive law reveals it. Adam violated a positive law, not a moral law. Any time a person violates a positive law, he repeats the trespass of Adam; every positive command, therefore, tends to increase the trespass. The law also made people see the enormity of sin and their helplessness under its reign. This would help them to realize more and more their need of some other means of deliverance. Sin abounded in that it triumphed over the sinner, made him feel his helplessness, and offered him no hope of deliverance. Where there was law, sin abounded. On the other hand, where sin abounded, much more did grace abound.

Verse 21: *"That, as sin reigned in death, even so might grace reign through righteousness unto eternal life through Jesus Christ our Lord."* Sin caused death, but that is not what Paul here has in mind. Sin reigned in death—in the sphere or realm of death. That Paul is here referring to spiritual life and spiritual death is made clear by the verses that immediately follow in the next chapter. In spiritual death sin's reign is absolute; it is the reigning monarch in every man who is dead in sins. But grace reigns through righteousness—that is, through this gospel plan of righteousness. It is God's grace that produced this plan of righteousness; it is the power that banishes sin from the heart and leads a man in devoted service to God. The ultimate result of its reign is eternal life through Jesus Christ our Lord.

Chapter 6

6:1 What shall we say then? Shall we continue in sin, that grace may abound? 2 God forbid. We who died to sin, how shall we any longer live therein? 3 Or are ye ignorant that all we who were baptized into Christ Jesus were baptized into his death? 4 We were buried therefore with him through baptism into death: that like as Christ was raised from the dead through the glory of the Father, so we also might walk in newness of life. 5 For if we have become united with *him* in the likeness of his death, we shall be also *in the likeness* of his resurrection; 6 knowing this, that our old man was crucified with *him*, that the body of sin might be done away, that so we should no longer be in bondage to sin; 7 for he that hath died is justified from sin. 8 But if we died with Christ, we believe that we shall also live with him; 9 knowing that Christ being raised from| the dead dieth no more; death no more hath dominion over him. 10 For the death that he died, he died unto sin once: but the life that he liveth, he liveth unto God. 11 Even so reckon ye also yourselves to be dead unto sin, but alive unto God in Christ Jesus.

12 Let not sin therefore reign in your mortal body, that ye should obey the lusts thereof; 13 neither present your members unto sin *as* instruments of unrighteousness; but present yourselves unto God, as alive from the dead, and your members *as* instruments of righteousness unto God. 14 For sin shall not have dominion over you: for ye are not under law, but under grace.

15' What then? shall we sin, because we are not under law, but under grace? God forbid. 16 Know ye not, that to whom ye present yourselves *as* servants unto obedience, his servants ye are whom ye obey; whether of sin unto death, or of obedience unto righteousness? 17 But thanks be to God, that, whereas ye were servants of sin, ye became obedient from the heart to that form of teaching whereunto ye were delivered; 18 and being made free from sin, ye became servants of righteousness. 19 I speak after the manner of men because of the infirmity of your flesh: for as ye presented your members *as* servants to uncleanness and to iniquity unto iniquity, even so now present your members *as* servants to righteousness unto sanctification. 20 For when ye were servants of sin, ye were free in regard of righteousness. 21 What fruit then had ye at that time in the things whereof ye are now ashamed? for the end of those things is death. 22 But now being made free from sin and become servants to God, ye have your fruit unto sanctification, and the end eternal life. 23 For the wages of sin is death; but the free gift of God is eternal life in Christ Jesus our Lord.

Verse 1: *What shall we say then? Shall we continue in sin, that grace may abound?* If where sin abounded, grace abounded more exceedingly, what is the consequence, or what should we do about it? Here Paul deals with a possible objection. "Shall we continue in sin, that grace may abound?" That question would naturally arise in the minds of the uninformed. Besides, some people would like to have an excuse to indulge in sin. If God's grace abounds where sin abounds, why not keep on sinning, so that grace may abound the more?

Verse 2: *God forbid. We who died to sin, how shall we any longer live therein?* In physical death a person no longer lives the life which he formerly lived. And so the sinner dies to the life of sin; in that life he no longer lives. A sinner dies to sin, and there is one less sinner in this world. Paul says: "I have been crucified with Christ; and it is no longer I that live, but Christ liveth in me" (Gal. 2:20). When Paul became a Christian, there was one less sinner in the world as certainly and definitely as if he had died physically and been buried at Damascus. And that death is repeated every time a person becomes a Christian. How shall we continue in sin, since we are dead to sin?

Verse 3: *Or are ye ignorant that all we who were baptized into Christ Jesus were baptized into his death?* Paul takes for granted that they knew they had been baptized into Christ, but asks if they were ignorant of the fact that, in being baptized into Christ, they were thereby baptized into his death. He plainly implies that if they knew they had been baptized into the death of Christ, they should know that they should no longer continue in sin. To be baptized into Christ is the same as to be baptized into the name of Christ, into the name of the Father and of the Son and of the Holy Spirit, into the remission of sins, and into the death of Christ. We are not baptized into the literal death of Christ, but into the benefits of his death, including the freedom from sin. A person is not completely dead to sin till he is separated from it, and that separation takes place in baptism.

Verse 4: *We were buried therefore with him through baptism into death: that like as Christ was raised up from the dead through the glory of the father, so we also might walk in newness of life.* In baptism there is a burial, an immersion in water. No other act would so fitly represent the complete ending of a life of sin. If there was no other source of knowledge as to how baptism was performed, this text should settle the matter beyond doubt. There is no burial in sprinkling and pouring a little water on a person's head, but there is a burial in immersion in water. Without going into a lengthy discussion of the subject, we call attention to three lines of evidence, each one independent of the others and each conclusive within itself.

The Lexicons. Thayer defines *baptisma:* "Immersion, submersion." Thayer is a recognized standard authority. As other lexicons agree with Thayer, it is useless to fill our limited space with quotations from them.

History. Concerning baptism in the first century, Mosheim says: "In this century *baptism* was administered in convenient places, without the public assemblies; and by immersing the candidate wholly in water." With this testimony other historians agree.

Circumstantial Evidence. If we could step back to the days of the apostles and see them baptize people, the matter would be settled. But we cannot be eye-witnesses to a first-century baptism. However, the circumstances connected with baptism then are so fully recorded that we should have no trouble in seeing that people were then immersed in water. Many a man has been convicted on circumstantial evidence less conclusive than can be presented in favor of immersion.

John the Baptist baptized the people in the river
Jordan (Mark 1:5). If you notice the marginal reading in verse 9, you will see that John baptized Jesus
into the Jordan. (See American Standard Version).
John could have dipped Jesus into the Jordan, but he
could not have sprinkled or poured him into the Jordan. And verse 10 says he came up out of the water.
Later "John was baptizing in Ænon near to Salim,
because there was much water there" (John 3:23).
It does not require much water to sprinkle or pour, but
it does require much water to immerse. When Philip
baptized the eunuch, they came to a certain water, they
both went down into the water, the baptizing was
done while they were in the water, then they came up
out of the water (Acts 8:36-39). When people are
immersed, they go to the water, the administrator and
candidate both go down into the water, the baptizing
is done while they are in the water, they then come up
out of the water; but not so when people are sprinkled
or poured. In baptism the body is washed in water
(Heb. 10:22). The evidence is conclusive. Add to
this Paul's statement that we are buried in baptism,
and assurance is made doubly sure, even though we
did not know the meaning of the Greek word for baptism, nor what the historians, commentators, and
critics say.

The New Life. Christ was raised from the dead by
the glorious power of the Father; even so are we raised
up from our burial in baptism to walk in newness of
life, or in a new life. We begin to walk in the new life
after we are baptized. We were baptized into death,
and are raised to a new life. We are baptized into
Christ, "in whom we have our redemption through his

blood, the forgiveness of our trespasses, according to
the riches of his grace." In Paul's language, redemption is forgiveness of sins. It is according to God's
grace that we have the forgiveness of our sins in
Christ, and not out of him. When a person is forgiven, there is nothing then against him. He then
stands justified in God's sight—"being justified freely
by his grace through the redemption (forgiveness) that
is in Christ Jesus" (Rom. 3:24)   But it is faith that
leads us to be baptized into Christ, in whom we have
forgiveness and consequent justification. It is by such
faith that we are justified, and it is according to grace
that it should be so. "For ye are all sons of God,
through faith, in Christ Jesus. For as many of you
as were baptized into Christ did put on Christ" (Gal.
3:26, 27). They were sons of God through faith in
Christ Jesus, for their faith had led them to put on
Christ in baptism. In baptism, therefore, we become
closely united with Christ.

Verse 5: *"For if we have become united with him
in the likeness of his death, we shall be also in the likeness of his resurrection."* In being buried in baptism
there is a likeness of his death; so also there is a likeness of his resurrection in our being raised from baptism to a new life. Hence, in being baptized we are
united with him in the likeness of his death and resurrection. We are, therefore, partakers with him in
death, and also in being raised to a new life. Jesus
was buried and arose to a new life; we are buried in
baptism and arise to a new life. These verses show
the act of baptism, and also its spiritual value.

Verse 6: *"Knowing this, that our old man was
crucified with him, that the body of sin might be done*

away, that so we should no longer be in bondage to sin."
Paul continues the analogy between Christ's death
and our death to sin. Christ was crucified—"our old
man was crucified." What is the *old man* that was
crucified? Some say: "Our corrupt nature." But
Paul does not view our nature as corrupt. Besides,
our nature is not put to death in the process of conversion to Christ. Read the verse again and you will
see that "our old man" and "the body of sin" are the
same thing, for certainly "our old man" is not crucified
in order that something else might be put to death. If
we will keep in mind what Paul had been saying, we
will see that to crucify the old man is the same thing
as to die to sin. Of himself Paul said: "I have been
crucified with Christ" (Gal. 2:20). Paul the sinner
died. What was true of him is true of every one who
becomes a Christian. The old man, the body of sin,
is the sinner. Every time a person becomes a Christian, a sinner dies. We die as sinners and are raised
up as saints. In verse 2, Paul affirms that we died—
died to sin; we are then raised to a new life. We are
then no longer the bondservants of sin. When a bond-
servant, or a slave, dies, he passes from under his master. His master no longer has dominion over him.

Verse 7: *For he that hath died is justified from sin.*
Or, according to the marginal reading in the American
Standard Version, "For he that hath died is released
from sin." Meyer translates it, "Whosoever is dead, is
acquitted from sin." If a slave died, he is free from
service to his master. If a slave of sin dies to sin, he
is free from service to his master. Sin rules him no
more.

Thus, in verses 2-7, Paul answers the question of the

first verse—namely, "Shall we continue in sin, that grace may abound?"

Verse 8: *But if we died with Christ, we believe that we shall also live with him.* Paul is not here referring to life with Christ in the world to come. He is stating a present, general truth. "The future tense does not necessitate a reference to the future life, and in the context such a reference is very unnatural; it is rather the logical future tense marking the new life as fulfilling a promise or natural consequence." Note in Cambridge Greek Testament. We died to sin, and were raised to a new life. This new life we live with Christ. We must live with him as our guide, as our Teacher, as our High Priest, and as our King. We cannot, therefore, continue in sin.

Verse 9: *Knowing that Christ being raised from the dead dieth no more; death no more hath dominion over him.* Knowing that Christ was raised from the dead to die no more gives us assurance that we shall live with him. If we feared that he would die again, our faith would be too defective to sustain us in our Christian life; we would certainly fall by the wayside, and cease to live with him. In fact, if a person does not believe that Christ arose from the dead to die no more, he does not believe in him as the Christ, the Son of the living God. Death had dominion over Christ while he was in the grave. He forever threw off that dominion when he arose from the dead. Spiritual death lost its dominion over us when we died to sin and arose to righteousness.

Verse 10: *For the death that he died, he died unto sin once: but the life that he liveth, he liveth unto God.* "Once" is from a word that means *once for all,* as may seen by noticing the marginal reading in the American Standard Version. It denies a repetition of the act. Jesus died once for all time. "But he, when he had offered one sacrifice for sins for ever, sat down on the right hand of God" (Heb. 10:12). This verse connects directly with the preceding verse. Jesus will die no more, for in the death that he died, he died for sins once for all time. He now lives unto God—unto the glory and honor of God. As Christians live with Christ, they also live so as to honor God. Hence, the admonition of the next verse.

Verse 11: *"Even so reckon ye also yourselves to be dead unto sin, but alive unto God in Christ Jesus."* A person is either dead to sin or he is not. If he is dead to sin, he is admonished to so consider himself. If we have not died to sin, we cannot in truth reckon ourselves dead to sin; but the person who is dead to sin should so count himself, and act accordingly. We are also to reckon ourselves alive to God in Christ. We are, therefore, to reckon ourselves as both dead and alive—dead to sin and alive to God. Hence, we cannot continue in sin.

Verse 12: *"Let not sin therefore reign in your mortal body, that ye should obey the lusts thereof."* Paul addresses that part of man which has the control of the body and which is, therefore, responsible for what the body does. The body is a mere instrument to be used by the inner man, the spirit, for good or bad. The spirit is charged not to let sin control the body. Our natural appetites and passions are not evil within themselves. They are God-given, and become evil only when they become the master, and thereby lead us into sinful thoughts and deeds. Now, since we died to sin, we are not to allow sin to reestablish its reign in our bodies. We must control the lusts of our bodies, not obey them. The mortal body, the body which must die, must not be allowed to cause spiritual and eternal death.

Verse 13: *"Neither present your members unto sin as instruments of unrighteousness; but present yourselves unto God, as alive from the dead, and your members as instruments of righteousness unto God."* This language shows plainly that when we sin, the members of our body are mere instruments through which the inner man accomplishes its purposes. The instrument used in committing a crime cannot be blamed for the crime. God gave the human being certain appetites and passions for his own preservation and for the perpetuity of the human race; but the purpose to hold them in check, or the plans to gratify them either in a lawful or unlawful way, are formed in the heart. "Keep thy heart with all diligence; for out of it are the issues of life" (Prov. 4:23). Obedience is from the heart. The spirit expresses itself through the body. Not one thing can be done in service to God without the use of the body. Hence, we are commanded to present our "members as instruments of righteousness unto God." And so also does the spirit sin through the instrumentality of the body. Though committed through the instrumentality of the body, sin comes from the heart. "For from within, out of the heart of men, evil thoughts proceed, fornications, thefts, murders, adulteries, covetings, wickedness, deceit, lasciviousness, an evil eye, railing, pride, foolishness: all these evil things proceed from within, and defile the man (Mark 7:21-23). As all sins come from the heart, or spirit, of man, it is absurd in the extreme for any one to claim, as some do, that the body of a regenerated man may sin, but his spirit remains pure and sinless. Certainly the body, being merely an instrument, is not responsible for the sin; and if the spirit of the regenerate is not responsible for the sin, it would seem that a regenerate man is not in any sense responsible for any wrong that he does!

Verse 14: *For sin shall not have dominion over you: for ye are not under law, but under grace.* The reign of sin over us has been broken by our death to sin, and through grace our sins have been forgiven. We are free from sin, and can, therefore, present our members to God as instruments of righteousness. It is not as if we had no escape from sin; for we are under grace, not law. Sin would have dominion over us if we had no means of escape from it, but through grace there is a way of escape from sin. Law does not free us from sin; it condemns the sinner. Under the reign of Christ sin does not have dominion over any one till he submits to its control and does not seek forgiveness. How can sin have dominion over one who abhors it, turns from it, and seeks forgiveness in God's appointed way? This verse does not mean that we are free from all law. Grace predominates. Where law condemns, grace makes pardon possible. If we were under no law, we would be guilty of no sin, and there would be no need of grace to forgive our sin. This verse is a figure of speech in which the less is denied so as to emphasize the greater. We are not merely under law, but more especially under grace.

Verse 15: *What then? shall we sin, because we are not under law, but under grace? God forbid.*

As Paul proceeds with his argument in this letter, he anticipates and meets arguments or objections that might be presented by Judaizing teachers. Since we are under grace, not law, some one might contend that this would give us liberty to go on sinning. But grace to forgive our sins and to help us overcome sin is not license to indulge in sin. Grace does not grant indulgences. Grace does not give license to indulge in sin, but grants to us a way of escape from sin.

The gospel teaching that we are not under law, but under grace, does not give liberty to continue in sin. Certainly the gospel of God's grace, which is God's power to save people from sin, would not encourage people to sin. Besides, those who think that the gospel teaching concerning law and grace gives license to sin overlook the fact that there is a principle of service involved. Whose servant are you? Whom do you serve?

Verse 16: *Know ye not, that to whom ye present yourselves as servants unto obedience, his servants ye are whom ye obey; whether of sin unto death, or of obedience unto righteousness?* Although we have been bought from the bondage of sin by the blood of Christ, God does not force us to accept the freedom bought for us. In those days captives in war were forced into slavery. Such men had no choice. But it is not so under the reign of Christ. We are not forced to be servants of sin, nor does God force us to be servants of righteousness. A man presents himself as a servant of sin or as a servant of righteousness. But Paul was here writing to Christians, and his language is a warning to us not to indulge in sin on the grounds that we are not under law, but under grace.

To do so is to become servants of sin. The life we live determines whose servants we are. To become servants of sin leads to death, but gospel obedience leads to righteousness. And the language of Paul shows that the Christian is as free to choose whom he will serve as is the alien sinner. To say that the Christian will always choose to continue his service to God is to beg the question, and to make this verse and the remaining part of the sixth chapter without point or reason.

Verses 17, 18: *But thanks be to God, that, whereas ye were servants of sin, ye became obedient from the heart to that form of teaching whereunto ye were delivered; and being made free from sin, ye became servants of righteousness.* The King James Version: "But God be thanked, that ye were servants of sin, but ye have obeyed," etc. Paul did not thank God for the fact that they had been sinners, but for the fact that the sinful part of their lives was a thing of the past. They had been servants of sin, but were not now; they had been delivered from sin. When they became free from sin, they became servants of righteousness; and they became free from sin by obeying from the heart the form, pattern, or mold, of doctrine into which they had been delivered. James Macknight makes this comment: "The original word *tupos*, among other things, signifies *a mold* into which melted metals are poured to receive the form of the mold. The apostle represents the gospel doctrine as a mold, into which the Romans were put by their baptism, in order to their being fashioned anew. And he thanks God that from the heart—that is, most willingly and sincerely —they yielded to the forming efficacy of that mold

of doctrine, and were made new men, both in principle and practice." The mold of doctrine is something
to which they had already become obedient, and by
that obedience had been delivered from the slavery of
sin and had become the slaves of righteousness. In
other words, by this obedience they had changed masters. It was not simply an inner condition of the heart
that had made this change, but obedience that came
from the heart. That obedience is spoken of in verses
3-6. The death, burial, and resurrection is the fundamental doctrine. In his death he was buried, and
then arose from the dead. In our death to sin we are
buried with him, and then are raised up to a new life.
The thing that caused Paul to be thankful to God was
the fact that, in their obedience from the heart to this
mold of doctrine, they had been made free from the
slavery of sin and had become slaves of righteousness.

Verse 19: *I speak after the manner of men because
of the infirmity of your flesh: for as ye presented
your members as servants to uncleanness and to iniquity unto iniquity, even so now present your members
as servants to righteousness unto sanctification.* Because they were slow to comprehend spiritual relations, he uses the customs of men as an illustration to
enable them to see that, though they were not under
law, but under grace, they had no more liberty to continue to serve sin than a man had to continue to serve
one master after he had been transferred to another.
Formerly they had presented their members as servants to uncleanness and to iniquity. Uncleanness has
reference to the degrading immoral practices so common among sinners, such as lewdness, drunkenness,
etc. The word from which we have "iniquity" means

lawlessness, and has reference to their former attitude toward God. They did not regard his law. As they formerly lived an unclean and lawless life, they are now to present their members as servants to righteousness unto sanctification. Formerly their members had been used in worldly living; now they are to separate them from such worldly uses and dedicate them to the service of God. And that is sanctification. In so doing, they, as Paul admonishes in Rom. 12:1, present their bodies a living sacrifice, holy, well-pleasing to God.

Verse 20: *For when ye were servants of sin, ye were free in regard of righteousness.* This does not mean that there was then no obligation resting upon them to do right, for in that case they would not have committed sin in not doing right. They were free from righteousness in the sense that they were not practicing righteousness. The implication is: since they have become servants of righteousness, they should live free from the practice of sin, just as they were once free from righteousness.

Verse 21: *What fruit then had ye at that time in the things whereof ye are now ashamed? for the end of those things is death.* Why should any one think of living in sin because he is not under law, but under grace? What advantage did you get out of that sort of life? The end—that is, the result—of such a life is death—eternal death.

Verse 22: *But now being made free from sin and become servants to God, ye have your fruit unto sanctification, and the end eternal life.* The fruit of being made free from sin and becoming servants to God is sanctification here and eternal life in the world to come.

Even if you were permitted to go back under sin, would it pay? Compare the fruits of righteousness and the fruits of sin.

Verse 23: *For the wages of sin is death; but the free gift of God is eternal life in Christ Jesus our Lord.* Sin pays wages—God makes a free gift. If you serve sin, you need not doubt as to what your wages are to be, nor as to whether you will be paid in full. The final reward for your service to sin is eternal death. And if you serve sin, you must look to sin for your wages. Eternal life is a free gift of God. No man can perform service that will entitle him to eternal life as wages; it comes as a free gift to those who love and serve the Lord. No, a man should not sin, even if he is not under law, but grace.

Chapter 7

7:1 Or are ye ignorant, brethren, (for I speak to men who know the law), that the law hath dominion over a man for so long time as he liveth? 2 For the woman that hath a husband is bound by law to the husband while he liveth; but if the husband die, she is discharged from the law of the husband. 3 So then if, while the husband liveth, she be joined to another man, she shall be called an adulteress: but if the husband die, she is free from the law, so that she is no adulteress, though she be joined to another man. 4 Wherefore, my brethren, ye also were made dead to the law through the body of Christ; that ye should be joined to another, even to him who was raised from the dead, that we might bring forth fruit unto God. 5 For when we were in the flesh, the sinful passions, which were through the law, wrought in our members to bring forth fruit unto death. 6 But now we have been discharged from the law, having died to that wherein we were held; so that we serve in newness of the spirit, and not in oldness of the letter. 7 What shall we say then? Is the law sin? God forbid. Howbeit, I had not known sin, except through the law: for I had not known coveting, except the law had said, Thou shalt not covet: 8 but sin, finding occasion, wrought in me through the commandment all manner of coveting: for apart from the law sin is dead. 9 And I was alive apart from the law once: but when the commandment came, sin revived, and I died; 10 and the commandment, which was unto life, this I found to be unto death: 11 for sin, finding occasion, through the commandment beguiled me, and through it slew me. 12 So that the law is holy, and the commandment holy, and righteous, and good. 13 Did then that which is good become death unto me? God forbid. But sin, that it might be shown to be sin, by working death to me through that which is good;—that through the commandment sin might become exceeding sinful. 14 For we know that the law is spiritual: but I am carnal, sold under sin. 15 For that which I do I know not: for not what I would, that do I practise; but what I hate, that I do. 16 But if what I would not, that I do, I consent unto the law that it is good. 17 So now it is no more I that do it, but sin which dwelleth in me. 18 For I know that in me, that is, in my flesh, dwelleth no good thing: for to will is present with me, but to do that which is good is not. 19 For the good which I would I do not: but the evil which I would not, that I practise. 20 But if what I would not, that I do, it is no more I that do it, but sin which dwelleth in me. 21 I find then the law, that, to me would do good, evil is present. 22 For I delight in the law of God after the inward man: 23 but I see a different law in my members, warring against the law of my mind, and bringing me into captivity under the law of sin which is in my members. 24 Wretched man that I am! who shall deliver me out of the body of this death? 25 I thank God through Jesus Christ our Lord. So then I of myself with the mind, indeed, serve the law of God; but with the flesh the law of sin.

Note.—Some of the efforts to explain Rom. 7:1-6 have not been very helpful. The meaning is sometimes obscured by injection into the passage things that the Holy Spirit did not put into it. Paul was not teaching a lesson on the relation of husband and wife, but was using that well-known relationship as an illustra-

tion to show the brethren their relation to the law and
to Christ.   There is always one main point of comparison in an illustration, and to seek to extend the
illustration to points not intended by the user is con-
fusing.   What is the purpose of Paul's marriage illustration?   He still has in mind freedom from the law,
and whether that freedom permits the Christian to sin
(Rom. 6:14, 15).   His illustration not only shows that
we are free from the law, but that Christians are
bound to Christ.   He now is our master.

Verse 1:   *Or are ye ignorant, brethren (for I speak
to men who know the law), that the law hath dominion
over a man for so long time as he liveth?*   Law, in the
parentheses, has no *the* before it in the Greek: "I
speak to those who know law"—who know both the
purpose and the limits of law, any and all law, including the law of Moses.   Paul credits them with knowing
that the law has dominion over a man so long as he
lives, and no longer.   *The law* is the law of Moses,
though what is here affirmed of the law of Moses is
true of any law under which a man lives.   When a man
dies, the law governs him no longer—he is dead to the
law, and the law is dead to him.

Verse 2:   *For the woman that hath a husband is
bound by law to the husband while he liveth; but if the
husband die, she is discharged from the law of the
husband.*   This is the general law of marriage.   Whatever exceptions there might be are not here taken into consideration, for they had no part in the truth
that Paul was illustrating.   It was intended that both
parties to a marriage should be faithful to their marriage vows, and that only death should separate them.
If they remained true to each other, only death could

separate them. As Paul was using this illustration to show that the brethren were released from the law so as to be married to Christ, it is easy to see why he speaks of the wife's obligations instead of the husband's. The death of the husband releases the wife from the law of her husband—that is, it releases her from the law that bound her to that husband.

Verse 3: *So then if, while the husband liveth, she be joined to another man, she shall be called an adulteress: but if the husband die, she is free from the law, so that she is no adulteress, though she be joined to another man.* Here again is a fixed law concerning the marriage relation. When one pledges one's self to another in marriage, it is a base thing to break the marriage vows by immoral practices. But let us not forget that Paul is using this marriage relation to illustrate a principle that is involved in our relations to the law and to the Christ. Our close union with the Lord Jesus Christ, Paul, by a figure of speech, speaks of as marriage to him. The relation of the people of Israel to Jehovah under the Old Testament was frequently spoken of under the same figure of speech. When the people then turned from Jehovah to worship idols and to mix in the religions of other people, Jehovah accused them of being guilty of whoredom and adultery. "She committed adultery with stones and with stocks" (Jer. 3:9). "With their idols have they committed adultery" (Ezek. 23:37). So long as the law was of force, they could not be married to another.

Verse 4: *Wherefore, my brethren, ye also were made dead to the law through the body of Christ; that ye should be joined to another, even to him who was*

*raised from the dead, that we might bring forth fruit
unto God.* This is the application of the principle set
forth in the marriage illustration. They became dead
to the law that they might be joined, or married, to
Christ. They became dead to the law through the
body of Christ—that is, through the death of the body
of Christ. It would be difficult to understand how
they became dead to the law through the body of Christ
were it not for light gained from other passages. People became dead to the law when it ended, or was abolished. "For he is our peace, who made both one, and
brake down the middle wall of partition, having abolished in his flesh the enmity, even the law of commandments contained in ordinances; that he might create in
himself of the two one new man, so making peace; and
might reconcile them both in one body unto God
through the cross, having slain the enmity thereby"
(Eph. 2:14-16). The law of Moses is here called the
enmity between Jew and Gentile, because it acted as
a barrier between them. Paul here affirms that this
enmity was slain by the cross, or by the death of Christ
on the cross. "Having blotted out the bond written
in ordinances that was against us, which was contrary
to us: and he hath taken it out of the way, nailing
it to the cross" (Col. 2:14). The law had dominion
over those under it so long as it lived, but it was abolished at the cross. They then became dead to it, for
it no longer had dominion over them. It is well to
notice that this passage definitely settles two things:
(1) They were not married to Christ before his death
—the law was taken out of the way at the cross that
they might be joined to the risen Christ. (2) When
Paul wrote this letter, these Roman brethren had been

joined to Christ. That is made clear by the fact stated: that they were joined to Christ that they might bring forth fruit unto God   It is certain that Christians are expected to bear fruit in this life. But the marriage, or joining, to Christ precedes the fruit bearing. Verse 6 shows that the bearing of fruit is done in serving God in newness of the spirit. Besides, if the closeness of the relationship that existed between Jehovah and the Jews was spoken of as a marriage, certainly the closer union between Christ and his followers would also be spoken of as a marriage. In another place Paul uses the marriage relationship to illustrate the close union between Christ and the church (See Eph. 5:22-33). Notice specially verse 23: "For the husband is the head of the wife, as Christ also is the head of the Church, being himself the Savior of the body." Here is a comparison: The husband is head of the wife, as Christ is head of the church— in the same manner as Christ is head of the church. How could that be if, as some say, the church is now only espoused to Christ? That Paul in this entire passage is using the marriage relation to illustrate the relationship existing between Christ and the church is evident to any unbiased reader. Verse 32 shows conclusively that such is his purpose: "This mystery is great: but I speak in regard of Christ and of the church." So, then, in speaking of husband and wife, he was by way of illustration speaking of Christ and the church

Verses 5, 6: *For when we were in the flesh, the sinful passions, which were through the law, wrought in our members to bring forth fruit unto death. But now we have been discharged from the law, having*

died to that wherein we were held, so that we serve in
newness of the spirit, and not in the oldness of the let-
ter. "Flesh" here does not mean the human body, for
their being "in the flesh" was a thing of the past.
Paul's marriage illustration to show their relation to
the law and to Christ shows that he had in mind the
Jewish brethren. No others were delivered from the
law that they might be joined to Christ. "In the flesh"
refers to the time they were under the law of Moses,
for Paul immediately adds by way of contrast: "But
now we have been discharged from the law." They
had been "in the flesh" but had been "discharged from
the law." It is not strange that Paul spoke of them
as "in the flesh" during the time they were under the
law. The old covenant was a flesh covenant. They
were members of the covenant by virtue of their flesh
connection with Abraham, and circumcision in the
flesh was a sign of membership in that covenant.

"Sinful passions," or passions of sin. Our passions
are not essentially sinful, and they certainly did not
come to us through the law of Moses—the law of
Moses did not create passions. They are sinful only
when they lead us to do things contrary to God's will.
In this way they became sinful through the law—that
is, through the violation of the law. These sinful passions work through our bodies to bring forth fruit unto death.

The statement that they had been discharged from
the law is a positive declaration that they were no
longer under the law. They had died to that wherein
they were held, and had no longer any connection with
it. "Newness of the spirit" is the new life of the
spirit into which they were raised at their baptism

(6:4). The "oldness of the letter" was the old law. They were not then serving God in the law of Moses. But Sabbatarians tell us that the term *law* in these verses does not include the Ten Commandments. The next verse shows them to be wrong.

Verse 7: *What shall we say then? Is the law sin? God forbid. Howbeit, I had not known sin, except through the law: for I had not known coveting, except the law had said, Thou shalt not covet.* Hence, the law Paul had in mind included the command, "Thou shalt not covet," which itself was one of the Ten Commandments. The Ten Commandments were a part of that law from which these brethren had been delivered. Because people violated the law, and thereby became sinful, did not prove the law to be sinful. The law defined and condemned sin. Paul had not known coveting—that is, he had not known the real nature of coveting—had not the law said, "Thou shalt not covet." Then he knew coveting—knew the nature of it, knew it to be sin. At the time Paul learned coveting to be sinful he was under the law of Moses, and it was his only source from which to learn the nature of coveting. Any one can now learn from the gospel of Christ the sinfulness of coveting. In fact, the gospel of Christ condemns coveting as idolatry, and thus condemns coveting more severely than does the law.

Verse 8: *But sin, finding occasion, wrought in me through the commandment all manner of coveting: for apart from the law sin is dead.* James Macknight translates this verse: "But I say that sin taking opportunity under the commandment, wrought effectually in me all strong desire. For without law sin is dead." The Authorized Version reads: "But sin, taking occasion by the commandment, wrought in me all manner of concupiscence. For without the law sin was dead." Many others render the verse substantially the same as do Macknight and the Authorized Version. It is a fact that the phrase, "by the commandment," or "through the commandment," in the Greek text, comes before *wrought,* and seems to connect directly with "taking occasion." This makes the commandment only the occasion for sin to assert itself. The commandment was only the occasion for sin to override the authority of God. It is certain that God's command was not the source of the evil desires. Let it be remembered that sin is here personified, and represented as an enemy that is trying to get us into trouble. There is no occasion for any one to think that a command of God creates or stirs up evil desires. The desire was there, even if God had issued no command, but became an evil desire when it sought to override the command. Hence, "without the law sin was dead." As sin is lawlessness, sin would not be operative where there is no law. Neither does law apply to a person who is not responsible for his deeds. To such a person there is really no law, and, therefore, no sin.

Verse 9: *And I was alive apart from the law once: but when the commandment came, sin revived, and I died.* The only time Paul was without law was during the years of his childhood, before he reached the years of accountability. On this verse the Cambridge Greek Testament makes the following clear comment: " 'I was living unaffected by law once.' He goes back to a pre-moral state—not necessarily in actual memory of a complete non-moral experience, but comparatively; his life as a child was untouched by numberless demands of law, which accumulated with his moral development; at that period whole regions of his life were purely impulsive; one after another they came under the touch of law, and with each new pressure of law upon his consciousness, the sphere, in which it was possible to sin, was enlarged. It was easy to carry this retrospect one step beyond memory, and to see himself living a life of pure impulse before the very first voice of law reached him, and to regard such a stage as a typical stage in the general development of the moral sense in man." The command came to Paul when he began to realize his own individual responsibility in the matter of obeying God. Then "sin revived." Sin sprang to life. It does not mean that sin came to life again. The Greek student will recognize the perfective function of the preposition prefixed to the word translated *revived*, and that instead of changing the meaning of the verb, adds to it force and vividness—sin came much alive. And then he died spiritually. But we are told that a person is born totally depraved—born dead in trespasses and sins. It would be interesting to hear one of those advocates of hereditary total depravity tell us when Paul was alive without the law and when he died spiritually.

Verse 10: *And the commandment, which was unto life, this I found to be unto death.* The commandment was meant to lead him in the way of life; but when he disobeyed that commandment, the curse of the law, the penalty of death, came upon him. Obedience to the commandment was life; disobedience brought

death. This is not strange, for many things that are
essential to life bring death when abused. The decree
of the law was: Obey, and live; disobey, and die.

Verse 11: *For sin, finding occasion, through the
commandment beguiled me, and through it slew me.*
In the King James Version this verse reads: "For
sin, taking occasion by the commandment, deceived
me, and by it slew me." Notice the difference in the
punctuation. The reader of the Bible should know that
punctuation marks were not in use when the Bible
was written, and that in using them now the translators place them so as to show what seems to them the
proper construction of the sentence. The translators
of the American Standard Version thought the phrase,
"through the commandment," should modify "deceived"—deceived through the commandment; the
King James translators thought it should modify "taking occasion"—taking occasion by the commandment.
In this instance I prefer the King James Version, for I
can see how the devil would take occasion through a
command of God to lead a person to disobey that command, but I cannot see how he could deceive a person
through a command of God. Yet some seriously argue
that Paul was deceived through the commandment,
and yet we wonder if the person who so argues does
not have any misgivings as to the correctness of his
contention. There is another peculiarity in the contention of those who so argue. Without seeming to
be conscious that they shift their ground a little, the
advocates of this position tell us that a command of
God stirs up in a sinner a feeling of rebellion against
whatever God commands. But if a person is led by
deception to disobey God, then he does not disobey

through a rebellious spirit. But do God's commands really stir in the sinner a determination not to do what God commands and to do what he forbids? Does any one really think that the command, "Thou shalt not kill," ever made any one want to commit murder? Did the command, "Thou shalt not steal," ever make any one want to slip out at night and steal?

Paul used his own experience as typical of the experiences of all other people. The truth he set forth is illustrated in the case of Eve. Concerning the fruit of the tree of the knowledge of good and evil God said to Adam and Eve: "Thou shalt not eat of it." By his lying speech Satan deceived her. He did not deceive her by means of the commandment, but took the commandment as an occasion to approach her, and to deceive her into believing it would be greatly to her advantage to eat the fruit. Death was the penalty for that disobedience. Hence, the devil seized the occasion, or opportunity, presented by that command, and by his artful speech deceived her, and by the command slew her. It certainly was not inherent depravity that caused her to sin. So nearly did her case parallel Paul's that we can say of her substantially what Paul said of himself: Satan, taking occasion through the commandment, deceived Eve, and by it slew her. And so of all others.

Verse 12: *So that the law is holy, and the commandment holy, and righteous, and good.* This is the conclusion to his answer to the question a Jew might ask: "If we had to be delivered from the law before we could be made free from sin, does that mean that the law is sin?" Sin and death had come through a failure to keep the law. But what is the difference between *the law* and *the commandment?* *Law* includes all the rules and regulations covering man's duties and obligations; *commandment* is any specific requirement. The law was given to promote holiness, and so was any specific commandment. The commandment was also just in its demands, and good in its results. But this raises another question.

Verse 13: *Did then that which is good become death unto me? God forbid. But sin, that it might be shown to be sin, by working death to me through that which is good;—that through the commandment sin might become exceeding sinful.* The commandment which was just, and intended for good, did not work death. Sin brought death through the good commandment that sin might appear in its true nature, and in that way appear to be exceeding sinful. Not only does sin by deceit make the good commands of God instruments of death, but also by deceit converts the choicest gifts of nature into instruments of sin, and even death. In its results sin shows its destructiveness. A good law is not to blame, if people disobey it and bring punishment upon themselves.

Verse 14: *For we know that the law is spiritual: but I am carnal, sold under sin.* The law is spiritual, because it appeals to the inner man—the spirit of man. Likely the worldly-minded Jew saw nothing in the law but forms and ceremonies, but the pious and faithful recognized its appeal to the heart. The first and fundamental requirement of the law is stated in these words: "Thou shalt love Jehovah thy God with all thy heart, and with all thy soul, and with all thy might. And these words, which I command thee this day, shall be upon thy heart" (Deut. 6:5, 6). "But I

am carnal, sold under sin." Was Paul here speaking
of himself as a Christian? Was he as a Christian
"sold under sin"? In verse 9 he spoke of the time
when sin entered his life, and he died. He then explains that sin, not the law, caused this spiritual
death. Sin is here personified, and Paul represents
himself as having been sold to sin as a slave. But if
he referred to his past experience, why did he use
the present tense? Because he was merely speaking
of himself as a type of all who were under the bondage
of sin. The following from Macknight is worth considering: "Because the apostle in this passage uses
the first person, 'I am sold,' etc., Augustine in the latter part of his life, and most of the commentators
after his time, with many of the moderns, especially the Calvinists, contend that in this, and in what
follows, to the end of the chapter, the apostle describes
his own state at the time he wrote this epistle, consequently the state of every regenerated person. But
most of the ancient Greek commentators, all the Ar-
minians, and some Calvinists, held that though the
apostle speaks in the first person, he by no means
describes his own state, but the state of an unregenerated sinner awakened, by the operation of law, to a
sense of his sin and misery. And this opinion they
support by observing that in his writings the apostle
often personates others (See Rom. 13:11-13). Wherefore, to determine the question, the reader must consider to which of the two characters the things written in this chapter best agree; and, in particular,
whether the apostle would say of himself, or other
regenerated persons, that 'they are carnal, and sold
under sin.' " Would he also say of himself as a Chris-

tian, "Wretched man that I am"? And would he as
a Christian exclaim, "Who shall deliver me out of the
body of this death"? (See verse 24). Then notice that
in the next verse he thanks God that deliverance
comes through Jesus Christ our Lord. To take it that
Paul in his own person describes the condition of the
unregenerated sinner presents less difficulties than to
suppose that he was describing his condition as a
Christian. The sinner's conflict is next described.

Verse 15: *For that which I do I know not: for
not what I would, that do I practice; but what I hate,
that I do.* Some commentators think the first clause
should read: "For what I do I approve not." But
that has the appearance of being a translation made
to escape a seeming difficulty. Lard thinks that
ginosko sometimes, though rarely, means *to approve*,
and adds: "Now, I hold that to render the word
know, in the present clause, is to make the apostle not
only contradict himself, but speak like a simpleton.
'For what I do, I know not.' If a man know not what
he is doing, he is demented. This will not do for Paul."
But Lard, with others, misses the significance of the
word *know*. It does not mean simply to be conscious
of the particular act one is performing, but also to
grasp the nature and consequences of what one is doing. No sinner does that. When Paul was persecuting Christians, he was conscious of his acts, but was
utterly ignorant of the nature and consequences of
his deeds. "Howbeit I obtained mercy, because I did
it ignorantly in unbelief" (1 Tim. 1:13). He did not
know that every act he performed in persecuting the
church was a crime against God and man; he thought
he was doing right. He, therefore, did not know what

he was doing—what he was accomplishing. When Jesus was on the cross, he prayed: "Father, forgive them; for they know not what they do." These men knew they were engaged in the act of crucifying a man called Jesus; they did not know that they were crucifying the Son of God. They did not know what they were doing. "And now, brethren, I know that in ignorance ye did it, as did also your rulers" (Acts 3:17). "For had they known it, they would not have crucified the Lord of Glory" (1 Cor. 2:8). Now, these men were not demented. They knew they were putting a person to death; yet they did not know what they were doing. If a sinner really knew the full nature and awful consequences of the life he is living, he would quickly turn away from it.

The correctness of the foregoing remarks will be more easily seen if the reader is able to note a peculiarity of this verse. "Do" occurs twice, and each time from a different Greek word, and "practice" is from still another word, and these words are:

katergadzomai—to effect, accomplish, achieve, etc.

Prasso—to exercise, practice, be busy with, carry on, etc.

poieo—to produce, construct, form, fashion, to make, etc.

And so it is seen that these words mean more than simply to perform one act. It will be helpful exercise if you will take your pencil and reconstruct this verse, using different definitions each time you write it. Try this: "For that which I accomplish I know not: for not what I would, that do I practice; but what I hate, that I produce." The sinner does not know what he accomplishes by a life of sin. He cannot so much as

know how far reaching is the influence of his life of
sin. In his thoughtful moments he desires a different
life from the things he practices, but without Christ,
sin has him under its dominion. He may delight in
gratifying his flesh, but he hates the results produced
by his dissipation.

Verse 16: *But if what I would not, that I do, I consent unto the law that it is good.* The law demands a
decent, upright life. He wished to live that kind of
life, knowing that it is really the best life; and so he
agreed that the law was good. But the sinner, helpless without Christ, goes contrary to what his better
self desires.

Verse 17: *So now it is no more I that do it, but sin
which dwelleth in me.* This verse furnishes conclusive
evidence that Paul is not, in these verses, represent-
ing the condition of the Christian, for it certainly cannot be said that sin dwells in the Christian. The Holy
Spirit dwells in the Christian, and it is not possible
that the Holy Spirit and sin inhabit the same dwelling
place. True, sin slips in at times when the Christian
is off guard, as a thief might slip into your dwelling
place. He who dwells in a house has charge of the
house. To say that sin dwells in a person is to say
that sin has the control of him. When sin enters into
a Christian, it enters as an intruder and not as a
dweller.

But Paul's language does not free the sinner from
responsibility for his conduct. His language is a figure of speech, often found in the Bible, in which one
member of a sentence is negative in order to emphasize the other member. Here is an illustration: "He
that believeth on me, believeth not on me, but on him

that sent me" (John 12:44). We would say: "He that believeth on me, believeth not on me alone, but also on him that sent me." And so with Paul: "So now it is not I alone that do evil, but rather it is sin that dwells in me." His urge to follow the flesh was greater than his desire to do what his moral judgment dictated.

Paul makes a distinction between his real self and the sin which dwelt in him. Had he held to the doctrine that total depravity was an inherent part of everybody born into the world, he could not have made that distinction. If sin is a part of our nature, then no one could think of himself as distinct from sin. I dwell in a house, but the house was not made with me in it. Paul locates the time when sin enters a person. "I was alive apart from the law once: but when the commandment came, sin revived, and I died" (Verse 9). Sin enters a person when he first becomes responsible before God and violates his law, and then it dwells in him till he is redeemed from its bondage.

Verse 18: *For I know that in me, that is, in my flesh, dwelleth no good thing: for to will is present with me, but to do that which is good is not.* Paul affirms that no good thing dwells in his flesh. Here again he makes a distinction between the inner man and the flesh. In and of itself, aside from the intellect, the flesh is neither morally good nor morally bad. The flesh, the animal part of man, is a bundle of appetites and passions, which lead to sin only when they have enlisted the mind to plan and execute methods of self-gratification in an unlawful way. For that reason an idiot or a crazy person is not responsible for his deeds. The mind must have a part in any deed

for it to be either morally good or morally evil. A
normal person under law, whether the moral law or the
law of Moses, but without Christ, has a desire to do
good, but has not the ability to throw off sin and lead
a pure life. Paul used himself as an example of all
such characters. To make the lesson forceful, he pic-
tures himself as under the law, and without redemption through Christ.

Verse 19: *For the good which I would I do not:
but the evil which I would not, that I practice.* Practically a repetition of verse 15. That could not be
said of Paul as a Christian. Of himself as a Christian
he said: "Ye are witnesses, and God also, how holily
and righteously and unblamably we behaved ourselves
toward you that believed" (1 Thess. 2:10).

Verse 20: *But if what I would not, that I do, it is
no more I that do it, but sin that dwelleth in me.* This
verse is almost a repetition of verse 17. Even when
the alien sinner would do good, he finds that sin hin-
ders him. Paul is picturing the helplessness of the
sinner without Christ—without the regenerating and
saving power of the gospel. Here again is emphasized
the need of the power of the gospel. The inward man,
the spirit, in its contest with the passions of the flesh
is helpless without the gospel.

Verse 21: *I find then the law, that, to me who would
do good, evil is present.* This verse has given commentators no end of trouble. Some think that *the law* is
the law of Moses; others, that it is the rule of sin.
But to say that it means the rule of sin involves Paul
in great confusion in the use of the term *the law.* By
that term, when not restricted by other words, he had
constantly designated the law of Moses. There is no

indication that Paul meant anything else in this verse. But to take it that he referred to the law of Moses involves us in a difficulty as to what the verse means, unless we adopt the marginal reading of the American Standard Version, or a similar reading. If we adopt the marginal reading, we have: "I find then in regard of the law, that to me who would do good, evil is present." This is in harmony with what Paul had said about the condition of a person under the law and, without Christ. Such a person endorsed the law, but sin hindered him from carrying out what he knew to be right. Every normal person out of Christ finds himself wishing for a better, cleaner life; but without Christ he finds himself unable to free himself from the dominion of sin. But the doctrine of hereditary total depravity, that by inheritance "we are utterly indisposed, disabled, and made opposite unto all that is spiritually good, and wholly inclined to all evil, and that continually," makes it impossible for an advocate of that doctrine to see how an unconverted person can ever approve purity and holiness, or have the least desire to do any good deed. With them a sinner is opposed to everything that is right and wholly inclined to commit every crime known to man. Hence, commentators who are thoroughly wedded to that theory become confused in trying to explain verses 14-23. They cannot understand how a sinner could desire to do good, or delight in any good thing.

Verse 22: *For I delight in the law of God after the inward man.* There is an inward man and an outward man. The inner man is the seat of the mind and will. Even the inner man of the sinner is pleased with the law of God, though he does not practice it. If there

were nothing good in an unconverted man, the good
that is in God's law would not appeal to him.   Beauty
does not appeal to him who has no eye for the beautiful; music does not appeal to him who has no ear for
music; and the goodness in the gospel would have no
attraction to him who is "opposite to all good and
wholly inclined to all evil."   People who reach that
stage of depravity are utterly beyond the hope of redemption.   Such were the people before the flood, and
such were the people of Sodom and Gomorrah.   To be
totally depraved means to be totally lost now and in
the world to come.

Verse 23: *But I see a different law in my members,
warring against the law of my mind, and bringing me
into captivity under the law of sin which is in my
members.*   "Members" here stands for the sum total
of the body.   The different law—different from the
one he has been discussing—is the rule of sin in his
members.   The law of the mind is the law of God, the
law addressed to the mind.   It is through the mind—
the inner man—that God seeks by his law to control
the body.   Hence, there is a warfare.   If the spirit
under the influence of the law of God controls the
body, the person lives a spiritual life.   If the appetites
and passions of the body control the person, he is
brought into captivity to the law of sin in his members.   In verse 14 Paul speaks of this condition as
being sold under sin.   Such a person is a slave of sin.
It could not be said of a Christian that he was sold
under sin—brought into captivity to the rule of sin.
Such language as Paul here uses shows the complete
helplessness of a person under the dominion of sin and
without Christ.

Verse 24: *Wretched man that I am! who shall deliver me out of the body of this death?* This moral and
spiritual death, to which the appetites and passions
of the body had led. To be sold under sin, to be dead
in sin, is the same thing. Paul here presents the condition of the man who first finds himself completely
under the dominion of sin and helpless in his desire
to free himself, and yet knows no way of escape, till
Christ is revealed to him; then he exclaims, "I thank
God that through our Lord Jesus Christ" deliverance
comes. In Christ Jesus our Lord there is peace with
God, life from spiritual death, and rest from the intol-
erable burden of sin.

Verse 25: *I thank God through Jesus Christ our
Lord. So then I of myself with the mind, indeed,
serve the law of God; but with the flesh the law of sin.*
It seems to me that the commentators fail entirely
to grasp the meaning of this verse. Some of them
take it for granted that Paul is speaking of the condition of the Christian. In their estimation the mind
of the redeemed man serves God, but the flesh serves
the law of sin. When they seek to explain this idea by
dwelling on the warfare in the Christian between the
spirit and the flesh, they miss the point entirely, for
the verse says nothing about such a warfare. Paul
spoke of service, and not of fighting. And there is no
such thing as serving God with the mind while the
body serves sin. The idea is absurd. No man can
serve two masters at the same time. Recognizing this
truth, Lard says, "Now of course, I cannot serve both
the law of God, with the mind, and the law of sin,
with the flesh, at one and the same time. To serve
the one is to slight the other. And since I cannot serve

the law of sin continually and be a Christian; it follows that the service of sin is only occasional and exceptional. Hence, the meaning must be that with the flesh, and not with the mind, I serve the law of sin whenever I sin at all. I sin but seldom, suppose, but whenever I do sin, it is with the flesh as an instrument, or through its influence." But Lard misses the mark, for the word here translated "serve" means *to be a slave,* or *subject.* An occasional act does not constitute slavery in any relationship. You do not become a slave to your neighbor by helping him occasionally. An occasional sin does not make one a slave of sin. A person becomes a slave of sin only when he gives himself up to the rule of sin.

Paul contrasts the two kinds of service. He had been a slave of sin, but was redeemed to the service of God. The Christian serves with the mind the law of God; the sinner with the flesh serves the law of sin. In the life of a Christian, the mind—the inner man—dominates the flesh; in the sinner's life the flesh dominates the mind. But in either case the mind does the planning and willing. In the sinful life the mind yields to the appetites and passions of the flesh, and plans for their gratification; in the Christian life the mind keeps the body under, and uses it in acts of service to God. Hence, the use we make of the members of our bodies determines whose servants we are. "Know ye not, that to whom ye present yourselves as servants unto obedience, his servants ye are whom ye obey; whether of sin unto death, or of obedience unto righteousness?" (6:16).

Chapter 8

8:1 There is therefore now no condemnation to them that are in Christ Jesus. 2 For the law of the Spirit in Christ Jesus made me free from the law of sin and of death. 3 For what the law could not do, in that it was weak through the flesh, God, sending his own Son in the likeness of sinful flesh and for sin, condemned sin in the flesh: 4 that the ordinance of the law might be fulfilled in us, who walk not after the flesh, but after the Spirit. 5 For they that are after the flesh mind the things of the flesh; but they that are after the Spirit the things of the Spirit. 6 For the mind of the flesh is death: but the mind of the Spirit is life and peace: 7 because the mind of the flesh is enmity against God; for it is not subject to the law of God, neither indeed can it be: 8 and they that are in the flesh cannot please God. 9 But ye are not in the flesh but in the Spirit, if so be that the Spirit of God dwelleth in you. But if any man hath not the Spirit of Christ, he is none of his. 10 And if Christ is in you, the body is dead because of sin; but the spirit is life because of righteousness. 11 But if the Spirit of him that raised up Jesus from the dead dwelleth[1] in you, he that raised up Christ Jesus from the dead shall give life also to your mortal bodies through his Spirit that dwelleth in you.

12 So then, brethren, we are debtors, not to the flesh, to live after the flesh: 13 for if ye live after the flesh, ye must die; but if by the Spirit ye put to death the deeds of the body, ye shall live. 14 For as many as are led by the Spirit of God, these are sons of God. 15 For ye received not the spirit of bondage again unto fear; but ye received the spirit of adoption, whereby we cry, Abba, Father. 16 The Spirit himself beareth witness with our spirit, that we are children of God: 17 and if children, then heirs; heirs of God, and joint-heirs with Christ; if so be that we suffer with him, that we may be also glorified with *him.*

18 For I reckon that the sufferings of this present time are not worthy to be compared with the glory which shall be revealed to us-ward. 19 For the earnest expectation of the creation waiteth for the revealing of the sons of God. 20 For the creation was subjected to vanity, not of its own will, but by reason of him who subjected it, in hope 21 that the creation itself also shall be delivered from the bondage of corruption into the liberty of the glory of the children of God. 22 For we know that the whole creation groaneth and travaileth in pain together until now. 23 And not only so, but ourselves also, who have the first-fruits of the Spirit, even we ourselves groan within ourselves, waiting for our adoption, *to wit,* the redemption of our body. 24 For in hope were we saved: but hope that is seen is not hope: for who hopeth for that which he seeth? 25 But if we hope for that which we see not, *then* do we with patience wait for it.

26 And in like manner the Spirit also helpeth our infirmity: for we know not how to pray as we ought: but the Spirit himself maketh intercession for us with groanings which cannot be uttered: 27 and he that searcheth the hearts knoweth what is the mind of the Spirit, because he maketh intercession for the saints according to *the will of* God. 28 And we know that to them that love God all things work together for good, *even* to them that are called according to *his* purpose. 29 For whom he foreknew, he also foreordained *to be* conformed to the image of his Son, that he might be the firstborn among many brethren: 30 and whom he foreordained, them he also called: and whom he called, them he also justified: and whom he justified, them he also glorified.

31 What then shall we say to these things? If God *is* for us, who *is* against us? 32 He that spared not his own Son, but delivered him up for us all, how shall he not also with him freely give us all things? 33 Who shall lay anything to the charge of God's elect? It is God that justifieth; 34 who is he that condemneth?

It is Christ Jesus that died, yea rather, that was raised from the dead, who is at the right hand of God, who also maketh intercession for us. 35 Who shall separate us from the love of Christ? shall tribulation, or anguish, or persecution, or famine, or nakedness, or peril, or sword? 36 Even as it is written,

For thy sake we are killed all the day long;
We were accounted as sheep for the slaughter.

37 Nay, in all these things we are more than conquerors through him that loved us. 38 For I am persuaded, that neither death, nor life, nor angels, nor principalities, nor things present, nor things to come, nor powers, 39 nor height, nor depth, nor any other creature, shall be able to separate us from the love of God, which is in Christ Jesus our Lord.

Verse 1: *There is therefore now no condemnation to them that are in Christ Jesus.* Now in this gospel dispensation, there is no condemnation to them that are in Christ Jesus. Under law it was different; all sinned and were under condemnation. The law could not save; it condemned, and made people realize their sinfulness and their helplessness. Conscious of this helplessness, the doomed man cried out: "Who shall deliver me?" But when the light of the gospel of Jesus Christ broke in upon him, he joyously exclaimed: "I thank God that through Jesus Christ there is deliverance." Now, being in Christ, having been forgiven of his sins and made righteous, he is free from the condemnation that formerly rested upon him. As to whether he may or may not again come into condemnation is not the matter under consideration; and one does violence to Paul's line of reasoning to try to make his language apply to anything more than the fact that the person who has come into Christ is free from his former condemnation. A person might run into a cave and be free from the storm that raged without, but that does not guarantee future safety. Hence, we must not conclude that this freedom from our former condemnation insures us against falling again into condemnation. To free a person from the condemnation formerly resting upon him does not rob him of personal responsibility for his conduct in the future. In the very nature of things, sin must be condemned anywhere, at any time, and in any place. No government could stand if sin were not condemned and punished. But in Christ condemnation can always be avoided.

Verse 2: *For the law of the Spirit of life in Christ Jesus made me free from the law of sin and of death.* It seems to me that the phrase "in Christ Jesus" modifies "made free," for it is in Christ that we are made free. To connect this phrase with the "law of the Spirit of life" leaves us in doubt as to its significance. "For" connects this verse with the preceding verse, and assigns the reason as to why there is no condemnation in Christ Jesus. There is no condemnation in Christ Jesus, for in Christ Jesus we have been made free from that which causes condemnation—namely, the law of sin and of death. This freedom is accomplished by the law of the Spirit of life. Many descriptive titles are applied to the Holy Spirit, each such title growing out of some particular work the Holy Spirit does, or some office he fills. "It is the spirit that giveth life" (John 6:63). Hence, the Spirit of life. But what is the law of the Spirit of life? If we can determine what the law of sin and death is, from which the law of the Spirit delivers us, we should be able to see what the law of the Spirit is. The death here mentioned is spiritual death, for in becoming a Christian a person is not delivered from the law of physical death. This law of sin and death cannot be the law of Moses; for, taking verses 2 and 3 together, we see that the law of Moses could not do what the law of the Spirit had done. If the law of sin and death

is the law of Moses, then we have Paul making the
absurd statement that the law of Moses could not deliver us from the law of Moses! But Paul never wrote
such foolishness. The law of sin and death is the law
set forth in 7:23: "But I see a different law in my
members, warring against the law of my mind, and
bringing me into captivity under the law of sin, which
is in my members." To be in captivity under the
law of sin is to be dead spiritually. Hence, this law
of sin in our members is also the law of death. Freedom
from that law is salvation. But the law of the Spirit
of life makes us free from the law of sin and death—
that is, it is that by which we are saved. In chapter
1:16, Paul tells us that the gospel is God's power for
saving people. We conclude, therefore, that the law of
the Spirit of life is the gospel. This conclusion har-
monizes with Paul's line of reasoning. It would be
absurd to think that Paul started in to prove that the
gospel is God's power for saving people, and then
reached the conclusion that some other law saves us,
or frees us, from sin and spiritual death.

Verse 3: *"For what the law could not do, in that it
was weak through the flesh, God, sending his own Son
in the likeness of sinful flesh and for sin, condemned
sin in the flesh."* The main thought in this verse seems
clear enough, but the grammatical construction is
difficult. As it stands, the first part—"for what the
law could not do, in that it was weak through the flesh"
—has no grammatical connection with the rest of the
sentence. The meaning of the verse may be expressed
somewhat as follows: For what the law could not accomplish, in that it was weak through the flesh, God
accomplished by sending his own Son in the likeness of

sinful flesh, and for sin (or, *and as an offering for sin* —marginal reading) condemned sin in the flesh. The law of Moses could not free a person from the law of sin and death, but God did that very thing by the plan of salvation perfected by the mission of his Son into the world, including his death as a sin offering. The death of Christ procured for all who accept him release from the condemnation that rests upon all sinners. And thus in his flesh he condemned sin. Formerly sin reigned as master, and held the sinner in captivity. When a person accepts Christ, sin as his master is destroyed—blotted out. So far as we know, there was no way to destroy the reign of sin except through the death of Jesus Christ; but that death benefits only those who yield obedience to him as their King. He came in the likeness of sinful flesh. Human flesh is not sinful in and of itself; if so the flesh of Jesus was sinful. But some commentators seek to evade this by stressing the word "likeness." His flesh, they say, was not sinful, but was like sinful flesh! But he was man (1 Tim. 2:5), and frequently spoke of himself as the Son of man. He, therefore, had in his nature all that the word "man" implies. "Since then the children are sharers in flesh and blood, he also himself in like manner partook of the same" (Heb. 2:14). "Wherefore it behooved him in all things to be made like unto his brethren" (Heb. 2:17). If his brethren were born sinful and he was not, then he was not like them in all things. But as Jesus was made in all things like his brethren and was without sin, it shows conclusively that sin is not a part of man's nature. When Adam and Eve were first created, they had all that belongs to human nature. Sin came into their lives as

a foreign element. Sin is no more a part of your nature than dust in your eye is a part of the nature of
your eye. Because the desires, appetites, and passions
of the flesh so often lead to sin, flesh is called sinful.
But we should remember always that fleshly desires
lead to sin only when the mind, or heart, purposes to
gratify the flesh in an unlawful way.

The law was not weak in itself; it was weak because
in man's folly the urgings of the flesh are stronger
than man's regard for law, and because in his ignorance and selfishness man could not meet its requirements.

Verse 4: *That the ordinance of the law might be
fulfilled in us, who walk not after the flesh, but after
the Spirit.* Commentators are not agreed as to whether
the Greek word translated "ordinance" should be
translated *ordinance, requirement, righteousness,* or
justification. They are, therefore, not agreed as to
what is fulfilled in us, nor as to how it is done. Neither
are they agreed as to whether it is fulfilled *in us* or *by
us.* Macknight thinks the law here referred to is the
gospel. It seems to me that the context—the trend of
Paul's argument—must decide the whole matter. Of
course, due regard must be had to the truths set forth
in other parts of the Scriptures. Let us notice the trend
of Paul's reasoning.

Under the law, the righteousness of the law could
be fulfilled only by perfect obedience. In such obedience there would have been no sin—God would have
had nothing against one who so lived. Now, it is the
mission of the gospel to take sinners and make them
righteous. When a person's sins are forgiven he is
freed from all guilt, and is then as righteous as if he

had never sinned. There is then no guilt attached to him—God has nothing against him. And so the thing that the law required, but could not accomplish, is fulfilled in those who obey the gospel. If this is not a correct exegesis of the first part of verse 4, it is certainly in harmony with Paul's line of reasoning and also with the general teaching of the Scriptures. Paul certainly did not mean that we were delivered from sin by the gospel that we might obey the ordinance of the law of Moses, but that the gospel, in freeing us from sin and making us righteous, accomplished in us exactly what the law was unable to accomplish, but what it would have accomplished in us had there been no transgression of it.

"Who walk not after the flesh, but after the Spirit." There is no "if" about this. The clause is descriptive of the characters in whom the righteousness of the law is fulfilled. "Walk" refers to manner of life. As flesh and spirit are here contrasted, it seems certain that Paul meant the human spirit, and not the Holy Spirit. To walk according to the flesh is to lead an animal life. Such a one may be an immoral wretch, or he may be a respected citizen. No matter what his character is, he is one who lives a worldly life. He lives as if this life were all that is worth while. To walk according to the spirit is to keep the flesh under control so as to promote spiritual growth in the service of God.

Verse 5: *For they that are after the flesh mind the things of the flesh; but they that are after the Spirit the things of the Spirit.* To mind the things of the flesh is to give our time and attention to the things of this life. To do so is to leave God and our eternal welfare out of consideration. We need to be careful, for it is easy for us in our struggles to make a living to forget God and look only to our material interests. To mind the things of the spirit is to look to the things that fit the spirit for acceptable service to God in this life and that will prepare it for the joys of the next life.

Verse 6: *For the mind of the flesh is death; but the mind of the Spirit is life and peace.* The mind of the flesh, as the connection shows, is the mind devoted to the flesh. The minding the flesh is death. To be devoted to the things of the flesh is death. Such a state not only tends to death, it is death itself. The one who thus lives is dead to God. For the mind to be devoted to the things of the spirit—to the needs of the spirit— is life and peace. It is life from spiritual death and peace with God and conscience. The phrases, "mind of the flesh" and "mind of the spirit," do not mean that a person has two distinct minds—that is, that the flesh has a mind and the spirit has a mind. If so, the flesh would always be dead to God, for the mind of the flesh is death; and the spirit would always be alive to God, whether in righteousness or sin, for the mind of the spirit is life. In that case the spirit would never need conversion, and the flesh could not be converted.

Verses 7, 8: *Because the mind of the flesh is enmity against God; for it is not subject to the law of God, neither indeed can it be: and they that are in the flesh cannot please God.* Minding the flesh is spiritual death, because it is enmity against God. While devoted to the flesh, while minding the flesh, a person is not subject to the will of God, and in that state a person cannot be subject to God, for such a life is in direct conflict with his will. It does not mean that a person

who lives a worldly life cannot turn from it and himself become subject to the law of God; but it does mean
that a person cannot live for the things of this life
and at the same time be subject to God. If you live a
worldly life, you are not living a Christian life. To
live a worldly life—a life devoted to the flesh—is to
be in the flesh. As Paul uses the terms in this connection, to walk according to the flesh, to be after the
things of the flesh, to mind the things of the flesh, and
to be in the flesh, are all one and the same thing. But
Christians are not in the flesh—that is, they are not
living a life devoted to the flesh.

Verse 9: *But ye are not in the flesh but in the Spirit, if so be that the Spirit of God dwelleth in you.* The
contrast, "not in the flesh but in the Spirit," shows
that the human spirit is meant. Lard's comment on
this verse seems to be to the point: "Not to be in the
flesh is not to live according to it, and not to live according to it is not to allow it to control us; it is, in a
word, not to sin under the pressure of its influence.
But in the Spirit.' The word 'spirit' here denotes the
human spirit; nor can I see how any one ever comes to
think otherwise. It is sheer assumption to say that it
denotes the Holy Spirit. To be in the flesh is to live
the life of a sinner; to be in the spirit, to live the life
of the Christian. . . . It is virtual tautology to say that
we are governed by the Holy Spirit provided the Holy
Spirit dwells in us, for the very purpose for which the
Holy Spirit dwells in us is to control us." But the
Spirit of God is the Holy Spirit. He dwells in the
Christian; that is plainly affirmed. And I dare not
deny what Paul here affirms. The Holy Spirit is also
called the Spirit of Christ. "But if any man hath not

the Spirit of Christ, he is none of his." That statement should engage the serious attention of every professed Christian.

Verse 10: *And if Christ is in you, the body is dead
because of sin; but the spirit is life because of righteousness.* This verse has given no end of trouble to
commentators. They are not agreed as to what is
meant by the clause, "the body is dead because of sin."
Lard thinks it means that the body is dead on account
of sin in the sense that it is doomed to death on account of Adam's sin. Some others hold practically
the same idea. But it sounds foolish to say: "If Christ
is in you, the body is doomed to death on account of
Adam's sin." That would imply that if Christ did not
dwell in us the body would not be doomed to death on
account of Adam's sin. As a matter of fact, the body
is doomed to die physically, whether Christ dwells in
us or does not dwell in us. Besides, that construction
does not agree with the context. In the latter part of
chapter 7, Paul spoke of the flesh as the source of sin.
Because the appetites and passions of the flesh lead to
so much sin Paul calls it "sinful flesh" (verse 3). For
that reason the flesh is crucified—put to death as to sin.
"And they that are of Christ Jesus have crucified the
flesh with the passions and lusts thereof" (Gal. 5:24).
Hence, "if Christ be in you, the body is dead because
of the sin to which it leads"; or, more exactly, "the
body is dead on account of sin that dwells in it." "But
the spirit is life because of righteousness"—that is, on
account of the righteousness to which we attain in the
forgiveness, or blotting out, of our sins. Hence, if
Christ is in you, the body is dead on account of sin to

which it tends, but the spirit is life on account of the righteousness to which we attain in Christ.

Verse 11: *But if the Spirit of him that raised up Jesus from the dead dwelleth in you, he that raised up Christ Jesus from the dead shall give life also to your mortal bodies through his Spirit that dwelleth in you.* Here again we have a condition stated. The making alive of our mortal bodies depends upon his Spirit's dwelling in us. Does this refer to the resurrection? Some think so. But does our resurrection from the dead depend upon the Spirit's dwelling in us? Do not the Scriptures plainly teach that the wicked, as well as the righteous, will be raised? The future resurrection from the dead is not the matter under discussion at this point. He had just stated that the body was dead because of sin. That means that it is no longer active in sin—no longer an instrument of sin. But is it to remain altogether inactive? Is it not to be brought into any kind of activity in the life of the Christian? If the Spirit of God dwells in you, he will make your bodies alive to righteousness. That seems to be in harmony with the context. Besides, I am not sure that in the resurrection God will give life to our mortal bodies. Here our bodies are mortal; they are subject to death and decay; they return to dust. In the resurrection will God again form the dust into a mortal body and then give it life? Are we to be mortal when raised from the dead? If not, then this verse is not talking about the resurrection from the dead. "Shall give life also to your mortal bodies" is stated in the future tense, because there are conditions to be performed by man. The word "also" connects this giving life to our mortal bodies with the life already given to the spirit.

The fact that Jesus was raised from the dead that we might be saved—might be made alive to his service—is a guarantee that even our bodies, as well as our spirits, shall be made alive to righteousness. By the teaching of the Holy Spirit we are required to present our bodies a living sacrifice. So if the Spirit of God dwells in us, not only are our spirits alive to righteousness, but our bodies will also be made alive to the service of God. "For we who live are always delivered unto death for Jesus' sake, that the life also of Jesus may be manifested in our mortal flesh" (2 Cor. 4:11).

The following note seems to be worth inserting here: "The section (8:1-11) balances the preceding section (7:7-25). There the inability of the law by itself to produce the higher spiritual life was shown, and the argument dealt primarily and mainly with human life as it is now. Here the whole object is to show that the gospel provides just such a power as law lacks—that is, to revive and renew the human spirit so as to enable it to mold and master the whole life. The life and death spoken of are the spiritual life and death already described; the raising is the present liberation of the spirit which affects the body also, making it, too, serve its true ends and live its true life. The raising of Jesus is a proof both of the will and character and power of that Spirit, which operated then and operates now through the risen life communicated now to man (cf. 6:2-11). The future resurrection is not referred to; but it is, of course, implied as a consequence of the whole relation thus described between God and man." (Cambridge Greek Testament).

Verse 12: *So, then, brethren, we are debtors, not to the flesh, to live after the flesh.* "So then" seems to cover the whole argument beginning at chapter 5:12. "We are debtors" to what? Not to the flesh; we have already learned that attending to the flesh leads to death. We could not be under obligation to follow a course that leads to our own destruction. To live after the flesh is to live a worldly life. If we are not debtors to the flesh, then what? Evidently to our spirits— that is, we are obligated to attend to the things of the spirit. As the spirit controls the body, we must keep our spirits pure. Also, the spirit endures to eternity. We must guard it well, lest we fail of eternal life.

Verse 13: *For if ye live after the flesh, ye must die; but if by the spirit ye put to death the deeds of the body, ye shall live.* It is certain that the death here mentioned is spiritual death, for we shall die physically, no matter how we live. To live after the flesh results in spiritual death. All the arguing that an advocate of the impossibility of apostasy can do cannot change what Paul says. A person must accept it or reject it; he cannot explain it away. But if the spirit gains the ascendency and subdues the flesh and makes it serve God, we shall live.

Verse 14: *For as many as are led by the Spirit of God, these are sons of God.* And only such are children of God. The statement indicates a continuous process. Nothing is here said as to how the Spirit leads people; but as Paul is still developing his theme that the gospel is God's power to save, it is certain that the Spirit leads through the power of the gospel. The gospel was revealed by the Spirit. In that revelation the Spirit tells us how to live, and sets motives before us to induce us to follow his directions. But if the Spirit, independent of the gospel, leads people to become chil-

dren of God, then the gospel is not God's power to save.
We are sure Paul did not make an assertion about the
Holy Spirit that contradicted his theme and his argu-
ment.

Verse 15: *For ye received not the spirit of bondage
again unto fear; but ye received the spirit of adoption
whereby we cry, Abba, Father.* Notice the word
"again." In becoming children of God we do not again
enter into a bondage wherein we serve through fear.
The Jew under the law was moved principally through
fear, and idol worshippers were moved by fear. But
not so with the Christian. "But ye received the spirit
of adoption;" or, more exact, "Ye received the spirit
of sonship." A Christian is one who has been born
again; he is a child of God by birth, rather than by
adoption. He serves God, not through a spirit of slav-
ish fear, but through a spirit of filial obedience. "Spirit" as used in this verse does not refer to an individual
personal intelligence, but to disposition or attitude. Instead of being moved by fear as slaves, the child of God
renders trusting obedience to God, and confidently
calls upon him as Father. The spirit of fear is dis-
placed by a spirit of reverence, trust, and worship. The
term "Abba" means "Father." It seems that the two
terms are here used for emphasis.

Verses 16, 17: *The Spirit himself beareth witness
with our spirit, that we are children of God: and if children, then heirs; heirs of God and joint-heirs with
Christ; if so be that we suffer with him, that we may be
also glorified with him.* These verses do not seem to express thoughts additional to those expressed in verses
14 and 15, for there is no connecting conjunction; they
seem rather to be an explanation or further develop-

ment of what had just been said. All who are led by
the Spirit of God are sons of God; and yet, though
they are children of God, they are also servants of God.
But these children of God, though they are also servants, serve in the spirit of children, not in the spirit
of slaves. They have received the spirit, or disposition
of sons. Serving in the spirit of sons, they have assurance that God is in reality their Father. "The Spirit
himself beareth witness with our spirit, that we are
children of God." In Barnes commentary on Romans
we have this: "Beareth witness, testifies, gives evidence. With our spirit. To our spirit. This pertains
to the adoption; and it means that the Holy Spirit furnishes evidence to our minds that we are adopted into
the family of God." Barnes thus changes "with" to
"to," and yet there is quite a difference in the meaning
of the two prepositions. Besides, the language of the
verse shows that our spirit is one of two witnesses. To
say that the Holy Spirit bears witness to our spirit
is to make our spirit a judge, and not in any sense a
witness. Many who hold this theory regard what they
feel as superior to what God says. A theory that discredits the word of God is wrong. Then another idea
is presented, namely, that the Holy Spirit has given
his testimony as to what one must do to become a child
of God, and our spirit testifies that we have done those
things; and thus the two witnesses bear witness together, that we are children of God. This idea has this
merit: It does not discredit the word of God, nor encourage disobedience; but does it set forth the meaning
of verse 16? Does the term "our spirit" refer to our
inner man, or to the spirit, or disposition of the Christian? Notice the context. The preceding verse spoke

of the "spirit of bondage" and the "spirit of adoption,"
or sonship. The "spirit of bondage" did not refer to an
intelligent being, but to a disposition, or an attitude;
and so also did the "spirit of adoption." Then why
should not "our spirit" refer to the disposition, or attitude, of the Christian? Our spirit as Christians is the
spirit of faithful sons, the spirit of loving obedience.
That is the spirit Paul had just mentioned, and that is
our spirit—the Christian spirit. The Holy Spirit gives
testimony as to what one must do and be to be a child
of God, and our spirit of filial submission shows that
we possess the characteristics of sonship. In this way
we prove, not only to ourselves, but to the world also,
that we are children of God. A life of devotion guided
by the testimony of the Holy Spirit is double evidence
that we are children of God. It is convincing evidence
to right thinking people of the world. Jesus said:
"Even so let your light shine before men; that they
may see your good works, and glorify your Father who
is in heaven" (Matt. 5:16). The fruits of sonship;
Heirs of God—joint-heirs with Christ. But this is not
an unconditional inheritance. Weigh well the condition
—"if so be that we suffer with him, that we may also
be glorified with him." This however does not mean—
cannot mean—that we will have the same degree of
glory that he has.

Verse 18: *For I reckon that the sufferings of this
present time are not worthy to be compared with the
glory which shall be revealed to usward.* In verses 16-
18 Paul reaches the climax of his argument on the
theme that the gospel is the power of God for saving
people. Even the sufferings which we undergo for
the gospel serve a purpose in helping to fit us for the

glory that shall be revealed to usward. "For our light affliction, which is for the moment, worketh for us more and more exceedingly an eternal weight of glory" (2 Cor. 4:17). The time of our suffering is short, but the glory and bliss of the reward are eternal. The greatness of the reward encourages the Christian to undergo the suffering that comes upon him, even though the suffering is not according to his will nor of his own choosing. To draw back on account of suffering is to fail of the reward. "Faithful is the saying: For if we died with him, we shall also live with him: if we endure, we shall also reign with him: if we shall deny him, he also will deny us" (2 Tim. 2:11,12).

Verses 19-23: *For the earnest expectation of the creation waiteth for the revealing of the sons of God. For the creation was subjected to vanity, not of its own will, but by reason of him who subjected it, in hope that the creation itself also shall be delivered from the bondage of corruption into the liberty of the glory of the children of God. For we know that the whole creation groaneth and travaileth in pain together until now. And not only so, but ourselves also, who have the first-fruits of the Spirit, even we ourselves groan within ourselves, waiting for our adoption, to wit, the redemption of our body.* Verses 19-23 have given commentators no end of trouble. No one has given an explanation that was satisfactory to all. Where students differ so, it is not well for any one to be overly dogmatic. The main trouble is in determining the meaning and application of the terms, "the creation," "the whole creation," "the first-fruits of the Spirit," and "we ourselves." Some assume that "the creation" and the "whole creation" are the same in extent of meaning and refer to all living things below man; that all living things, both animal and vegetable, suffer the curse of death along with man; and that they are represented as looking forward to the time when the curse of death shall have been removed. But it seems to me that there are insurmountable difficulties in the way of this interpretation. Where did any one get the idea that death came upon animals and vegetables as a result of Adam's sin? Upon what did the animal and fish feed before Adam sinned, and on what would they have continued to feed had he not sinned? What did Adam and Eve eat before they sinned? Any living thing that becomes food must die, whether that thing be animal or vegetable. The thing that kept Adam and Eve alive before they sinned was the fruit of the tree of life. It can hardly be conceived that the fishes and animals and vegetables were kept alive by the same means. It does not seem possible that Paul had in mind the lower creation in verses 19-21. It seems unreasonable that he should, by a figure of speech, represent animals and vegetables as expecting and awaiting the revealing of the sons of God; and it seems especially strange that he would affirm that animals and vegetables "shall be delivered from the bondage of corruption into the liberty of the glory of the children of God," or that they were subject to vanity, "not of their own will." Every statement indicates that he was talking about intelligent beings who had a real interest in the resurrection and glorification of the children of God. The verses are closely connected with verse 18, and evidently were written to encourage the Christian to endure the suffering for the sake of the glory that shall be revealed to usward.

It would not help me to endure suffering to be told that the lower creation was longing to be delivered from suffering into the liberty of the glory of the children of God.

What, then, is the creation of verses 19-21? Who or what is it that with earnest expectation—strong hope—waits for the revealing of the sons of God? Who but Christians are so hopefully interested in that event? Of what creation could it be said that it hopes to be "delivered from the bondage of corruption into the liberty of the glory of the children of God"? Who but Christians have such hopes? But are Christians, either as individuals or as a group, ever referred to as a creation? Paul says: "Wherefore if any man is in Christ, he is a new creature" (2 Cor. 5:17). The marginal reading has new creation. The Greek word for "creature" in this verse is the same as the word for "creation" in Rom. 8:19, 21. The church is said to have been created. "That he might create in himself of the two one new man" (Eph. 2:15). Here we have the verb form of the word from which we have creation. Jesus created the church; hence, it is a creation. And the things Paul says of the creation are true of the church—true of its members. The same things are elsewhere said of the sufferings, the hope, and the final glory of faithful Christians. If this view is not correct, it at least has the merit of being in harmony with what the scriptures elsewhere say concerning the present condition and future destiny of Christians. In verse 22, Paul speaks of the whole human race. He reminds Christians that sufferings, death, and decay are not peculiar to Christians, but are the common lot of all human beings. But the reader will notice that no hope—no future outlook—is attributed to the whole creation.

But who is referred to in verse 23? and what are the "first-fruits of the Spirit"? It seems to be taken for granted by many commentators that all Christians are here referred to and the "first-fruits of the Spirit" is the same as the "earnest of the Spirit" as mentioned in 2 Cor. 1:22; 5:5; Eph. 1:13, 14. But I cannot see how in any sense the indwelling of the Holy Spirit in the Christian can be called the "first-fruits of the Spirit." It rather seems that the "first-fruits of the Spirit" in the Christian dispensation were the miraculous powers conferred on the apostles. Hence, to encourage Christians to endure their sufferings he reminds them that suffering is the common lot of the whole human family, and that even we, the apostles, who have all these miraculous endowments of the Spirit, also groan within ourselves on account of our burdens and afflictions, "waiting for our adoption, to wit, the redemption of our bodies."

Verses 24, 25: *For in hope were we saved: but hope that is seen is not hope: for who hopeth for that which he seeth? But if we hope for that which we see not, then do we with patience wait for it.* The "for" shows close connection with the preceding verses. Christians are now subject to vanity, the bondage of corruption; but they hope to be "delivered from the bondage of corruption into the liberty of the glory of the children of God" (verses 20, 21). In this hope we were saved. In the Greek text there is an article before *hope* in the first clause which equals *this hope.* In the hope of such glorious deliverance we are saved; not saved by this hope, but in this hope. In salvation, which is a process and which began at conversion, faith guides and hope stimulates us to patient endurance. The whole process is carried on in an element of hope, and culminates in our full deliverance into the liberty of the glory of the children of God. "But hope that is seen is not hope." The word *see* frequently means to possess, to enjoy, to suffer, to experience. That is true even in our everyday speech. We see a good time; we see much sorrow; we see much pain. We experience these things. A person does not hope for what he sees —that is, for what he already has or experiences. If our redemption was already complete, if there was nothing yet to be desired or expected, there would be no hope. But we desire and expect a glorious future, and this hope for full deliverance from the bondage of corruption into the glorious liberty of the children of God causes us to be patient during our period of waiting. Without hope we would not endure—we would not strive. Hope anchors our soul to the eternal world. "Hope lost, all is lost."

Verse 26: *And in like manner the Spirit also helpeth our infirmity: for we know not how to pray as we ought; but the Spirit himself maketh intercession for us with groanings which cannot be uttered.* Or unutterable groanings. Hope helps us to endure afflictions, and in like manner the Spirit helps us in our infirmities. Perhaps there is more in this than we know. The infirmity here mentioned is that we know not how to pray as we ought to pray. What we already know about how to pray we learned through the teaching of the Holy Spirit. And there are urgings and longings in the heart of a sincere child of God that he cannot express. He has a feeling of helplessness, or of a deep

need, without knowing what that need really is, or
what would meet the need. It is what Paul calls "unutterable groanings." It is the groaning within ourselves mentioned in verse 23. These groanings are
silent groanings—unutterable feelings of need. The
Spirit helps us in these groanings, for he understands
our needs and longings and can make them known to
God.

Verse 27: *And he that searcheth the hearts knoweth what is the mind of the Spirit, because he maketh
intercession for the saints according to the will of God.*
God is the great heart searcher. He knows our light-
est thoughts and purposes and the deepest longings of
our hearts. But what is meant by *the mind of the
Spirit?* Mind may refer to the intellectual faculty or to
the mental disposition, or mood. It is foreign to Paul's
line of reasoning to make *mind of the Spirit* refer to
the intellectual faculty of the Spirit or to the mental
disposition of the Spirit. Verse 6 may help us out:
"For the mind of the flesh is death; but the mind of
the Spirit is life and peace." "Mind of the flesh" is
evidently the mental disposition, or mood, of the person dominated by the flesh—the disposition of mind
produced by the flesh. And so the "mind of the Spirit"
is the mental disposition, or mood, produced by the
Spirit. All that the gospel contains stirs up in the
heart of the honest believer feelings and aspirations
that he cannot express in words. But God, the heart
searcher, knows the mental disposition, the feelings,
and aspirations thus produced by the Spirit. It is easy
to understand Paul, if we understand him to mean
that God, who searches the hearts, knows the mental
disposition produced by the Spirit. It is probable that

God searches the heart through the agency of the Holy Spirit; "for the Spirit searcheth all things, yea, the deep things of God" (1 Cor. 2:10).

Verse 28: *And we know that to them that love God all things work together for good, even to them that are called according to his purpose.* The expressions "them that love God" and "them that are called according to his purpose," refer to the same persons. What is included in the *all things* of the verse? Does Paul include the devil and all his works and agents? Does he include the lusts of the flesh, which war against the soul, and to our infirmities in which we need help? It seems to me that the context and the very nature of the case demand that we take the *all things* in a limited sense. In all that he had said up to this point Paul was talking about what God had done and is doing for us through Christ and by the ministry of the Holy Spirit. He had also shown how hope sustains us and how the Holy Spirit interprets to God the unutterable longings of our hearts. Why not understand Paul to refer to the things he had been talking about? And all of God's dealings in the past with men and nations worked for the good of those who love God, and whom God called. Paul's statement is a sort of conclusion from what he had said. It is not fair to him to make his conclusion include things he had not mentioned. Why, then, should we conclude that he now speaks of every conceivable thing, every conceivable force and circumstance, and that he affirms that all these things, both good and bad, work together for good to those who love God? To do so is to entirely miss the trend of his thought.

Who are those who love God? "He that hath my

commandments, and keepeth them, he it is that loveth
me" (John 14:21). "This is the love of God, that we
keep his commandments" (1 John 5:3). "And this is
love that we should walk after his commandments"
(2 John 6). But what is meant by the words "called
according to his purpose"? God's purpose in sending
his Son into the world was to save those who believe
in him. He, therefore, purposed to save men through
his Son. It is his purpose to save all who want to do
right (Matt. 5:6). Hence, all who feel the burden of
sin and their need of righteousness, or justification,
are called. "Come unto me, all ye that labor and are
heavy laden, and I will give you rest" (Matt. 11:28).
Those who answer this call are *the called according to
his purpose*. This calling is spoken of in 2 Tim. 1:9:
"Who saved us, and called us with a holy calling, not
according to our works, but according to his own purpose and grace, which was given us in Christ Jesus
before times eternal."

Verses 29, 30: *For whom he foreknew, he also
foreordained to be conformed to the image of his Son,
that he might be the firstborn among many brethren:
and whom he foreordained, them he also called: and
whom he called, them he also justified: and whom he
justified, them he also glorified.* This is one of the
very difficult passages in the Roman letter. The terms
and scope of the passage are not so difficult to understand, but commentators have difficulty in deciding to
whom the language applies. Some have argued or assumed that the persons mentioned are the saints who
arose when Jesus arose from the dead (Matt. 27:52,
53). But that explanation seems far fetched. (1) It
does not fit in with Paul's line of thought. He was

showing what the gospel does for people, and not what became of certain Old Testament saints. To introduce them at this time would seem to have no point. (2) The record in Matthew does not say that the saints who arose ascended to heaven and were glorified. So far as we know, they may have died again. (3) Paul's language shows that all who were foreknown were also glorified; whereas Matthew tells us that many of the saints arose. Not all of them arose. This is further proved by the fact that Peter makes a point out of the fact that David had not been raised (Acts 2:29). There was a purpose in raising these saints. It helped to emphasize the claim that Jesus arose. If people of past ages, whom no one then living in Jerusalem knew, had been raised and had walked the streets of Jerusalem, they would have seemed to the people to be strangers who had come to Jerusalem to the passover; but if saints whom the people of Jerusalem had known, and whom they had known to be dead and buried, appeared on the streets of Jerusalem, it would have opened their eyes and prepared them to believe that Jesus also arose. (4) Verses 29 and 30 are a further development of the thought presented in verse 28. Verse 28 refers to those who are called by the gospel, called according to God's purpose. Notice that verse 29 begins with *for*, which shows that verses 29 and 30 are closely connected with verse 28, and that all three verses refer to the same class of people.

The verses are directly connected with God's purpose, as expressed in verse 28. The whole purpose of God with reference to the redemption of man through the gospel of Christ is viewed as completed, so as to show how all things do work together for good to those

who are called according to his purpose. The plans and
purposes of God which are certain of fulfillment are
sometimes spoken of as fulfilled when the fulfillment
is yet future. Before Isaac was born God said to Abraham: "The father of a multitude of nations have I
made thee" (Gen. 17:5). "For whom he foreknew."
To know (Greek, ginosko) a person is to approve him.
God approved certain characters before they were
actually called. Hence, there are certain conditions of
heart that God approves even in those who have not
yet become Christians. He approves the poor in spirit
—that is, those who feel their sinfulness and need of
salvation, and, therefore, hunger and thirst after
righteousness — justification (Matt. 5:3, 6). Such
characters were foreordained, or appointed, to become
conformed to the image of his Son. (This language
shows that Paul was speaking of people under the gospel dispensation). Jesus guaranteed, or foreordained,
that those who hunger and thirst after righteousness
shall be filled—that is, shall receive that for which
they hunger and thirst. Such characters are the ones
who are called, and no others. Jesus did not come to
call the self-righteous, who do not realize their sinfulness and need of salvation. The *called* are those who
have answered the gospel invitation, and not those to
whom the call has merely been issued. Those who are
actually called are justified—that is, forgiven and
made righteous. And these are the ones who, in the
final day of accounts, are glorified. These verses are
not so difficult if we understand Paul as viewing the
whole process of redemption through Christ. It is a
sublime conception.

Verses 31, 32: *What then shall we say to these*

*things? If God is for us, who is against us? He that
spared not his own Son, but delivered him up for us
all, how shall he not also with him freely give us all
things?* Here again we have "all things," as in verse
28. To all these things we can say: If God is for us,
it matters little who is against us. Certainly if God
gave us the greatest, the most precious gift, the gift
of his Son, he will not withhold any of the lesser things
that might be good for us; and are not the "all things"
which he gives us with Christ the "all things" that
work together for our good?

Verses 33, 34: *Who shall lay anything to the charge
of God's elect? It is God that justifieth; who is he that
condemneth? It is Christ that died, yea rather, that
was raised from the dead, who is at the right hand of
God, who also maketh intercession for us.* The word
elect has been much abused by religionists of the Cal-
vinistic type. The original word means, according to
Thayer, picked out, chosen. God does not choose at
random; there is a reason for the choice he makes. He
chooses, or elects, all who obey him, regardless of race,
social standing or financial rating. Certainly God will
not lay anything to the charge of his chosen ones; he
justifies them. Hence, no one can bring a charge
against God's elect, so as to induce him to condemn
them. Will Christ condemn them? It is he that is to
be judge (Matt. 25:31, 46; John 5:22; Acts 17:30, 31).
But certainly he will not condemn them that God justifies, for he died for them and now makes intercession
for them. Hence, only those whom God does not justify will be condemned.

Verses 35, 36: *Who shall separate us from the love
of Christ? shall tribulation, or anguish, or persecution,*

*or famine, or nakedness, or peril, or sword? Even as
it is written, For thy sake we are killed all the day
long; we are accounted as sheep for the slaughter.* The
phrase, "the love of Christ," can mean either the love
Christ has for us or the love we have for him. Here
it evidently means the love we have for him, for no one
would think that the harsh things we suffer for him
would separate his love from us; whereas it might appear reasonable to some that the sufferings we undergo in serving Christ might cause our love to grow cold,
and even vanish. It will be noticed that all the evils
mentioned are things that come upon us—things from
without. If a man loves Christ as he should, none of
the things mentioned will destroy that love; only the
conditions of our own heart can cause us to cease loving
him. Jesus shows how we can be led astray: "And
many false prophets shall arise, and shall lead many
astray. And because iniquity shall be multiplied, the
love of many shall wax cold" (Matt. 24:11, 12).

Verse 37: *Nay, in all these things we are more than
conquerers through him that loved us.* "In all these
things"—the sufferings and hardships just mentioned.
"More than conquerers"—if we successfully endure all
these things, we have done more than merely to
triumph over them; we have made a decided gain in
Christian character. In conquering we have grown
in character and in favor with God. Hence, even the
evil things with which our enemies meant to crush us
may be so used as to work to our good.

Verses 38, 39: *For I am persuaded, that neither
death, nor life, nor angels, nor principalities, nor things
present, nor things to come, nor powers, nor height,
nor depth, nor any other creature, shall be able to sepa-*

rate us from the love of God, which is in Christ Jesus our Lord. It will be noticed again that all the things mentioned are things without. Nothing here is said as to what corrupting influence might do to the heart. No powers or persecutions can force one to quit loving God. If he quits, he does it of his own accord. Love cannot be destroyed by force or by imperial command, but it may wax cold. Some even depart from their first love (Rev. 2:4). Paul recognized that people might depart from the faith, but he was persuaded that no evils coming on us from without could destroy the love of God. In Christ, God's love for us and our love for him meet.

Chapter 9

9:1 I say the truth in Christ, I lie not, my conscience bearing witness with me in the Holy Spirit. 2 that I have great sorrow and unceasing pain in my heart. 3 For I could wish that I myself were anathema from Christ for my brethren's sake, my kinsmen according to the flesh: 4 who are Israelites; whose is the adoption, and the glory, and the covenants, and the giving of the law, and the service of God, and the promises; 5 whose are the fathers, and of whom is Christ as concerning the flesh, who is over all, God blessed for ever. Amen.

6 But it is not as though the word of God hath come to nought. For they are not all Israel, that are of Israel: 7 neither, because they are Abraham's seed, are they all children: but, In Isaac shall thy seed be called. 8 That is, it is not the children of the flesh that are children of God; but the children of the promise are reckoned for a seed. 9 For this is a word of promise. According to this season will I come, and Sarah shall have a son. 10 And not only so; but Rebecca also having conceived by one, even by our father Isaac—11 for the children being not yet born, neither having done anything good or bad, that the purpose of God according to election might stand, not of works, but of him that calleth, 12 it was said unto her, The elder shall serve the younger. 13 Even as it is written, Jacob I loved, but Esau I hated.

14 What shall we say then? Is there unrighteousness with God? God forbid. 15 For he saith to Moses, I will have mercy on whom I have mercy, and I will have compassion on whom I have compassion. 16 So then it is not of him that willeth, nor of him that runneth, but of God that hath mercy. 17 For the scriptures saith unto Pharaoh, For this very purpose did I raise thee up, that I might show in thee my power, and that my name might be published abroad in all the earth. 18 So then he hath mercy on whom he will, and whom he will he hardeneth.

19 Thou wilt say then unto me, Why doth he still find fault? For who withstandeth his will? 20 Nay but, O man, who art thou that repliest against God? Shall the thing formed say to him that formed it, Why didst thou make me thus? 21 Or hath not the potter a right over the clay, from the same lump to make one part a vessel unto honor, and another unto dishonor? 22 What if God, willing to show his wrath, and to make his power known, endured with much longsuffering vessels of wrath fitted unto destruction: 23 and that he might make known the riches of his glory upon vessels of mercy, which he afore prepared unto glory, 24 even us, whom he also called, not from the Jews only, but also from the Gentiles? ɩ 25 As he saith also in Hosea,

> I will call that my people, which was not my people:
> And her beloved, that was not beloved.
>
> 26 And it shall be, that in the place where it was said unto them, Ye are not my people,
> There shall they be called sons of the living God.

27 And Isaiah crieth concerning Israel, If the number of the children of Israel be as the sand of the sea, it is the remnant that shall be saved: 28 for the Lord will execute his word upon the earth, finishing it and cutting it short. 29 And, as Isaiah hath said before,

> Except the Lord of Sabaoth had left us a seed,
> We had become as Sodom, and had been made like unto Gomorrah.

30 What shall we say then? That the Gentiles, who followed not after righteousness, attained to righteousness, even the righteousness which is of faith: 31 but Israel, following after a law of righteousness, did not arrive at that law. 32 Wherefore? Because they sought it not by faith, but as it were by works. They stumbled at the stone of stumbling; 33 even as it is written.

Behold, I lay in Zion a stone of stumbling and a rock of offence:
And he that believeth on him shall not be put to shame.

Introductory Note: In chapter 9, Paul enters on a new train of thought, which he continues to the close of the eleventh chapter. He has developed his theme that the gospel is God's power for saving men, and has shown that only through obedience to the gospel can men be saved, whether they be Jews or Gentiles. This would naturally lead to certain questions concerning the Jewish nation.

"The theme of 1:16, 17 has been worked out; it has been shown that the gospel is a power of God unto salvation for them that believe, a power needed by Gentile and Jew alike, guaranteed on condition of faith and in response to faith by the love of God, and adequate to man's needs as shown in history and in individual experience; and a brief description has been given of the actual state of the Christian in Christ and of the certainty and splendor of his hope, resting upon the love of God. Naturally at this point the question of the Jews arises; they were the typical instance of a people brought into close and peculiar relation to God, and they therefore afford a crucial case of God's dealings with such. How then did it come to pass that they rejected the gospel? What is their present state? their future destiny? and how does this affect Christians? The answer is found in the conditions under which God selects men for the executing of his purposes. It is important to bear in mind that the selection throughout is regarded as having reference not to the final salvation of persons, but to the execution of the purpose of God. Underlying the whole section is the special object of Saint Paul to justify himself in preaching the gospel to the Gentiles." (Cambridge Greek Testament).

Verses 1, 2: *I say the truth in Christ, I lie not, my*

*conscience bearing witness with me in the Holy Spirit,
that I have great sorrow and unceasing pain in my
heart.* There seems to me no just reason for saying, as
some commentators do, that Paul was making oath
that he was telling the truth. He was solemnly assert-
ing that, as a man in Christ—that is, as a Christian—
he was saying the truth. This use of the word *conscience* seems to be purely classical. Liddell and Scott
define the Greek word thus: *"A knowing with one's-
self, consciousness; conscience."* Of conscience Schaff-
Herzog say: "The word comes to us from the Latin
conscius, conscientia ('conscious,' 'consciousness') ; but
neither Greek nor Roman used it in our sense. It had
no religious bearing. It is unknown in the Old Testament, never used by our Lord, nor by the New Testament writers, except Paul (and those directly inspired
by him) and Peter." Hence, all that Paul knew of
himself, as enlightened by the Holy Spirit, bore witness that he was speaking the truth when he said that
he had great sorrow and unceasing pain in his heart.
He was conscious that he was telling the truth. Paul
did frequently use the word *conscience* in a moral and
religious sense, but not here. Bear in mind that where
we have two words—"consciousness" and "conscience"
—the Greeks had the one word.

Verse 3: *For I could wish that I myself were anathema from Christ for my brethren's sake, my kinsmen
according to the flesh.* Ever since Paul became a Christian the Jews had shamefully and cruelly persecuted
him. Even the Judaizing Christians had been bitter
toward him; yet he had the tenderest of feelings toward
his kinsmen according to the flesh. He did not actually
wish himself to be anathema from Christ for his breth-

ren's sake, for had he given up Christ it would not have brought his kinsmen to Christ; but he could so wish, if it would do any good, if it would save his kinsmen.

Verses 4, 5: *Who are Israelites; whose is the adoption, and the glory, and the covenants, and the giving of the law, and the service of God, and the promises; whose are the fathers, and of whom is Christ as concerning the flesh, who is over all, God blessed for ever.* Paul's brethren were descendants of Jacob, whom God named Israel. They had been adopted as God's special and chosen people. The *glory* perhaps includes all the manifestations of God's care for them, including also the Shekinah, the emblem of his presence in the Holy of Holies. From Abraham onward God had made covenants with no other people, nor had he given laws to any other people. As the laws were God-given, they were perfectly suited to their needs. And their greatest glory and distinction: "of whom is Christ as concerning the flesh." With all these blessings and distinctions, they murdered the Christ, whom they gave the world, and still continued, and do still continue, to reject him, "who is over all, God blessed for ever." The careful reader will not fail to notice that Christ is now over all. Nowhere does Paul give any hint that Christ is yet to be exalted to that high state.

Verse 6: *But it is not as though the word of God hath come to nought. For they are not all Israel, that are of Israel.* The condition of fleshly Israel, though not clearly stated in verses 1-5, was, nevertheless, implied. But the fact that fleshly Israel had rejected Christ, and were therefore anathema from Christ, did not show that the word of God—the promise to Abraham—had come to nought. Verse 7 shows that the

promise made to Abraham is the word of God that Paul
had in mind. Even though fleshly Israel had rejected
Christ, there was yet a spiritual Israel, and the promise
was fulfilled in them. Paul's language in these verses
shows that the promise made to Abraham terminated
in spiritual Israel. They do greatly err who think the
promise to Abraham is yet to be fulfilled in fleshly
Israel. Blood descent from Abraham does not entitle
one to share in the promise.

Verse 7 : *Neither, because they are Abraham's seed,*
are they all children: but, In Isaac shall thy seed be
called. In verses 6 and 7, Paul begins to show the Jews
that they had no right to complain, even if God did
reject them for another people. In working out his
plans, God had rejected the other sons of Abraham and
selected Isaac through whom the promised seed should
come. Other illustrations Paul gives later.

Verses 8, 9 : *That is, it is not the children of the*
flesh that are children of God; but the children of the
promise are reckoned for a seed. For this is a word of
promise, According to this season will I come, and
Sarah shall have a son. If it had been the children of
the flesh, then all Abraham's sons would have been included in the promise. But Isaac was a child of promise. Christians are now children of promise as much
as was Isaac. How Isaac was a child of promise is told
in verse 9.

Verses 10-12 : *And not only so; but Rebecca also*
having conceived by one, even by our father Isaac—
for the children being not yet born, neither having done
anything good or bad, that the purpose of God accord-
ing to election might stand, not of works, but of him
that calleth, it was said unto her, The elder shall serve

the younger. In working out his plan to bless the world through the seed of Abraham, God selected Isaac to be heir of the promise, and rejected the other sons of Abraham. The Jew might say that as Isaac was the only son of Abraham's real wife, his selection was natural and right. But it was different with his selection of Jacob over Esau. Jacob and Esau were full brothers; and though they were twins, Esau the first-born was the natural heir of the promise. Yet of the two, God selected Jacob, even before they were born, and therefore before they had done anything good or bad, "that the purpose of God according to election might stand." The purpose inhered in the promise. God was selecting his own instruments to work out his own plans.

In choosing Jacob, God chose his descendants; and every Jew gloried in that choice. But the selection of Jacob and the rejection of Esau had nothing to do with their salvation. If it had pertained to their salvation, there would have been no point in mentioning the fact that the younger was selected instead of the older; for even the most dogmatic predestinarian would not say that the oldest son is the natural heir of salvation and all the other sons reprobates. The fact is that the selection of Jacob was the selection of a people rather than an individual. Had it been the election to salvation, then the nations descending from Jacob were all elected to salvation, and Esau's descendants were all lost. Jehovah's language to Rebekah shows plainly that he was speaking of the descendants of Jacob and Esau rather than of them as individuals: "Two nations are in thy womb, and two peoples shall be separated from thy bowels: and the one people shall be stronger than the other people; and the elder shall serve the younger" (Gen. 25:23). Nor does the statement that the elder shall serve the younger apply to Jacob and Esau as individuals, for as individuals Jacob came nearer serving Esau. However, it did come to pass that the descendants of Esau served the descendants of Jacob (1 Chr. 18:12, 13).

Verse 13: *Even as it is written, Jacob I loved, but Esau I hated.* Some think this also was said before Jacob and Esau were born, but not so. No such language is found in what Jehovah said to Rebekah. The language quoted was written several hundred years after the days of Jacob and Esau. That the language refers to the two peoples instead of to Jacob and Esau as individuals is clearly seen by reading the connection from which the quotation was taken: "The burden of the word of Jehovah to Israel by Malachi. I have loved you, saith Jehovah. Yet ye say, Wherein hast thou loved us? Was not Esau Jacob's brother? saith Jehovah: yet I loved Jacob; but Esau I hated, and made his mountains a desolation, and gave his heritage to the jackals of the wilderness. Whereas Edom saith, we are beaten down, but we will return and build the waste places; thus saith Jehovah of hosts, They shall build but I will throw down; and men shall call them The border of wickedness, and The people against whom Jehovah hath indignation for ever" (Mal. 1:1-4).

Verse 14: *What shall we say then? Is there unrighteousness with God? God forbid.* There was no unrighteousness with God in the selection he had made. If God selected Isaac and Jacob because they would be the best instruments through which to work out his plans, and the Jews gloried in these selections, why should they think that it would be out of harmony with God's nature to reject the Jews because of unbelief and accept the Gentiles who believed in him? Even though God had rejected the Jewish nation as such, they had the same opportunity as did the Gentiles to become children of God.

Verse 15: *For he saith to Moses, I will have mercy on whom I have mercy, and I will have compassion on whom I have compassion.* It seems that Moses had grown somewhat discouraged on account of the waywardness of the children of Israel, and showed a reluctance to go on, unless God would show him some special favors. Was this a gentle reminder to Moses? God had shown mercy to his people in spite of all that Pharaoh could do, and he could, and would, continue to show them mercy even should Moses become discouraged. No one can keep God from showing mercy to whom he will. But to whom will he show mercy? "He that covereth his transgressions shall not prosper; but whoso confesseth and forsaketh them shall obtain mercy" (Prov. 28:13). And all the objections and efforts of the Jews would not keep him from having mercy on the Gentiles who turned to him. "Let the wicked forsake his way, and the unrighteous man his thoughts; and let him return unto Jehovah, and he will have mercy upon him; and to our God, for he will abundantly pardon" (Isa. 55:7).

Verse 16: *So then it is not of him that willeth, nor of him that runneth, but of God that hath mercy.* This is a conclusion, not so much from what is said in verse 15 as from the whole scope of Paul's argument. In bringing to maturity his plans to bless all nations through Abraham's seed, God had followed the counsel of his own will. The promised seed was Christ, and not the Jewish nation, as the Jews thought. These blessings would be bestowed according to God's good pleasure, and not according to any racial dinstinctions. The Jews willed that it should be otherwise. They would have no Gentile blessed unless he became circumcised and kept the law of Moses. Their striving earnestly, for so the word *run* implies, could not defeat the purpose of God, any more than Isaac and Esau could defeat God's purpose to bless Jacob. The working out of God's plan through the men Paul mentioned had nothing to do with their personal salvation. Someone had to be selected through whose seed the world would be blessed. God selected Abraham. Of Abraham's sons, one had to be an heir of the promise— as the progenitor of the Messiah, the promised seed; God selected Isaac; and so also with reference to Isaac's sons, Jacob and Esau; Jacob was selected. However, since the way of salvation through Christ has been opened, a man's own will is the deciding factor in his salvation. "And he that is athirst, let him come: he that will, let him take the water of life freely."

Verse 17: *For the scripture saith unto Pharaoh, For this very purpose did I raise thee up, that I might show in thee my power, and that my name might be published abroad in all the earth.* The "for" shows a close connection with what had just been said. When the time came for God to show mercy to his oppressed people in Egypt, Pharaoh determined not to let Israel go. Through Moses and Aaron, Jehovah said to Pharaoh: "Let my people go, that they may hold a feast unto me in the wilderness." Pharaoh replied: "Who is Jehovah, that I should hearken unto his voice to let

Israel go? I know not Jehovah, and moreover I will
not let Israel go." In so saying, Pharaoh openly de-
fied Jehovah. He arrogated to himself supreme authority. In his estimation, Jehovah did not have the
power to dictate to him what he should do, or not do;
hence, the demand that he let Israel go stirred in him a
full determination to do as he pleased with Israel, no
matter what Jerovah said or did. Instead of producing
in Pharaoh willing obedience, the demand of Jehovah
stirred up in him a great determination to defeat Jehovah's purpose to show mercy to Israel. He felt that
Israel belonged to him—they were the property of his
kingdom. Yes, he would pit his strength against Jehovah, and see that they did not go from him. Hence,
every demand of Jehovah to let them go aroused his
determination to keep them. These demands and his
attitude toward them served to harden his heart. This
shows how Jehovah hardened his heart, and also how
he hardened his own heart. Hence, it is said that Jehovah hardened his heart, and it is said a number of
times that he hardened his own heart. This contest
continued a sufficient length of time to attract attention through all Egypt, and the nations round about
Egypt; and when Jehovah, in his own time and in his
own way, triumphed over Pharaoh and all his gods,
his power was shown, and his name was "published
abroad in all the earth." If Pharaoh had immediately
let Israel go, there would have been no contest and
God's power would not have been displayed before the
world. Pharaoh would have been credited with being
good and kind to Israel.

The language quoted by Paul was spoken to Pharaoh
after miracles had been wrought before Pharaoh, and

after six of the ten plagues had been visited upon him and the Egyptians. Each plague further hardened his heart and stirred him to greater determination to hold Israel in bondage. The term *raise up* is from a Greek word which Liddell and Scott define as follows: *"To raise from the dead; to arouse, stir up; to kindle, as fire." To arouse, stir up,* is the only definition given here that will fit the case. God's demands stirred Pharaoh's antagonism toward God. No others ever had so much evidence that God's hand was in a matter as did Pharaoh and the Egyptians. God was long-suffering toward him, and that long-suffering contributed much to the hardening of his heart. "So then he hath mercy on whom he will, and whom he will he hardeneth." The whole circumstance shows that it is not necessary to conclude that God hardened Pharaoh's heart by any direct operation of the Spirit.

Verse 19: *Thou wilt say then unto me, Why doth he still find fault? For who withstandeth his will?* These questions would arise in the mind of some of the Jews. If God had mercy on the Israelites, no matter who tried to hinder him from doing so, why is he now finding fault with them? Or if he hardens some people, why does he then find fault with them? Paul does not intimate that the questions logically grow out of what he had said, but they are questions that quibblers would likely raise.

Verse 20: *Nay but, O man, who art thou that repliest against God? Shall the thing formed say to him that formed it, Why didst thou make me thus?* The questions of verse 19 do not imply any objections to Paul's statements concerning God's dealings with certain men in working out his plans, but rather to the methods of God himself. Verse 20 is not an answer to the questions, but rather a rebuke to those who raise such questions. Such questioners show a lack of reverence and respect for God. Such questions really charge God with being unfair and capricious. Who is man that he should find fault with God? Who is man that he should talk back at God? Man makes his own character, either according to God's directions and with his help, or else he makes a character against God's teaching and God's willingness to help. God then uses him as an agent of mercy, or else an instrument upon which to display his wrath. Pharaoh's character was bad; he made it so. God, therefore, made him an object upon which to display his wrath and to make his power known. He, therefore, had no grounds for complaint against God because of the plagues.

Verse 21: *Or hath not the potter a right over the clay, from the same lump to make one part a vessel unto honor, and another unto dishonor?* Let us not put such a strained construction on Paul's language as to make him teach that man has no freedom of will and of action, and, therefore, no personal responsibility. Paul is speaking of the use God makes of men and of nations; and whether God makes of a man or a nation a vessel unto honor or unto dishonor depends on the man or the nation. "Now in a great house there are not only vessels of gold and of silver, but also of wood and of earth; and some unto honor, and some unto dishonor. If a man therefore purge himself from these, he shall be a vessel unto honor, sanctified, meet for the master's use, prepared unto every good work" (2 Tim. 2:20, 21). Hence, as to whether a man is a vessel unto honor or unto dishonor, he alone is responsible. The same is true of nations, as the following lengthy quotation from Jeremiah clearly shows: "The word which came to Jeremiah from Jehovah, saying, Arise, and go down to the potter's house, and there I will cause thee to hear my words. Then I went down to the potter's house, and behold, he was making a work on the wheels. And when the vessel that he made of the clay was marred in the hand of the potter, he made it again another vessel, as seemed good to the potter to make it. Then the word of Jehovah came to me, saying, O house of Israel, cannot I do with you as this potter? saith Jehovah. Behold, as the clay in the potter's hand, so are ye in my hand, O house of Israel. At what instant I shall speak concerning a nation, and concerning a kingdom, to pluck up and to break down and to destroy it; if that nation, concerning which I have spoken, turn from their evil, I will repent of the evil that I thought to do unto them. And at what instant I shall speak concerning a nation, and concerning a kingdom, to build and to plant it; if they do that which is evil in my sight, that they obey not my voice, then I will repent of the good, wherewith I said I would benefit them. Now therefore, speak to the men of Judah, and to the inhabitants of Jerusalem, saying, Thus saith Jehovah: Behold, I frame evil against you, and devise a device against you: return ye now every one from his evil way, and amend your ways and your doings. But they say, It is in vain; for we will walk after our own devices, and we will do every one after the stubbornness of his evil heart" (Jer. 18:1-12). Isaiah had said: "Woe unto him that striveth with his maker! a potsherd among the potsherds of the earth! Shall the clay say to him that fashioneth it, What makest thou?" (Isa. 45:9).

Concerning the quotations from Isaiah and Jeremiah, Albert Barnes says: "The passage in Isaiah proves that God has the right of sovereign over guilty *individuals;* that in Jeremiah, that he has the same right over *nations;* thus meeting the whole case as it was in the mind of the apostle. These passages, however, assert only the right of God to do it, without affirming anything about the *manner* in which it is done. In fact, God bestows his favors in a mode very different from that in which a potter molds his clay. God does not create holiness by a mere act of power, but he produces it in a manner consistent with the moral agency of man; and bestows his favors not to *compel* men, but to incline them to be *willing* to receive them." God does not by any direct power make people either good or bad. God "would have all men to be saved" (1 Tim. 2:4).

Verse 22: *What if God, willing to show his wrath, and to make his power known, endured with much long- suffering vessels of wrath fitted unto destruction?* This is another point in Paul's reply to the questions of verse 19. If God wills to show his wrath against sin and his power to punish sin, why should anyone object? To say that God is not willing to do so is to accuse him of being indifferent to sin. His wrath is revealed from heaven against all ungodliness and unrighteousness of men (Rom. 1:18). Yet the Lord does not wish "that any should perish, but that all should come to repentance" (2 Pet. 3:9). Because he is not willing that any should perish, he is longsuffering, giving all sinners a full opportunity to repent. He endured with long-suffering the highhanded rebellion of Pharaoh, and also the sins of ungrateful Israel. This longsuffering is a manifestation of God's mercy and goodness to man, though many take advantage of it to indulge in more sin; but the day of wrath will come. "Or despisest thou the riches of his goodness and forbearance and long-suffering, not knowing that the goodness of God leadeth thee to repentance? but after thy hardness and impenitent heart treasurest up for thyself wrath in the day of wrath and revelation of the righteous judgment of God; who will render to every man according to his works" (Rom. 2:4-6). "Wherefore, beloved, seeing that ye look for these things, give diligence that ye may be found in peace, without spot and blameless in his sight. And account that the longsuffering of our Lord is salvation; even as our beloved brother Paul also, according to the wisdom given to him, wrote unto you; as also in all his epistles, speaking in them of these things" (2 Pet. 3:14-16). This comment of Peter shows the purpose of the longsuffering of which Paul speaks—its purpose is to lead to salvation.

The phrase "fitted for destruction" does not mean that God made them so. It could not be said that God endured with much longsuffering any character or thing that he, by his own direct power, had made. All people and things that God made by his own direct power were exactly as he wanted them. Certainly it could not be said that he endured with much longsuffering people or things that were exactly as he wanted them to be. Hence, God did not make these characters fit for destruction; they made themselves so, and God had endured them with much longsuffering. His power would be manifested in their destruction.

Verses 23, 24: *And that he might make known the riches of his glory upon vessels of mercy, which he afore prepared unto glory, even us, whom he also called, not from the Jews only, but also from the Gentiles.* The Jewish nation had long been fitted for destruction. Besides their general corruption and their arrogant self-righteousness, they had murdered the Son of God. This was a national crime, a national murder. The authorities hunted down Christians, and thus became guilty of wholesale murder. Death was and is the penalty for murder; and the nation was soon to suffer that penalty. God had endured them with much longsuffering, not for their sake, but "that he might make known the riches of his glory upon vessels of mercy, which he afore prepared unto glory, even us, whom he also called, not from the Jews only, but also from the Gentiles." Though the Jewish nation had for many years been ripe for destruction, God endured them with much long-suffering—spared them—till the gospel could be preached to the Gentiles and churches established among them. Think what would have been the fate of the churches when Jerusalem and the Jewish nation were destroyed, if that awful event had occurred before there were churches outside Judea. The riches of God's glory were the blessings of the gospel upon all, both of the Jews and of the Gentiles, who were called by the gospel into the service of God.

The Jews were upset because Paul, a Jew, was going among the Gentiles and preaching to them and teaching that God now put no difference between Jew and

Gentile. Even in the churches there were Jews who contended that Gentiles must be circumcised and keep the law—that is, they must become as Jews—or they could not be saved.

Verses 25, 26: *As he saith also in Hosea, I will call that my people, which was not my people; And her beloved, that was not beloved. And it shall be, that in the place where it was said unto them, Ye are not my people, There shall they be called sons of the living God.* Paul had shown that God dealt with men and nations according to their attitude toward him. He now quotes Hosea to show that it had been God's purpose to call faithful Gentiles his people, though Gentiles had not been his chosen people—they had not been his beloved people. Those who had not been his people were to become sons of the living God. Paul was showing that these prophecies concerning the Gentiles were being fulfilled in the gospel of Christ. Paul then devotes considerable space to a discussion of the condition of Israel under the gospel.

Verses 27, 28: *And Isaiah crieth concerning Israel, If the number of the children of Israel be as the sand of the sea, it is the remnant that shall be saved: for the Lord will execute his word upon the earth, finishing it and cutting it short.* Jews boasted, "We are Abraham's seed"; because of this they thought they had a right to all of God's richest blessings. But they had not believed their own prophets. They should have learned from Isaiah that only a remnant—a small portion—of Israel would be saved. The rest would be lost. To that end his word had gone forth, and that word would be executed, "finishing it and cutting it short."

(See Isa. 10:22, 23). Yet it was hard for a Jew to see himself as a sinner.

Verse 29: *And, as Isaiah hath said before, Except the Lord of Sabaoth had left us a seed, We had become as Sodom, and had been made like unto Gomorrah.* Because a few righteous people were not found in Sodom and Gomorrah, Jehovah utterly destroyed them. Even so the whole nation of Israel would have been destroyed in captivity had not there been some righteous people in the nation; these few righteous people in the nation were the seed mentioned in this quotation from Isaiah.

Verse 30: *What shall we say then? That the Gentiles, who followed not after righteousness, attained to righteousness, even the righteousness which is of faith.* When a man is forgiven, when his sins are blotted out, he is righteous. Men attain to that righteousness when they through faith become obedient to the Lord Jesus Christ. While the Gentiles did not seek righteousness according to the law, they became righteous by their obedience to the gospel. "But thanks be to God, that, whereas ye were servants of sin, ye became obedient from the heart to that form of teaching whereunto ye were delivered; and being made free from sin, ye became servants of righteousness" (Rom. 6:17, 18).

Verse 31: *But Israel, following after a law of righteousness, did not arrive at that law.* Israel professed adherence to the law of Moses, but they did not keep that law. Instead, therefore, of being righteous, they were sinners—transgressors of the law they professed to follow.

Verses 32, 33: *Wherefore? Because they sought it not by faith, but as it were by works. They stumbled at the stone of stumbling; even as it is written, Behold,*

I lay in Zion a stone of stumbling and a rock of offense: and he that believeth on him shall not be put to shame. The law could not make righteous the one who had transgressed it. The only hope, therefore, of the Jew, as well as of the Gentile, is to attain righteousness through faith in the Lord Jesus Christ; but because he was not what they expected in the Messiah, the Jews rejected him—to them he was a stone of stumbling. "We preach Christ crucified, unto the Jews a stumblingblock" (1 Cor. 1:23). But those who did believe in Christ were not put to shame, as men are when they find that they have been deceived into following a false leader. "And blessed is he, whosoever shall find no occasion of stumbling in me" (Matt. 11:6). Jesus fails no one who puts his trust in him; he is not slack concerning his promises.

Chapter 10

10:1 Brethren, my heart's desire and my supplication to God is for them, that they may be saved. 2 For I bear them witness that they have a zeal for God, but not according to knowledge. 3 For being ignorant of God's righteousness, and seeking to establish their own, they did not subject themselves to the righteousness of God. 4 For Christ is the end of the law unto righteousness to every one that believeth. 5 For Moses writeth that the man that doeth the righteousness which is of the law shall live thereby. 6 But the righteousness which is of faith saith thus, Say not in thy heart, Who shall ascend into heaven? (that is, to bring Christ down:) 7 or, Who shall descend into the abyss? (that is, to bring Christ up from the dead.) 8 But what saith it? The word is nigh thee, in thy mouth, and in thy heart: that is, the word of faith, which we preach: 9 because if thou shalt confess with thy mouth Jesus as Lord, and shalt believe in thy heart that God raised him from the dead, thou shalt be saved: 10 for with the heart man believeth unto righteousness; and with the mouth confession is made unto salvation. 11 For the scripture saith, Whosoever believeth on him shall not be put to shame. 12 For there is no distinction between Jew and Greek: for the same Lord is Lord of all, and is rich unto all that call upon him: 13 for, Whosoever shall call upon the name of the Lord shall be saved. 14 How then shall they call on him in whom they have not believed? and how shall they believe in him whom they have not heard? and how shall they hear without a preacher? 15 and how shall they preach, except they be sent? even as it is written, How beautiful are the feet of them that bring glad tidings of good things!
16 But they did not all hearken to the glad tidings. For Isaiah saith, Lord, who hath believed our report? 17 So belief cometh of hearing, and hearing by the word of Christ. 18 But I say, Did they not hear? Yea, verily,

Their sound went out into all the earth,
And their words unto the ends of the world.
19 But I say, Did Israel not know?
First Moses saith,

I will provoke you to jealousy with that which is no nation,
With a nation void of understanding will I anger you.
20 And Isaiah is very bold, and saith,

I was found of them that sought me not;
I became manifest unto them that asked not of me.
21 But as to Israel he saith, All the day long did I spread out my hands unto a disobedient and gainsaying people.

Verse 1: *Brethren, my heart's desire and my supplication to God is for them, that they may be saved.* The Jews regarded Paul as an apostate, a hater of their nation. In the beginning of Chapter 9, Paul expressed his deep devotion to his brethren, his kinsmen according to the flesh; but the Holy Spirit directed him in writing that only a remnant of Israel would be saved. The casting off the Jews was not an arbitrary act of God—he had not doomed them beyond remedy. Had Paul so understood it, he would not have been praying that they might be saved. His desire and prayer showed his deep interest in them. There was still a way for Jews as individuals to be saved; but knowing that salvation could be attained only through Christ, he did not pray for them to be saved in their unbelief—that was impossible.

Verse 2: *For I bear them witness that they have a zeal for God, but not according to knowledge.* They had not understood the purpose of the law nor the voice of the prophets (Acts 13:27). Had they understood their own Scriptures, they would have known that Jesus fulfilled both the law and the prophets. The Jews were full of zeal, but in willful ignorance crucified the Son of God.

Verse 3: *For being ignorant of God's righteousness, and seeking to establish their own, they did not subject themselves to the righteousness of God.* The Jews fully understood that God was a righteous being. It was not that of which they were ignorant. They were ignorant of God's plan, or way, of righteousness. This righteousness is something to which men should submit and to which the Jews had not submitted. This righteousness is revealed in the gospel; this they had repudiated, and were, therefore, in a lost condition.

Verse 4: *For Christ is the end of the law unto righteousness to every one that believeth.* The law demanded absolute righteousness, but could not free the transgressor of guilt. The law could not make the guilty righteous. It seems to me that commentators usually miss Paul's point. It is true that the law ended at the cross, but it ended at the cross regardless of whether

one believes or does not believe. The end of which
Paul here speaks is attained by those who believe in
Christ. The end, or aim, of the law was righteousness.
The believer in Christ is made righteous, and thus the
end of the law for righteousness is reached in Christ.
When a man's sins are all blotted out, when he is
cleansed from all sin, he is righteous; that condition
is reached in Christ by those who believe. The end,
or purpose, of the law was righteousness; that end is
reached in Christ by the believer. It will be noticed
that Paul says: "Christ is the end of the law unto
righteousness to every one that believeth." The modi-
fying phrase, "to every one that believeth," shows that
Paul was not speaking of the abrogation of the law;
that is taught abundantly elsewhere. And it was abro-
gated for all, believers and unbelievers alike.

Verse 5: *For Moses writeth that the man that doeth
the righteousness which is of the law shall live thereby.*
This refers to what Moses said in Lev. 18:5: "Ye shall
therefore keep my statutes, and mine ordinances; which
if a man do, he shall live in them." That meant strict
adherence to all that the law said—perfect obedience
to all its requirements. This no man ever did. Righteousness would have been of the law if there had been
perfect obedience to the law; and yet the law demanded
just that. Its end, or purpose, is realized in Christ to
all who believe. And that way of righteousness is not
hard to understand, nor to practice.

Verses 6-8: *But the righteousness which is of faith
saith thus, Say not in thy heart, Who shall ascend into
heaven? (that is, to bring Christ down:), or, Who shall
descend into the abyss? (that is, to bring Christ up
from the dead). But what saith it? The word is nigh*

thee, in thy mouth, and in thy heart: that is, the word of faith, which we preach. In the connection in which these words are used, they seem at first glance to be somewhat obscure. Paul was quoting Deut. 30:12-14, with parenthetical words of his own to adapt the words of Moses to his own purpose. But the words of Moses in the verse preceding the words Paul quotes, together with the last words quoted, help us to understand the significance of the passage: "For this commandment which I command thee this day, it is not too hard for thee, neither is it far off. . . . But the word is very nigh unto thee, in thy mouth, and in thy heart, that thou mayest do it." "This commandment" refers to the whole law, which Moses had just finished giving them in detail and in completeness. Hence, it was nigh them; so that it was not necessary to go to heaven to bring it down, nor across the sea to learn it. That law was not in heaven, but here among them. The law had been within easy reach, but righteousness had been unattainable. But the righteousness which is by faith in Christ is attainable, and is within easy reach. It does not require the impossible, such as ascending to heaven to bring Christ down or to bring him up from Hades. No such additional signs are necessary; nor do we now have to hear direct from heaven to enjoy this righteousness by faith. The word of faith, or the word which produces faith, was preached—that is, made known—by the apostles. The connection shows that this plan of righteousness made known by the apostles is all that is necessary—is, indeed, the only plan through which we may become righteous by faith in Christ. To pray for some additional power to come direct from heaven is to show a lack of faith in what

God has said. But to believe in Christ means more than to give mental assent to the truths and facts revealed about him; it means more than to have a passive trust in him; it must be an active faith—a faith made perfect by obedience to the commands of him in whom we believe.

Verses 8-11: *But what saith it? The word is nigh thee, in thy mouth, and in thy heart: that is, the word of faith, which we preach: because if thou shalt confess with thy mouth Jesus as Lord, and shalt believe in thy heart that God raised him from the dead, thou shalt be saved: for with the heart man believeth unto righteousness; and with the mouth confession is made unto salvation. For the scripture saith, Whosoever believeth on him shall not be put to shame.* We are told that the Jews spoke of a difficult or impossible thing as a thing afar off; an easy thing, as nigh. It was impossible, a thing afar off, to be justified by the law of Moses. To be justified by law requires perfect obedience, and no one rendered such obedience. But the Jews expected their Messiah to be here on earth in person—to remain here. This gospel system of righteousness by faith in Christ does not demand that he be brought down from heaven; nor does it, as if he were yet in the tomb, demand that he be brought up from the dead. It does not demand, nor require, his personal presence here on earth. But what does this gospel system of righteousness by faith say? "The word is nigh thee"; it is not a difficult matter—not a matter afar off. On the evidence given by his inspired teachers, you believe in the heart that he is the Messiah, and confess that faith with the mouth. That is the word of faith which the apostles preached, and that is the way

of righteousness through Christ. To believe in Christ
is to recognize him for what he is—to put our full trust
in him; to confess him is to pledge our allegiance to
him. A mere lip confession is worthless; we must ac-
knowledge him by word and deed as our Lord—our
Prophet, Priest, and King, as well as our Savior. This
sort of confession brings us finally to eternal life,
eternal salvation. And this announcement that salvation was now offered in the gospel to all, whether Jew
or Gentile, was a great blow to the Jew with his pride
of race. It is now whosoever—"whosoever believeth on
him shall not be put to shame." Sometimes we put our
trust or confidence in a man, and he betrays that confidence; he turns out bad, and we are put to shame.
But we can put our full confidence in Christ, and give
him our life's best service, without any fear that he
will betray us and put us to shame. We can glory in
him now and evermore.

Verses 12, 13: *For there is no distinction between
Jew and Greek: for the same Lord is Lord of all, and
rich unto all that call upon him: for, Whosoever shall
call upon the name of the Lord shall be saved.* Under
the law there was a distinction between Jew and Gentile, but this was not a matter of favoritism. God was
working out his greater plan, the plan in which Jew
and Gentile would have the same standing before Jehovah. But the law of Moses—all things Jewish—had
to be taken out of the way before both Jew and Gentile
could be brought together into one body, one worshiping
assembly (Eph. 2:13-18). In Paul's writings are many
arguments to show that the law of Moses ended at the
cross, but some of the professed Christians among the
Jews never did recognize that the Jew had no advan-

tage over the Gentile. His claim that God now made no distinction between Jew and Gentile, and his preaching to the Gentiles, made these Jews very bitter toward him. They would not recognize that the riches of God's grace were as abundant for the Gentiles, as for the Jew. It is: "Whosoever will." In this the gospel of Christ is much more glorious than the law, as it is also in many other respects.

Verses 14, 15: *How then shall they call on him in whom they have not believed? and how shall they believe in him whom they have not heard? and how shall they hear without a preacher? and how shall they preach, except they be sent? even as it is written, How beautiful are the feet of them that bring glad tidings of good things!* These are rhetorical questions, and are equal to direct statements. No one can call on one in whom he does not believe, and he cannot believe in one of whom he has never heard. And we never would have heard of Christ and his gospel had he not sent men to preach it. It had to be proclaimed in order that people might hear and believe. Paul is here speaking of the original proclamation of the gospel. It is a perversion of Paul's language to use it to prove that a preacher now cannot preach unless the church sends him. It is also an argument contrary to facts, for a man can go out now and present the gospel of Christ without being sent by any church or any man. But the original proclamation of the gospel required men whom the Lord qualified and sent. If Jesus had not sent them, they could not have proclaimed the gospel. We are now just as dependent upon the preaching of these men whom Jesus sent as the people were to whom they went personally. They are the ones who brought the message. The Lord selected them, gave them the message, and sent them to deliver it. Because this message is so precious and wonderful to those who accept it, it is said: "How beautiful are the feet of them that bring glad tidings of good things!"

Verses 16-18: *But they did not all hearken to the glad tidings. For Isaiah saith, Lord, who hath believed our report? So belief cometh of hearing, and hearing by the word of Christ. But I say, Did they not hear? Yea, verily, their sound went out into all the earth, and their words unto the ends of the world.* Personal responsibility is here plainly set forth. If any did not believe, it was because they did not hearken to the glad tidings proclaimed by the preachers whom the Lord sent, for their report went out into all the earth—to the ends of the world. The unsaved man, whether Jew or Gentile, has no one to blame but himself. And this report went out to all, that they might believe; for faith comes by hearing the word of God, and it comes in no other way. Some people hear, and do not believe, and are therefore not saved. In his explanation of the parable of the sower Jesus said: "The sower soweth the word." "The seed is the word of God. And those by the wayside are they that have heard; then cometh the devil, and taketh away the word from their heart, that they may not believe and be saved." The devil knows that the word of God in the heart is the only thing that will cause anyone to believe. "And it came to pass in Iconium that they entered together into the synagogue of the Jews, and so spake that a great multitude both of Jews and of Greeks believed" (Acts 14:1).

Verses 19-21: *But I say Did Israel not know? First Moses saith, I will provoke you to jealousy with that which is no nation, With a nation void of understanding will I anger you. And Isaiah is very bold, and saith, I was found of them that sought me not; I became manifest unto them that asked not of me. But as to Israel he saith, All the day long did I spread out my hands unto a disobedient and gainsaying people.* "Did Israel not know?" This refers to what is said in verse 18: "Yea, verily, their sound went out into all the earth, and their words unto the ends of the world." From this prophecy, quoted from Isaiah, Israel should have known that the gospel was to go "out into all the earth," "unto the ends of the world"—to the Gentiles as well as to the Jews. The Jews, therefore, should not have been angered, or even surprised, that the gospel was being preached to the Gentiles, as their own prophet had foretold. "But I say, Did Israel not know?" If they did not, it was because they were so blinded by their own conceits that they could not understand plain language. Even Moses had said: "I will provoke you to jealousy with that which is no nation, with a nation void of understanding will I anger you." The Jews were so opposed to the Gentiles that they wanted no consideration given them. Even many of the professed Christians of the Jews were enraged at Paul for his work among the Gentiles. "And Isaiah is very bold, and saith, I was found of them that sought me not; I became manifest unto them that asked not of me." It is true in a sense that men must seek after God, but they cannot do so unless they know something of him; and the Gentiles were so lost in ignorance that they did not know to seek

God until he was made known to them. Hence, it is
literally true that God first sought the Gentiles. They
could not ask anything of Jehovah of whom they knew
nothing. He had first to make himself manifest to
them. This he did by sending his preachers out among
them. But to Israel, who should have readily obeyed
the gospel, God said: "All the day long did I spread
out my hands unto a disobedient and gainsaying people." These Jews not only disobeyed, but spoke
against God's message to them. As an illustration of
this, see Acts 13:45; 18:5, 6.

Chapter 11

11:1 I say then, Did God cast off his people? God forbid. For I also am an Israelite, of the seed of Abraham, of the tribe of Benjamin. 2 God did not cast off his people which he foreknew. Or know ye not what the scripture saith of Elijah? how he pleadeth with God against Israel: 3 Lord, they have killed thy prophets, they have digged down thine altars; and I am left alone, and they seek my life. 4 But what saith the answer of God unto him? I have left for myself seven thousand men, who have not bowed the knee to Baal. 5 Even so then at this present time also there is a remnant according to the election of grace. 6 But if it is by grace, it is no more of works: otherwise grace is no more grace. 7 What then? That which Israel seeketh for, that he obtained not; but the election obtained it, and the rest were hardened: 8 according as it is written, God gave them a spirit of stupor, eyes that they should not see, and ears that they should not hear, unto this very day. 9 And David saith,

Let their table be made a snare, and a trap,
And a stumblingblock, and a recompense unto them:
10 Let their eyes be darkened, that they may not see,
And bow thou down their back alway.

11 I say then, Did they stumble that they might fall? God forbid: but by their fall salvation is come unto the Gentiles, to provoke them to jealousy. 12 Now if their fall is the riches of the world, and their loss the riches of the Gentiles: how much more their fulness? 13 But I speak to you that are Gentiles. Inasmuch then as I am an apostle of Gentiles, I glorify my ministry: 14 if by any means I may provoke to jealousy them that are my flesh, and may save some of them. 15 For if the casting away of them is the reconciling of the world, what shall the receiving of them be, but life from the dead? 16 And if the firstfruit is holy, so is the lump: and if the root is holy, so are the branches. 17 But if some of the branches were broken off, and thou, being a wild olive, wast grafted in among them, and didst become partaker with them of the root of the fatness of the olive tree; 18 glory not over the branches: but if thou gloriest, it is not thou that bearest the root, but the root thee. 19 Thou wilt say then, Branches were broken off, that I might be grafted in. 20 Well: by their unbelief they were broken off, and thou standest by thy faith. Be not highminded, but fear: 21 for if God spared not the natural branches, neither will he spare thee. 22 Behold then the goodness and severity of God: toward them that fell, severity; but toward thee, God's goodness, if thou continue in his goodness: otherwise thou also shalt be cut off. 23 And they also, if they continue not in their unbelief, shall be grafted in: for God is able to graft them in again. 24 For if thou wast cut out of that which is by nature a wild olive tree, and wast grafted contrary to nature into a good olive tree; how much more shall these, which are the natural branches, be grafted into their own olive tree?

25 For I would not, brethren, have you ignorant of this mystery, lest ye be wise in your own conceits, that a hardening in part hath befallen Israel, until the fulness of the Gentiles be come in: 26 and so all Israel shall be saved: even as it is written,

These shall come out of Zion the Deliverer;
He shall turn away ungodliness from Jacob:
27 And this is my covenant unto them,
When I shall take away their sins.

28 As touching the gospel, they are enemies for your sake: but as touching the election, they are beloved for the fathers' sake. 29 For the gifts and the calling of God are not repented of. 30 For as ye in time past were disobedient to God, but now have obtained mercy by their disobedience, 31 even so have these also now been disobedient, that by the mercy shown to you they also may now obtain mercy. 32

For God hath shut up all unto disobedience, that he might have mercy upon all.
33 O the depth of the riches both of the wisdom and the knowledge of God!
how unsearchable are his judgments, and his ways past tracing out! 34 For who
hath known the mind of the Lord? or who hath been his counsellor? 35 or who
hath first given to him, and it shall be recompensed unto him again? 36 For of
him, and through him, and unto him, are all things. To him be the glory for ever.
Amen.

Verses 1-6: *I say then, Did God cast off his people?
God forbid. For I also am an Israelite, of the seed of
Abraham, of the tribe of Benjamin. God did not cast
off his people which he foreknew. Or know ye not what
the scripture saith of Elijah? how he pleadeth with
God against Israel: Lord they have killed thy prophets,
they have digged down thine altars; and I am left
alone, and they seek my life. But what saith the answer of God unto him? I have left for myself seven
thousand men, who have not bowed the knee to Baal.
Even so then at this present time also there is a remnant according to the election of grace. But if it is by
grace, it is no more of works: otherwise grace is no
more grace.* "I say then, Did God cast off his people?" Paul's critics might claim that he was teaching
God's utter rejection of all Jews. "Be it not so." Paul
certainly would not propagate a theory that would put
himself outside the pale of salvation. He gives
himself as an example that the rejection of the
Jewish nation had nothing to do with the salvation of individual Jews. "For I am also an Israelite, of the seed of Abraham, of the tribe
of Benjamin." God did not, and does not, withhold salvation from any obedient Jew. "God did
not cast off his people which he foreknew." Let us not
get confused over this word *foreknew.* In the New
Testament this verb *know,* when it has a person for its
object, means to *recognize,* or *accept.* And Paul's language does not mean that God knew, or accepted, cer-

tain people before they were born; his language refers to those he accepted as his people under the former dispensation—that is, the obedient Jews. The connection, as well as the language itself, shows this to
be his meaning. He uses the complaint of Elijah and
God's answer to him to illustrate his point. Although
the great mass of Israel had forsaken Jehovah, and
were not therefore acceptable to him, there were yet
seven thousand whom he could and did accept. Paul's
language seems to indicate that there had always been
some of Israel that were acceptable to Jehovah. "Even
so then at this present time also there is a remnant
according to the election of grace." This refers to
those Jews who had become obedient to Christ. God
had rejected the whole Jewish system, and would soon
destroy what government the Romans had so far left
to them; but he had not barred the door of salvation
against any Jew that became obedient to the gospel of
grace through Christ. Under this system of grace he
makes no distinction between Jew and Gentile. "But
if it is by grace, it is no more of works: otherwise
grace is no more grace." No amount of works can
blot out sins already committed. Forgiveness is a
matter of grace, no matter how many conditions one
must fulfill in order to be forgiven. If a man's works
had always been perfect, he would have no sins to be
forgiven; he would stand justified on his own merit.
There is no grace when a man merits justification.
Works by which a man merits justification, and commands which one must obey to be saved, are distinct
matters. It is unfortunate that many religionists cannot, or will not, see this distinction, which should be
plainly seen by any Bible reader. Because they fail

to make this distinction they conclude that a sinner must do nothing in order to be saved. A man has no real understanding of either works or grace when he thinks conditions of forgiveness make salvation a matter of works and not of grace. Nothing that a sinner can do merits salvation. Many things are of grace, and yet conditional. Is anyone so simple as to think Naaman's healing of leprosy was any less a matter of grace because he had to dip seven times in the river Jordan? Is any so blind that he cannot see that giving sight to the blind man was a matter of grace, even though he had to go wash in the pool of Siloam? If so, he needs his eyes opened as badly as did the blind man.

Verses 7. 8: *What then? That which Israel seeketh for, that he obtained not; but the election obtained it, and the rest were hardened: according as it is written, God gave them a spirit of stupor, eyes that they should not see, and ears that they should not hear, unto this very day.* Here it seems that Paul begins to sum up his argument concerning Israel and God's dealings with them. The most of them had sought righteousness by the works of the law; but righteousness by works of law required perfect obedience to that law, and all had at some time sinned against that law. The law does not forgive; it cannot make the guilty righteous, or, what is the same, cannot justify the guilty. A remnant had sought forgiveness through Christ; these were the election, or the elect, that obtained righteousness. "The rest were hardened"—that is, dulled or blinded. Their will was hardened; their understanding was dulled. They, and not God, brought that condition upon themselves. Compare Matt. 13:14, 15: "And unto them is fulfilled the prophecy of Isaiah, which saith, By hearing ye shall hear, and shall in no wise understand; and seeing ye shall see, and shall in no wise perceive: for this people's heart is waxed gross, and their ears are dull of hearing, and their eyes they have closed; lest haply they should perceive with their eyes, and hear with their ears, and understand with their heart, and should turn again, and I should heal them."

Jesus did not offer the Jews what they wanted; they, therefore, turned a deaf ear to his teaching. They did not see in him anything they desired. They would not hear and they would not see, and, therefore, did not understand; and that condition prevailed to the time Paul wrote the Roman letter, and has not improved even until now. In verse 8 Paul makes a free translation of Deut. 29:4 and Isa. 29:10.

Verses 9, 10: *And David saith, Let their table be made a snare, and a trap, and a stumblingblock, and a recompense unto them: let their eyes be darkened, that they may not see, and bow thou down their back always.* "Their table" was put for their religious food. Instead of being led to Christ by the law they were entrapped by their blind adherence to the law; they were caught as in a snare. And their blind adherence to the law would be their recompense, and that would amount to condemnation. Their rejection of Christ and their blind devotion to the law was their ruin. Paul said such people judged themselves unworthy of eternal life (Acts 13:46). In clinging to the law and rejecting Christ, the Jews were wearing a yoke which they were not able to bear (Acts 15:10). Their course brought upon themselves the destruction of their nation and hard servitude.

Verse 11: *I say then, Did they stumble that they might fall? God forbid: but by their fall salvation is come unto the Gentiles, to provoke them to jealousy.* Commentators usually make Paul's question mean something like this: Did they stumble so as to fall away completely and finally, never to be restored? But that is making Paul say more than he really said. Now, in classic Greek the conjunction here translated *that* introduces a final clause of purpose, but we are told that in the New Testament it "ranges in its use from definite purpose to simple result." Let it here have its primary meaning, and Paul's question would have this meaning: Did they stumble in order that they might fall? Was that their purpose? Certainly not, but it led to their fall; that much is certain. Was it their final doom? As a nation, Yes. Whether any of them as individuals were brought back into favor with God depended on their own choice in the matter. Now, the only way to favor with God is through Christ, and that is an individual matter.

So long as the law stood, Gentiles as such could not have covenant relationship with God. The law stood as a barrier, a wall, between Jew and Gentile; but that wall was taken out of the way that God might make of Jews and Gentiles one new man, one new church (Eph. 2:13-18.) The Jews broke the covenant, and it was abolished (Heb. 8:7-9). Jews and Gentiles then stood on an equal footing; God makes no difference between them now. In fact, it had been God's purpose all along to offer the blessings of salvation through Christ to the Gentiles. To Abraham God said: "In thy seed shall all the nations of the earth be blessed" (Gen. 22:18). This promise refers to Christ (Gal. 3:16). Read the

Great Commission, "Make disciples of all the nations,"
"Preach the gospel to the whole creation," and learn
that the prophets had said that "repentance and remission of sins should be preached in his name unto
all the nations, beginning from Jerusalem." Because
of the hardness of the Jews at Antioch of Pisidia, "Paul
and Barnabas spake out boldly, and said, it was necessary that the word of God should first be spoken to
you. Seeing ye thrust it from you, and judge yourselves unworthy of eternal life, lo, we turn to the Gentiles" (Acts 13:46). This spreading of the gospel
among the Gentiles did provoke the Jews to jealousy;
but it was jealousy for Judaism, not for the gospel.
Yet some commentators think Paul meant that the
Jews would become jealous of the great blessings the
gospel brought to Gentiles, and would, therefore, become Christians; but that view is not in line with
Paul's argument nor with the effects preaching to
Gentiles had on the Jews. When Paul was rescued
from a mob by the Roman soldiers, from the stairway
of the castle he made a speech to the angry Jews, in
which he said: "And it came to pass, that, when I
had returned to Jerusalem, and while I prayed in the
temple, I fell into a trance, and saw him saying unto
me, Make haste, and get thee quickly out of Jerusalem;
because they will not receive of thee testimony concerning me. . . . And he said unto me, Depart: for I
will send thee forth far hence unto the Gentiles" (Acts
22:17-21). These last words of Paul sent these Jews
into an insane rage. In Rom. 10:19 Paul quotes this
from Deuteronomy: "I will provoke you to jealousy
with that which is no nation, with a nation void of understanding will I anger you."

Verse 12: *"Now if their fall is the riches of the world, and their loss the riches of the Gentiles; how much more their fulness?* The fall of the Jews and the abrogation of the law of Moses opened up the way for the blessings of the gospel to be carried to the whole world. The first meaning Liddell and Scott gives to the word here translated "loss" is *defeat,* and we are told by an eminent scholar that there is no justification for translating it by "loss." Anyway, it is a fact that the Jews were defeated in their effort to destroy Christ and his teaching by crucifying him, and in their efforts to destroy the church; and they were defeated in their efforts to please God by the course they pursued. Because of their defeat in all these efforts the riches of the blessings of salvation were offered to the Gentiles—in fact, to all the people of the earth. "How much more their fulness?" "Fulness" in what way? Commentators seem to take it for granted that Paul was speaking of the full—complete—return of the Jews to the favor of God, but Paul's reasoning in this chapter does not contemplate such a thing as the conversion of the Jewish nation. Besides, he was speaking of the fall, or defeat, of the Jews and not their conversion. Might he not, therefore, have meant their full and complete degradation which resulted in their full and complete destruction as a nation? Their complete overthrow as a nation did contribute to the spread of the gospel. The majority of the Jews, both in Palestine and in foreign countries, had been the bitterest enemies Christianity had. In foreign countries where they had a synagogue, they did all they could to stir up the people and Roman authorities against Christians; but their active persecution of Christians ceased when their nation was destroyed. And they lost all influence with the Roman authorities everywhere. And those Judaizing meddlers, who sought to stir up trouble in all churches where there were Gentile members, lost their influence for harm. Perhaps nothing outside the church helped the spread of the gospel among all peoples so much as the full destruction of the Jewish nation.

Verses 13. 14: *But I speak to you that are Gentiles. Inasmuch then as I am an apostle of Gentiles, I glorify my ministry; if by any means I may provoke to jealousy them that are my flesh, and may save some of them.* Though Paul was discussing at length the fate of the Jews, he would not have Gentile Christians think he was forgetting the Gentile people. He had been chosen as an apostle of the Gentiles, and he gloried in that ministry. He demonstrated that he was sent of God by the miracles he performed. He hoped that his preaching to the Gentiles and his miracles among them would stir some of the Jews to such a pitch of jealousy that they would so investigate the testimony concerning the Christ as to become believers in Jesus as the Christ. By so doing he would be an instrument in saving those who believed his preaching. By teaching, backed up by a godly life, any Christian may be an agent in saving others. "Take heed to thyself, and to thy teaching. Continue in these things; for in doing this thou shalt save both thyself and them that hear thee" (1 Tim. 4:16). Paul did not expect to save all the Jews, only some of them.

Verse 15: *For if the casting away of them is the reconciling of the world, what shall the receiving of them be, but life from the dead?* The casting away of the Jews did not bring about the reconciling of the whole world, nor does "the receiving of them" mean that all Jews would be restored to God's favor. Reconciliation was offered to the whole world, and all Jews have the opportunity to be saved. All Jews were dead to God—dead in their sins, just as were the Gentiles. Hence, receiving a Jew back into favor with God is as life from the dead. The conversion of any sinner to Christ is life from the dead. The Jews are not now God's people any more than are the Gentiles—all are dead in trespasses and sins till they are made alive in Christ.

Verse 16: *And if the firstfruit is holy, so is the lump: and if the root is holy, so are the branches.* The word *holy* does not here mean free from sin. The law of Moses said, "The first of the first-fruits of thy ground thou shalt bring into the house of Jehovah thy God (Ex. 23:19). "And Jehovah spake unto Moses, saying, Speak unto the children of Israel, and say unto them, When ye are come into the land which I give unto you, and shall reap the harvest thereof, then shall ye bring the sheaf of the first-fruits of your harvest unto the priest: and he shall wave the sheaf before Jehovah, to be accepted for you. . . . And ye shall eat neither bread, nor parched grain, nor parched ears, until this selfsame day, until ye have brought the oblation of your God" (Lev. 23:9-14). When the first-fruits were brought to the priest, then the whole harvest became holy to the people, that is, devoted to their use. When God acceped the first Jewish converts, the first-fruits of the gospel harvest, then the whole nation was holy, that is acceptable to God on the terms of the gospel.   Only in that sense was the whole Jewish race holy.

Verses 17, 18: *But if some of the branches were broken off, and thou, being a wild olive, wast grafted in among them, and didst become partaker with them of the root of the fatness of the olive tree; glory not over the branches: but if thou gloriest, it is not thou that bearest the root, but the root thee.* An illustration must not be pressed so far as to contradict the plain teaching of other passages of the scriptures. This illustration must not be made to teach that some of the Jews were not broken off from God's favor; "for we before laid to the charge both of Jews and Greeks, that they are all under sin" (Rom. 3:9).   Many Jews, broken off from God's favor, had been grafted in again through their faith in Christ.   The wild olive tree represented the Gentiles; Gentile converts had been grafted into God's favor, and thereby had become partakers with the believing Jews "of the root of the fatness of the olive tree."   The unbelieving Jews were not partakers "of the root of the fatness of the olive tree," any more than the unbelieving Gentiles; they had been broken off.   They had been broken off for good reasons: they had broken the covenant, which gave them national existence; they had killed the Messiah; they had rejected the gospel, and unmercifully persecuted the Lord's church.   But even so, the Gentile Christians should not glory over the broken-off branches; neither should they glory over believing Jews, for believing Jews are as acceptable to God as are believing Gentiles. In this illustration, or figure, it seems that Abraham is the root, for all Israel sprang from him.   He gained God's favor by faith, and so do we.   By changing the figure, Abraham is said to be "the father of all them that believe" (Rom. 4:10). In the true sense now unbelieving Jews are not the seed of Abraham (John 8:39).

Verses 19-21: *Thou wilt say then, Branches were broken off, that I might be grafted in. Well; by their unbelief they were broken off, and thou standest by thy faith. Be not high-minded, but fear: for if God spared not the natural branches, neither will he spare thee.* From what was said in verses 11 and 12, the Gentile Christian might conclude that the Jews were rejected for the definite purpose of granting salvation to the Gentiles.

The rejection of the Jews, which resulted from their sins, did hasten the preaching of the gospel to the Gentiles; they were not arbitrarily rejected for the special benefit of Gentiles. The term "unbelief" here stands for all their sin and rebellion. In reality they cut themselves loose from all relations with God. By their faith the Gentile Christians stood in God's favor. They did not obtain God's favor through God's partiality to them, nor through any merit of their own, but by grace through faith in the Lord Jesus Christ. Jews could obtain that favor in the same way. There was therefore no grounds nor occasion for their glorying over the Jews. Besides, these Gentile Christians might also be broken off from God's favor, as a result of unbelief. By a natural birth all Jews had been God's people—they had been born into covenant relationship with God; but that covenant ended at the cross, and that left the Jews in the same condition as the Gentiles. "For they continued not in my covenant, and I regarded them not, saith the Lord" (Heb. 8:9). This should be a warning to Gentile Christians—in fact to all members of the New Covenant, whether Jews or Gentiles; "for if God spared not the natural branches, neither will he spare thee." This shows conclusively that Christians may conduct themselves in such way as to sever themselves from God's favor.

Verses 22, 23: *Behold then the goodness and severity of God: toward them that fell, severity; but toward thee, God's goodness, if thou continue in his goodness: otherwise thou also shalt be cut off. And they also, if they continue not in their unbelief, shall be grafted in: for God is able to graft them in again.* This saving some through faith, and cutting off others because of their unbelief, shows both the mercy and justice of God, both the goodness and severity of God. And this leads Paul to exclaim: "Behold then the goodness and severity of God." God dealt severely with the Jews because they fell through unbelief. His goodness would be extended to the Gentile Christians so long as they did not fall through unbelief. In his goodness and in his severity God is neither tyrannical nor whimsical; the display of either his goodness or severity depends on man's attitude toward him. Let us not get a one-sided view of God. "God is love" (1 John 4:8). It is equally true that "our God is a consuming fire" (Heb. 12:29). Because of unbelief the Jews had been cut off from God's favor. Their only hope therefore was to come back to God through faith in Christ. Any among them could be grafted again into God's favor, "if they continue not in their unbelief." God was able to graft them in again; the only hindering cause was their unbelief.

Verse 24: *But if thou wast cut out of that which is*

*by nature a wild olive tree, and wast grafted contrary
to nature into a good olive tree; how much more shall
these, which are the natural branches, be grafted into
their own olive tree?*   A wild olive tree is an unculti-
vated olive tree, a tree of the woods. Its fruit would be
inferior; and it would not be natural to expect to im-
prove its fruit by grafting it into a good olive tree.
However the fruit of the Gentiles, here represented as
of a wild olive tree, would be improved by their being
grafted into the good olive tree, that is, into the favor
and service of God.   And if a branch of a wild olive
tree is grafted into the good olive tree, how much more
natural is the grafting in of the natural branches.

Paul's olive-tree parable, or illustration, has often
been used in an attempt to prove the perpetuity of the
church from Abraham on down through the Christian
dispensation; and this is done in an effort to prove infant membership in the church. But a careful consideration of the parable, or illustration, shows the argument to be fallacious.

1.   The language is only an illustration of God's
method of dealing with Jews and Gentiles. To make an
illustration do service beyond the point illustrated is
to do violence to language and reason.

2.   The perpetuity of a supposed Abrahamic church
was not under consideration; Paul was not therefore
giving an illustration to prove that point. He had not
so much as hinted at such a thought.

3.   Two olive trees are in the parable. If the tame
olive tree represents the church of God, what church
does the wild olive tree represent? What is the wild
church?

4.   If the church at Pentecost had been with the

Jews all along, who were the hold-over members? Jesus had told Nicodemus, one of the best of the Jews, that he had to be born again. In fact the language of Jesus includes all: "Except one"—*tis*, any one—"be born of water and the Spirit, he cannot enter into the kingdom of God." Hence a Jew, any Jew, had to be born again to enter—to be grafted in. As if to make sure that Nicodemus and all others would know that all Jews were included, Jesus said, "Ye"—notice the plural pronoun—"Ye must be born again."

5. If the church began with Abraham and the olive tree represents that church, then Jews were members by nature, and would not have to be born again to enter it—they were born into it; and all Jewish children are still members of it. If Jews who reached the years of accountability were broken off—turned out of the church—because of unbelief, that would not destroy the fact that they were born into it. If that assumption is correct, then all Jewish children are yet born into it. If not, why not? Can a pedobaptist answer? Natural branches were broken off because of unbelief, but that would not apply to infants. What broke off the Jewish infants? It will not do to say that Jewish infants were brought into the church by circumcision, but infants are now brought in by baptism, and that therefore unbaptized Jewish infants are now left out; for if Jews became members by circumcision, then they were not branches by nature. Any one can see this. Hence the pedobaptist argument on the olive tree compels them to say that Jews were members by nature—by a natural birth; but their argument that baptism came in the room of circumcision compels them

to say that Jews became members by circumcision. Their arguments cancel each other.

6.   As all grafting in is done by faith, infants cannot be grafted in—they cannot have faith. And as no Gentiles are born into this supposed Abrahamic church and Gentile infants cannot be grafted in by faith, it is certain that Gentile infant membership in such a church is impossible.

7.   A parable or any other figure of speech must not be pressed beyond what the writer meant to teach. This is done when it is argued that Paul's parable of the olive tree teaches the perpetuity of a supposed Abrahamic church. In Eph. 2:14-16 Paul tells us that God took the law out of the way that he might make of both Jews and Gentiles one new man—one new church. It does not meet the issue to say that the covenants were changed, but the church remained the same, for Paul plainly says the Old Covenant was abolished that the new church might be established.

8.   The olive tree is God's favor, God's goodness, as may be seen by giving attention to verse 22. As a people, the Hebrews had been the special object of God's favor—he had been good to them, till they were broken off because of unbelief, and thereby fell under the severity of God.   Gentile believers were grafted into God's favor, God's goodness; but they also must continue in God's goodness, or also be broken off.   In all the parable nothing is said about a church, or about infant membership in anything.

Verse 25: *For I would not, brethren, have you ignorant of this mystery, lest ye be wise in your own conceits, that a hardening in part hath befallen Israel, until the fulness of the Gentiles be come in.* In the

New Testament the word mystery usually refers to
things not before revealed, but not always. (See 1 Tim.
3:9, 16; 2 Thes. 2:7). Things too great for finite minds
to comprehend are mysteries. The mystery of this
verse 25 is, that "a hardening in part hath befallen
Israel, until the fulness of the Gentiles be come in."
That statement itself is somewhat of a mystery, for
Paul does not reveal to us what the coming in of the
fulness of the Gentiles is. What Paul does not say,
some commentators and other writers fill in with their
own assumptions. It is assumed by some that "the
fulness of the Gentiles" means that all Gentiles will be
finally converted to Christ, and that will be followed
by the conversion of the whole Jewish race. Some
future kingdom advocates interpret "the fulness of the
Gentiles" as the full count of the Gentiles; that is,
when the Lord gathered out of the Gentiles the full
number he wants for rulers in the supposed future
kingdom, then evangelism among them will cease, and
the Jews will then turn to Christ. These are baseless
assumptions. It is assumed that the preposition "until" shows that this hardening of a part of the Jews
would continue only "until the fulness of the Gentiles
be come in," then the whole Jewish race would turn
to Christ. But the preposition "until" does not tell
what will follow the event or events mentioned in the
phrase it introduces, or governs. Consider a few examples. "And the waters decreased continually until
the tenth month" (Gen. 8:5). That does not indicate
any change after the tenth month; the record shows
that the waters continued to decrease for some time.
"Thy servants have been keepers of cattle from our
youth even until now" (Gen. 46:34). This does not

mean that they would quit the cattle business at that
time, and turn to something else; but it was to be the
basis of a plea to Pharaoh that they be allowed to
continue in the same business. "And Samuel came no
more to see Saul until the day of his death" (1 Sam.
15:35). That implies nothing as to what Samuel did
after the death of Saul. "My Father worketh even
until now" (John 5:17). And of course he kept on
working as he had always done. "For we know that
the whole creation groaneth and travaileth together until now" (Rom. 8:22). And Paul did not mean that
any change would follow the writing of that letter.
The whole creation continues to groan and travail even
now as they did before Paul penned those words. And
so, what change took place, or whether any change
occurred, after the things mentioned in the "until"
phrase, cannot be determined by that phrase, nor by
the other part of the sentence. Now, if we must deal
in suppositions, and must draw conclusions about "until," why not suppose things that are in harmony with
what actually occurred? As the church became more
and more made up of Gentile members, hardness among
the Jews increased until the church became almost, if
not entirely, Gentile in membership—until the fulness
of the Gentiles came in; then the hardness among the
Jews apparently became complete. If this is not what
Paul meant, it is, at least, what really occurred. And
aside from inspired interpretations, are not develop-
ments the best commentary on a prophecy?

Verses 26, 27: *And so all Israel shall be saved:
even as it is written, There shall come out of Zion the
Deliverer; he shall turn away ungodliness from Jacob:
and this is my covenant unto them, when I shall take*

away their sins. "So" is an adverb of manner; it is here a translation of a Greek word, which means, "in this way (manner), so, under these circumstances." Paul had shown how Gentiles had been grafted into God's favor, and how the Jews, the broken-off branches, might also be grafted in again. And so, in this manner, or in this way, shall all Israel be saved. Paul had just said that they would be grafted in again, if they continued not in unbelief. The Holy Spirit did not expect all Jews to turn from their unbelief. Paul did not therefore mean that every person of fleshly Israel would be saved; many since then have died in unbelief, and unsaved. And Paul did not say that the time would come when all Jews then living would be saved. And yet some speak as if that is what he said. When Peter said (Acts 15:11) that the Jews would be saved even as the Gentiles, he did not mean that all of either class would be saved, but that all would be saved as others had been saved—salvation was open to all on the same terms. The Deliverer is Christ Jesus. "Jacob" here stands for the descendants of Jacob. Jesus came to turn away ungodliness from Jacob, and did that for all who accepted him. They were to turn from their ungodliness—their impiety, or irreverence, and he would take away their sins, and that was his covenant with them.

Verses 28, 29: *As touching the gospel, they are enemies for your sake: but as touching the election, they are beloved for the fathers' sake. For the gifts and the calling of God are not repented of.* The Jews considered the Gentiles so far beneath them, that they considered themselves unclean if they touched a Gentile. From the start the Jews opposed the gospel, because it did not meet their expectations, and because it condemned them as sinners and as murderers. To be told that they were no better than Gentiles intensified their enmity. When Paul told the Jews in Jerusalem that the Lord had told him to depart from them and go and preach to the Gentiles, they said, "Away with such a fellow from the earth: for it is not fit that he should live" (Acts 22:17-22). The preaching of the gospel to Gentiles, and their acceptance into the church further hardened them from giving it any consideration. Of course no proud Pharisee would think of becoming a member of a body made up largely of Gentiles. And so, because of the Gentile Christians, the Jews were enemies of the gospel. God had selected the fathers, Abraham, Isaac, and Jacob, and their descendants as the line through which the Christ would come, and he had not repented of that selection; and even though these descendants had so sinned as to be broken off from his favor, they were beloved on account of the fathers, and not on their own account.

Verses 30, 31: *For as ye in time past were disobedient to God, but now have obtained mercy by their disobedience, even so have these also now been disobedient, that by the mercy shown to you they also may now obtain mercy.* Here it seems that Paul speaks especially to Gentile Christians. Though the Gentiles had not been under the law of Moses, yet they had been disobedient to God. If, as some say, Gentiles were not under any law of God, how could Paul say they had been disobedient to God? The truth is, all people are, and have always been, under God's eternal moral law, a law inherent in the nature of our relations to one another. The Gentiles, in disobeying this moral law, had sinned against God. For a list of their sinful practices see Romans 1:18-32. They were therefore under condemnation, as much so as were disobedient Jews. But mercy had been extended to these Gentile sinners; the opportunity to turn from their sins and be saved had been granted to them in the gospel. And this was a guaranty that disobedient Jews also could obtain mercy.

Verse 32: *For God hath shut up all unto disobedience, that he might have mercy upon all.* This does not mean that God had shut up all, both Jews and Gentiles, under such conditions that they had to be disobedient, but that he counted all as disobedient; "for we before laid to the charge both of Jews and Greeks, that they are all under sin" (Rom. 3:9) And for this reason he commands all men everywhere to repent (Acts 17:30, 31). Christ came to save sinners, not to cause men to be sinners. People are not made sinners by hearing the gospel, but the gospel is preached to them because they are sinners. People are sinners, and they need to realize that they are under condemnation, that they may obtain God's mercy. In this verse Paul ends his argument on the theme that the gospel is the power of God for salvation.

Verses 33-36: *O the depth of the riches both of the wisdom and the knowledge of God! how unsearchable are his judgments, and his ways past tracing out! For who hath known the mind of the Lord? or who hath been his counsellor? or who hath first given to him, and it shall be recompensed unto him again? For of him, and through him, and unto him, are all things. To him be the glory for ever. Amen.* How sublime are these words! They refer to the provisions for salvation as revealed in the gospel, including God's use of men and nations in the development of this plan of salvation, as had been set forth in this letter, and not merely, as some think, to what was said in verses 30 and 31.

In the Bible use of the term "knowledge of God" that phrase does not refer to what God knows, but to what is known, or may be known, about him; that is, it refers to the things revealed about him and his plans. Here are some examples of the use of the phrase: "Then shalt thou understand the fear of Jehovah, and find the knowledge of God (Prov. 2:5). " . . . there is no truth, nor goodness, nor knowledge of God in the land" (Hosea 4:1). "Some have no knowledge of God" (1 Cor. 15:34). Paul prayed that the Colossians be "increasing in the knowledge of God" (Col. 1:9-10). "But grow in the grace and knowledge of our Lord and Savior Jesus Christ" (2 Pet. 3:18). (See also Hosea 6:6; 2 Cor. 10:5; 2 Pet. 1:2, 3, 8). In not one passage does the phrase refer to what God knows, any more than the phrase "knowledge of mathematics" refers to what mathematics knows. No uninspired man could search out and discern the judgments of God, nor trace out his ways down through the ages as he used men and nations in working out his plans and purposes. And no one can know the mind of God, save as he reveals it. By man's unaided powers he cannot find out these glorious things. "But unto us God revealed them through the Spirit: for the Spirit searcheth all things, yea, the deep things of God. For who among men knoweth the things of a man, save the spirit of the man, which is in him? Even so the things of God none knoweth, save the Spirit of God. But we received, not the spirit of the world, but the Spirit which is from

God; that we might know the things that were freely given to us of God. Which things also we speak, not in words which man's wisdom teacheth, but which the Spirit teacheth" (1 Cor. 2:9-13). Only as God reveals himself may we know his mind. And no one has ever given anything to God, so as to bring God under obligation to recompense him; for all things are of him, through him, and unto him. We cannot therefore enrich him by giving him that which is already his; but we can, with Paul, say, "To him be glory for ever."

Chapter 12

12:1 I beseech you therefore, brethren, by the mercies of God, to present your bodies a living sacrifice, holy, acceptable to God, *which is* your spiritual service. 2 And be not fashioned according to this world: but be ye transformed by the renewing of your mind, that ye may prove what is the good and acceptable and perfect will of God.

3 For I say, through the grace that was given me, to every man that is among you, not to think of himself more highly than he ought to think; but so to think as to think soberly, according as God hath dealt to each man a measure of faith. 4 For even as we have many members in one body, and all the members have not the same office: 5 so we, who are many, are one body in Christ, and severally members one of another. 6 And having gifts differing according to the grace that was given to us, whether prophecy, *let us prophesy* according to the proportion of our faith; 7 or ministry, *let us give ourselves* to our ministry; or he that teacheth, to his teaching; 8 or he that exhorteth, to his exhorting; he that giveth, *let him do it* with liberality; he that ruleth, with diligence; he that showeth mercy, with cheerfulness.

9 Let love be without hypocrisy. Abhor that which is evil; cleave to that which is good. 10 In love of the brethren be tenderly affectioned one to another; in honor preferring one another; 11 in diligence not slothful; fervent in spirit; serving the Lord; 12 rejoicing in hope; patient in tribulation; continuing stedfastly in prayer; 13 communicating to the necessities of the saints; given to hospitality. 14 Bless them that persecute you; bless, and curse not. 15 Rejoice with them that rejoice; weep with them that weep. 16 Be of the same mind one toward another. Set not your mind on high things, but condescend to things that are lowly. Be not wise in your own conceits. 17 Render to no man evil for evil. Take thought for things honorable in the sight of all men. 18 If it be possible, as much as in you lieth, be at peace with all men. 19 Avenge not yourselves, beloved, but give place unto the wrath of God: for it is written, Vengeance belongeth unto me; I will recompense, saith the Lord. 20 But if thine enemy hunger, feed him; if he thirst, give him to drink: for in so doing thou shalt heap coals of fire upon his head. 21 Be not overcome of evil, but overcome evil with good.

Verse 1: *I beseech you therefore, brethren, by the mercies of God, to present your bodies a living sacrifice, holy, acceptable to God, which is your spiritual service.* Instead of giving a command Paul put forth all his apostolic authority in this tender appeal—"I beseech you." The riches of God's mercy as manifested in his provisions for man's salvation in and through the gospel should be a mighty appeal to man to give him all his powers. "Or know ye not that your body is a temple of the Holy Spirit which is in you, which ye have from God? and ye are not your own; for ye were bought with a price: glorify God therefore in your body" (1 Cor. 6:19, 20). Our bodies are to be presented as living sacrifices. This is not said, as so many suppose, "in contrast with dead sacrifices of the Old Testament"; for no Jew ever offered a dead animal as a sacrifice. Living animals were brought to the altar. Paul commands, "Present yourselves unto God, as alive from the dead, and your members as instruments of righteousness unto God" " . . . even so now present your members as servants to righteousness unto sanctification" (Rom. 6:13, 19). So the meaning is, present your bodies alive to righteousness—alive to God. The body is dead to sin. "But if the Spirit of him that raised up Jesus from the dead dwelleth in you, he that raised up Christ Jesus from the dead shall give life also to your mortal bodies through the Spirit that dwelleth in you" (Rom. 8:11). This does not refer to the resurrection of the body, but to its use in the service of God now. Our bodies, once dead in sin, are now, by the Holy Spirit that dwells in us, made alive in the service of God; they are to be presented to God as living, active instruments in his service. "Holy." With the Greeks the word here translated "holy" meant, "devoted to the gods." Any gift made to their gods was said to be *devoted, holy.* It is easy to see its application. Our bodies, as living sacrifices, are devoted to the worship and service of God. Anything taken out of common use and devoted to God is holy. Our bodies are therefore important; in fact, no command can be obeyed, and no kind of service to God can be rendered, without the use of the body. And as the spirit of man thus uses his body, it is called a spiritual service. The common version has, "reasonable service."

Some have concluded that Paul was urging the brethren to do what God said on the grounds that his demands were just and equitable, as if one should advise another to buy a piece of property because the price was reasonable, that is, just and right! That no inspired writer would do. The word occurs one other time in the New Testament; there King James has *sincere*, the American Standard has *spiritual* (1 Pet. 2:2). There are no carnal ordinances in Christianity; every acceptable service is a spiritual service. And to thus devote our bodies as instruments of service to him is acceptable to him, a spiritual service.

Verse 2: *And be not fashioned according to this world: but be ye transformed by the renewing of your mind, that ye may prove what is the good and acceptable and perfect will of God.* Some Christians, like the children of Israel, want to copy the ways and practices of other people. This Paul forbids. His language also bans our drifting into the customs prevailing about us; and Christians will drift into the customs of other religious people, if they do not study the Bible, and make it their guide in speech and action. The Christian should make the Bible his guide, and give no thought as to whether it makes him like or unlike others. " . . . as children of obedience, not fashioning yourselves according to your former lusts in the time of your ignorance: but like as he who called you is holy, be ye yourselves also holy in all manner of living" (1 Pet. 1:14, 15). Fashion yourselves according to the life of Christ and the gospel, not the world. "But be ye transformed." This demands a radical change in the thinking and the conduct of those who become Christians. The Greek word here rendered *transformed* is rendered *transfigured* in Matt. 17:2 and Mark 9:2. The Christian is made responsible for this change; the change is not brought about suddenly. "Though our outward man is decaying, yet our inward man is renewed day by day" (2 Cor. 4:16). This transformation can be brought about only by renewing the mind, the inward man, day by day. No one can transform his character while holding to the same old stock of ideas and ideals. Study the Bible — make God's thoughts and ideals your thoughts and ideals, and a transformation naturally follows. The gospel in the heart works the change. And because the will of God cherished in the heart works such a change in character, the thoughtful person therefore by actual experience proves to himself that the will of God is good, well-pleasing, and perfect.

Verse 3: *For I say, through the grace that was given me, to every man that is among you, not to think of himself more highly than he ought to think; but so to think as to think soberly, according as God hath dealt to each man a measure of faith.* Paul speaks of his being made an apostle as the grace that was given him. The same thought is expressed in chapter 15:15, 16; 1 Cor. 3:10; 15:10; Gal. 2:7-9; Eph. 3:7. He warns Christians against thinking too highly of themselves. To think soberly is to think sensibly—to think of our proper relations with God and our fellowmen. No one should feel himself to be wise above what is written, nor feel so important as to be domineering. Neither should he, like Moses, feel that he is too insignificant to do what God commands him to do. "A measure of faith." It does not seem to me that "measure" here means portion. R. St. John Parry, in his

notes in the Cambridge Greek Testament, says of the
Greek term here translated "measure," "In N. T. it
always has its proper significance of 'a measuring
instrument.'" Faith is the measuring instrument, the
instrument by which we are to measure our thinking.
Whether faith in this place refers to the gospel, as it
does in some places, or to our own faith in the gospel,
makes no difference; for our faith includes a whole-
hearted belief in the gospel. It equals the idea that
the gospel is the measuring instrument; for our faith
cannot go beyond the gospel, and should not fall short
of it. Our faith is the gospel written in our hearts.

Verses 4, 5: *For even as we have many members in
one body, and all the members have not the same office: so we, who are many, are one body in Christ,
and severally members one of another.* As all Christians are one body in Christ, and members one of another, no member should think himself to be above another. The word "office" in verse 4 refers to function.
Each member of the body of Christ has an office, a
function, just as does each member of our own body,
and is an essential part of the body. It is a sobering
thought. Paul dwells on this same illustration in
greater length in 1 Cor. 12:12-27.

Verses 6-8: *And having gifts differing according
to the grace that was given to us, whether prophecy,
let us prophesy according to the proportion of our faith;
or ministry, let us give ourselves to our ministry; or
he that teacheth, to his teaching; or he that exhorteth,
to his exhortation; he that giveth, let him do it with*

liberality; he that ruleth, with diligence; he that show-eth mercy, with cheerfulness.

The human body is a unit, though it has many members; and each member has an office, or function. So it is in the church, the body of Christ. People have certain natural gifts, but no natural gift will enable a man to prophesy. A prophet was one who spoke for God; that is, God spoke through him to the people. Foretelling future events was not his main work; God delivered through him whatever teaching the people needed. He was an inspired teacher. Certain other activities in the early church required special endowments; these special endowments were called spiritual gifts. These are mentioned more specifically in 1 Cor. 12:1-11, 28-30. It seems that teachers did not reveal, but taught what had been revealed. As the New Testament had not been completed, these teachers would need a degree of inspiration to enable them to remember what they had been taught and to guard them against error. But ministry is service, and it seems that service could be rendered without inspiration; and so with exhorting and giving. The ruler needed diligence, but too many give very little time or attention to the responsibility placed upon them. And no one should attempt to show mercy in a half-hearted or indifferent way. Showing mercy in a helpful way is a fine art.

Verses 9, 10: *Let love be without hypocrisy. Abhor that which is evil; cleave to that which is good. In love of the brethren be tenderly affectioned one to another; in honor preferring one another.* There should be no pretended love; pretended love is hypocrisy. The man who does not abhor that which is evil neither loves the

good ·nor cleaves to it. "Hate the evil, and love the
good" (Amos 5:15). Jehovah said concerning Christ,
"Thou hast loved righteousness, and hated iniquity,
therefore God, thy God, hath anointed thee with the oil
of gladness above thy fellows" (Heb. 1:9). Because
Jesus loved man, he hated evil; and so must the Christian. If we love our fellowman, we hate that which is
hurtful to him. When Christians are "tenderly affectioned one to another," they will fight against everything that is hurtful to others. And in all social and
business affairs Christians should prefer one another.

Verses 11-13:   ... *in diligence not slothful; fervent*
in spirit; serving the Lord; rejoicing in hope; patient
in tribulation; continuing stedfastly in prayer; com-
municating to the necessities of the saints; given to
hospitality. "Slothful implies excessive and sluggish
indolence." The Christian must be industrious in the
Lord's service; otherwise he can have no hope. Hope
sustains people in all their undertakings; and to the
Christian hope of future bliss brings joy and happiness
even in his tribulations and difficulties. Patience is
steadfastness—endurance. Hope helps the Christian to
be patient, or steadfast, in tribulation; for without hope
we would not endure trials and persecutions. Patience
holds on; it does not quit. Realizing our continuous dependence on the Lord leads to steadfastness in prayer.
Indifference and a feeling of self-sufficiency causes
a neglect of prayer. To communicate to the necessities of the saints is to help them in their needs. Hospitality is the receiving and entertaining of guests gen-
erously and kindly, or to be generous toward any who
needs, and that includes strangers. If all these traits

of character are manifested by all the members of a church, that church is a power for good.

Verses 14, 15: *"Bless them that persecute you; bless, and curse not. Rejoice with them that rejoice; weep with them that weep.* Persecutions are the common lot of Christians. "Yea, and all that would live godly in Christ Jesus shall suffer persecution" (2 Tim. 3:12). It is living godly as a Christian that brings persecution. It is not personal enmity; it is enmity against Christ. This should cause the Christian to pity the persecutor for his blind rage. The greatest blessing we can confer upon the persecutor is to lead him to be a Christian. To curse does not mean to use ordinary profanity; it is a call for calamity to befall a person. If a fellow-Christian has a righteous cause for rejoicing, we should rejoice with him. Too often we envy the good fortune of others. And we should enter into full sympathy with others in their sorrows.

Verse 16: *Be of the same mind one toward another. Set not your mind on high things, but condescend to things that are lowly. Be not wise in your own conceits.* The admonition to be of the same mind is directly connected with what is said in verse 15. It does not seem to refer to unity in gospel teaching, but rather of sentiment, or disposition, of one toward another— each one to enter into the rejoicings and sorrows of the other. Be not ambitious to appear to be greater or better than others. In reading this verse the marginal reading in the American Standard Version should be carefully noted. The marginal reading informs us that the Greek word here translated *condescend* means, *be carried away with.* For *things* the marginal reading has *them.* This gives, "be carried away with them that

are lowly." Conybeare and Howson has, "suffer yourselves to be borne along with the lowly." James Macknight: "associate with lowly men." The Cambridge
Greek Testament says the Greek word equals, "put
yourselves on a level with, accommodate yourselves
to." Barnes says, "Literally, 'being led away by, or
being conducted by.' It does not properly mean to
condescend, but denotes a *yielding,* or being guided and
led in the thoughts, feelings, plans, by humble objects."
In a note on synonyms under the definition of condescend Webster says, "Condescend implies a courteous
or patronizing waiving of real or assumed superiority;
as, his insolent *condescension.*" And so it seems that
condescend is the wrong word, and that it expresses a
wrong idea. The truth is, we Christians are all members of one family. One child of God does not condescend when he associates with another member of the
family, and he should not feel that he does. The egotist
feels that he condescends when he associates with the
lowly, but the genuine Christian does not so feel. "Be
not wise in your own conceits." Such a condition of
mind makes a person feel superior to other children
of God.

Verse 17: *Render to no man evil for evil. Take
thought for things honorable in the sight of all men.*
Returning evil for evil settles nothing, but usually
makes bad matters worse. Besides, to return evil for
evil puts one in the class of evil doers. Spite work is
of the devil. Even men of the world look upon retalia-
tion as beneath the dignity of a gentleman, and therefore not honorable. "There is a common standard of
honor which Christians must by no means ignore."
When a Christian so far forgets himself as to violate

the world's standard of honor, he loses his influence for good. And this does not mean that we must be men-pleasers. The Greek word for "take thought" means to pre-think—to think before you adopt a certain course of action. The Christian lowers himself in the estimation of men when he engages in things that the world thinks beneath the Christian profession; he also disobeys Paul's injunction.

Verse 18: *If it be possible, as much as in you lieth, be at peace with all men.* Christians should strive especially to be at peace among themselves. And we should do our best, without sacrificing truth and duty, to be at peace with all men. We should not be meddlers in other men's affairs; but if we preach the truth, rebuke, and exhort, somebody will not like it. It is impossible therefore to be at peace with all men. Neither Jesus nor Paul could be at peace with the enemies of Christ. We must contend earnestly for the faith— we must fight the good fight of faith. But the Christian can afford to sacrifice his own personal rights and preferences rather than stir up trouble. The Christian should certainly not stir up trouble over things of no vital importance.

Verses 19-21: *Avenge not yourselves, beloved, but give place unto the wrath of God: for it is written, Vengeance belongeth unto me; I will recompense saith the Lord. But if thine enemy hunger, feed him; if he thirst, give him to drink: for in so doing thou shalt heap coals of fire upon his head. Be not overcome of evil, but overcome evil with good.* Paul's addressing them as "beloved" would remind them that they should feel the same way toward one another. That feeling would promote peace and good fellowship among them,

for people do not indulge in strife and harsh words
with those they love. But there is inherent in man a
sense of justice, a feeling that evil-doers should be punished. Taking vengeance is the savage's way of exact-
ing justice, but not the Lord's way. Neither is that
sort of punishment tolerated by civilized governments.
"Avenge not yourselves." The individual should not
with his own hands try to take satisfaction for injuries.
To punish evil doers is God's prerogative; let him do
the punishing in his own appointed way. Paul quotes
from Deut. 32:35: "Vengeance belongeth unto me; I
will recompense, saith the Lord." Paul's quoting that
statement did not change its meaning nor its application. It does not refer to the vengeance God will take
on sinners at the final judgment. Under the law of
Moses God took vengeance on evil-doers by the agency
of chosen authorities. Paul's quoting that part of the
law did not change its application, and the vengeance
here mentioned will be taken in the same way. A little
later Paul will show how this is to be done. Instead
of taking personal vengeance on an enemy, give him
food and drink as his needs may require. If there is
any degree of manhood in him, this course will fill him
with shame and remorse—figuratively it will heap
coals of fire on his head, and may entirely melt down
his enmity. If it does not do this, it will make him
feel uncomfortable, in that he has no evil thing he can
say about you. By following the course outlined in
verses 19 and 20, the Christian overcomes evil with
good; if he seeks with his own hands to inflict punishment on an enemy, he is overcome of evil—he himself
becomes evil.

Chapter 13

13:1 Let every soul be in subjection to the higher powers: for there is no power but of God: and the *powers* that be are ordained of God. 2 Therefore he that resisteth the power, withstandeth the ordinance of God: and they that withstand shall receive to themselves judgment. 3 For rulers are not a terror to the good work, but to the evil. And wouldest thou have no fear of the power? do that which is good. and thou shalt have praise from the same: 4 for he is a minister of God to thee for good. But if thou do that which is evil, be afraid; for he beareth not the sword in vain: for he is a minister of God, an avenger for wrath to him that doeth evil. 5 Wherefore *ye* must needs be in subjection, not only because of the wrath, but also for conscience' sake. 6 For for this cause ye pay tribute also; for they are ministers of God's service, attending continually upon this very thing. 7 Render to all their dues: tribute to whom tribute *is due;* custom to whom custom; fear to whom fear; honor to whom honor.

8 Owe no man anything, save to love one another: for he that loveth his neighbor hath fulfilled the law. 9 For this, Thou shalt not commit adultery, Thou shalt not kill, Thou shalt not steal, Thou shalt not covet, and if there be any other commandment, it is summed up in this word, namely, Thou shalt love thy neighbor as thyself. 10 Love worketh no ill to his neighbor: love therefore is the fulfilment of the law.

11 And this knowing the season, that already it is time for you to awake out of sleep: for now is salvation nearer to us than when we *first* believed. 12 The night is far spent, and the day is at hand: let us therefore cast off the works of darkness, and let us put on the armor of light. 13 Let us walk becomingly, as in the day; not in revelling and drunkenness, not in chambering and wantonness, not in strife and jealousy. 14 But put ye on the Lord Jesus Christ, and make not provision for the flesh, to *fulfil* the lusts *thereof.*

Verse 1: *Let every soul be in subjection to the higher powers: for there is no power but of God; and the powers that be are ordained of God.* Paul here speaks of civil governments, human governments. These injunctions apply to all men, especially to all Christians, in all times and places; but there was then a special need for such teaching. Christianity was new, and was regarded by some as antagonistic to human governments. There was likely to be such a notion among Christians. The Jews were especially averse to being subject to the Roman government, and Jews who became Christians would likely hold to their former prejudice against being subject to Rome. And converts from heathenism might feel that, having confessed Jesus Christ as their king, they were not subject to any other government. Hence the special need for Paul's plain and emphatic teaching. To make such submission to earthly governments seem more reasonable and necessary he informs them that all power is of God, and that civil governments are ordained of God. He who denies this fact denies the voice of inspiration. The fact that governments sometimes turn out bad, and do unjust things, does not prove Paul's statement to be untrue. The devil sometimes controls the actions of governments, but that does not prove that all governments belong to the devil. The devil sometimes gets into churches and causes them to do evil and unjust things, but that does not prove that the devil owns and controls all churches. The design of civil government is to promote the security and the well-being of its citizens; and there would be no security of life and property, if there were no human governments. And so obedience to civil authorities is a fundamental requirement of the gospel. "Put them in mind to be in subjection to rulers, to authorities, to be obedient, to be ready unto every good work" (Tit. 3:1). "Be subject to every ordinance of man for the Lord's sake: whether to the king, as supreme; or unto governors, as sent by him for vengeance on evil-doers and for praise to them that do well. For so is the will of God, that by well-doing ye should put to silence the ignorance of foolish men" (1 Pet. 2:13-15). One can scarcely imagine a government that would be worse than none. In all he says, Paul assumed that governments would carry out their God-appointed mission. Of course, if a government demands that a Christian must do anything against the will of God, he must obey

God rather than man. Aside from this one thing, the Christian should be the best of all citizens; for "the powers that be are ordained of God."

Verse 2: *Therefore he that resisteth the power, withstandeth the ordinance of God: and they that withstand shall receive to themselves judgment.* Because these powers are ordained of God, the one who resisteth—takes his stand against—the power resists the ordinance of God. To resist the government does not simply mean to fail sometimes to obey a law; it is to take a stand against the government—to defy the authority of the government. To do this is to array oneself against both God and the government, and in so doing brings upon himself the judgment of both.

Verses 3, 4: *For rulers are not a terror to the good work, but to the evil. And wouldest thou have no fear of the power? do that which is good, and thou shalt have praise from the same: for he is a minister of God to thee for good. But if thou do that which is evil, be afraid; for he beareth not the sword in vain: for he is a minister of God, an avenger for wrath to him that doeth evil.* The Roman authorities later put Paul to death; yet he says, "Rulers are not a terror to the good work, but to the evil." On this point Conybeare and Howson have this to say: "We must remember that this was written before the imperial government had begun to persecute Christians. It is a testimony in favor of the general administration of the Roman criminal law." But that seems to imply that Paul's statement applied only to the Roman government, and only up to the time the Roman government began to persecute Christians. But was not Paul laying down principles that would apply to all Christians under estab-

lished governments in all ages? So it seems to me.
Paul was stating the proper functions of civil governments. His statements are a guide to the duties and
limitations of governments, and a rebuke to those who
overstep the bounds of their proper functions. Governments sometimes fail to function within their proper
limits, just as churches sometimes fail to function as
they should. The failure of a church to function as it
should does not prove that the devil originated it, nor
that all churches are owned and controlled by the devil;
neither does a persecuting government prove that the
devil controls all governments. No human government is perfect, and certainly the Roman government
was far from perfection; but try to imagine the fate of
the early Christians and of all other decent people,
had there been no government at all. All governments are pleased with law-abiding citizens. The trouble was, the Roman government had some laws concerning religion, which Christians could not obey; and
this caused the trouble. Monsters of cruelty like Nero
made it hard on Christians. Civil governments were
meant to be ministers of God for the good of the people; but they sometimes swerve from their God-appointed mission, and become instruments of cruelty.
The sword, as here used, is a symbol of power—the
power, or authority, to inflict the death penalty. The
death penalty for certain crimes is one of God's fundamental requirements. Long before the law of Moses
was given God said to Noah, "Whoso sheddeth man's
blood, by man shall his blood he shed: for in the image
of God made he man" (Gen. 9:6). This decree of God
has always had to be carried out in a legal way; otherwise it would be murder. "He beareth not the sword in

vain; for he is a minister of God, an avenger for wrath to him that doeth evil." No person should therefore take vengeance with his own hands.

Verse 5: *Wherefore ye must needs be in subjection, not only because of the wrath, but also for conscience' sake.* Two reasons or motives are here given for submission to government authorities, namely, the penalty the government would inflict for failure to be in subjection; and a Christian must obey the authorities in order to have a clear conscience. A man who can disobey the laws of his government without having any remorse of conscience is lacking in respect for God's commands. The requirement that Christians must be in subjection to the laws of the land, has been used by some as proof that Christians can have no part in government affairs; but that is an unwarranted conclusion. The fact is, every citizen, whether he takes part in political affairs or does not, is expected to be in subjection to the laws of the country. From the humblest citizen to the Chief Executive all are subject to the laws of the government. It would be a curious thing to say that those who take part in the affairs of government are not to be in subjection to its laws.

Verses 6, 7: *For this cause ye pay tribute also: for they are ministers of God's service, attending continually upon this very thing. Render to all their dues: tribute to whom tribute is due; custom to whom custom; fear to whom fear; honor to whom honor.* Tribute has special reference to "the annual tax levied upon houses, lands, and persons." The Christian must pay his taxes; the officers of the government must be paid, "for they are ministers of God's service." No Christian should try to avoid paying his just share of

government expenses; it is common honesty, as well
as a Christian duty. Our Lord taught the Jews to pay
their taxes (Matt. 22:15-22). "Render to all their
dues"; or, Pay to all what you owe. Pay tribute and
custom to whom they are due. Tribute—direct taxes
on a person and his property; custom is revenue levied
on imports and trades. So long as we live in the flesh,
even if all people were Christians, we need civil governments; for there are things that must be done, that
the church as a body is not authorized to do.

Verses 8-10: *Owe no man anything, save to love
one another: for he that loveth his neighbor hath fulfilled the law. For this, Thou shalt not commit adultery, Thou shalt not kill, Thou shalt not steal, Thou
shalt not covet, and if there be any other commandment,
it is summed up in this word, namely, Thou shalt love
thy neighbor as thyself. Love worketh no ill to his
neighbor: love therefore is the fulfilment of the law.*
If a man pays promptly according to contract, he owes
nothing. "Render to all their dues"—pay what is due.
When therefore the time comes to meet an obligation,
meet it promptly. But the obligation to love one another is always due, and is never fully paid; it is a
perpetual debt. The marginal reading in the American Standard Version informs us that the Greek word
translated *neighbor* in verse 8 means, *the other.* So
the verse would read, "Owe no man anything, save to
love one another: for he that loveth the other hath fulfilled the law." But the law is not fulfilled by mere
sentiment, or feeling, but by deeds of helpfulness; and
it means, as well, refraining from doing any harm. It
means that one must refrain from doing the evil things
mentioned in verse 9. "For this"—this is the sum of

fulfilling the law of love, namely, refrain from the evils mentioned, and love your neighbor as yourself; really it is all summed in the one command: "Thou shalt love thy neighbor as thyself." And we love our neighbor as ourselves when we treat him as well as we would have him treat us. If a man loves his neighbor as himself, he will not do him any harm, but always good. This is real love.

Verse 11. *And this, knowing the season, that it is already time for you to awake out of sleep; for now is salvation nearer to us than when we first believed.* "And this" additional matter, "knowing the season"—knowing the character of the time in which they lived—it was time for them to arouse from their indifference and lethargy. Few Christians are ever as wide awake as they should be. "Wherefore he saith, Awake thou that sleepest, and arise from the dead, and Christ shall shine upon thee" (Eph. 5:14). "Salvation nearer." This seems to refer to their eternal salvation; for they were already in possession of salvation in Christ from their alien sins. As time passes eternal salvation comes nearer. It is now nearer than when we first believed.

Verse 12: *The night is far spent, and the day is at at hand: let us therefore cast off the works of darkness, and let us put on the armor of light.* There are some difficulties in this verse, but its general meaning seems clear enough. Sin and ignorance are both represented as darkness—night. Christians are all more or less under the influence of both. Paul's language in this verse shows this to be so: "Let us therefore cast off the works of darkness." Without the gospel of Christ darkness covered the world; but the darkness, or night, was far spent, for the full revelation of the gospel was nearing completion. The day—the full light of the gospel—was at hand. Now men walk in darkness only by choice. Christians have a responsibility. The gospel is light only to those who open their eyes to it. We must cast off the works of darkness, and put on the armor of light. Light of the gospel is the armor; we put that armor on by learning the gospel and cherishing it. The gospel is light to us only in so far as we know its teaching. In connection with verses 11-14 read 1 Thes. 5:7-10.

Verses 13, 14: *Let us walk becomingly, as in the day; not in revelling and drunkenness, not in chambering and wantonness, not in strife and jealousy. But put ye on the Lord Jesus Christ, and make no provision for the flesh, to fulfil the lusts thereof.* No Christian should be guilty of unseemly conduct. Love does not behave itself unseemly (1 Cor. 13:5): A Christian man should be a gentleman—a gentle man. He should not stumble, as if he were walking in the dark; he should walk uprightly, as in the day. But if he does not walk in the light of the gospel, he is sure to stumble. He should not be guilty of revelling and drunkenness; the two usually go together. To revel is to engage in hilarious conduct, and the drunkard usually does that. "Not in chambering"—not in unchaste conduct with the opposite sex; "and wantonness"—lewdness. Strife and jealousy usually grow out of such conduct. Verse 14 is in contrast with verse 13. Instead of indulging in such things as mentioned in verse 13, we are to clothe ourselves with the characteristics manifested by our Lord while he was in the flesh—put ourselves completely under his authority, and let him always be our guide. We are to make his life our life.

We must make provision for the needs of our body, but not to fulfill its lusts. In short, the Christian must lead a clean life.

Chapter 14

14:1 But him that is weak in faith receive ye. yet not for decision of scruples
2 One man hath faith to eat all things: but he that is weak eateth herbs. 3 Let
not him that eateth set at nought him that eateth not; and let not him that eateth
not judge him that eateth: for God hath received him. 4 Who art thou that judgest
the servant of another? to his own lord he standeth or falleth. Yea, he shall be
made to stand; for the Lord hath power to make him stand. 5 One man esteemeth
one day above another: another esteemeth every day *alike.* Let each man be fully
assured in his own mind. 6 He that regardeth the day, regardeth it unto the
Lord: and he that eateth, eateth unto the Lord, for he giveth God thanks; and
he that eateth not, unto the Lord he eateth not, and giveth God thanks. 7 For
none of us liveth to himself, and none dieth to himself. 8 For whether we live, we
live unto the Lord; or whether we die, we die unto the Lord: whether we live
therefore, or die, we are the Lord's. 9 For to this end Christ died and lived *again.*
that he might be Lord of both the dead and the living. 10 But thou, why dost
thou judge thy brother? or thou again, why dost thou set at nought thy brother?
for we shall all stand before the judgment-seat of God.
    11 For it is written,
         As I live, saith the Lord, to me every knee shall bow,
         And every tongue shall confess to God.
    12 So then each one of us shall give account of himself to God.
    13. Let us not therefore judge one another any more: but judge ye this rather
that no man put a stumbling-block in his brother's way, or an occasion of falling
14 I know, and am persuaded in the Lord Jesus, that nothing is unclean of itself:
save that to him who accounteth anything to be unclean, to him it is unclean. 15
For if because of meat thy brother is grieved, thou walkest no longer in love. Destroy not with thy meat him for whom Christ died. 16 Let not then your good
be evil spoken of: 17 for the kingdom of God is not eating and drinking, but
righteousness and peace and joy in the Holy Spirit. 18 For he that herein serveth
Christ is well-pleasing to God, and approved of men. 19 So then let us follow
after things which make for peace, and things whereby we may edify one another.
20 Overthrow not for meat's sake the work of God. All things indeed are clean;
howbeit it is evil for that man who eateth with offence. 21 It is good not to eat
flesh, nor to drink wine, nor *to do anything* whereby thy brother stumbleth. 22
The faith which thou hast, have thou to thyself before God. Happy is he that
judgeth not himself in that which he approveth. 23 But he that doubteth is condemned if he eat, because *he eateth* not of faith; and whatsoever is not of faith
is sin.

In this chapter and in 1 Cor., chapters 8 and 10:14-33, Paul discusses the matter of eating meat; but in the main the points of emphasis in the two letters are different. In Corinthians he warns brethren against eating meat under circumstances that might lead others to eat certain meat in honor of an idol, but the main point in this fourteenth chapter is somewhat different.

The Christian Jews, at least, many of them, had not entirely broken away from the law of Moses. They observed certain days, and were disposed to condemn the Gentile Christians for not doing so. They would not eat meat that the law declared unclean. Some ate only herbs, lest they might eat meat that had been dedicated to an idol. The Gentile Christians would consider their conduct as foolishness. Perhaps some Gentile converts, having been used to eating certain meats dedicated to idols, feared to eat any meat, lest they honor an idol in so doing. All these matters were grounds for a lot of criticisms and strife.

Verses 1-4: *But him that is weak in faith receive ye, yet not for decision of scruples. One man hath faith to eat all things; but he that is weak eateth herbs. Let not him that eateth set at nought him that eateth not; and let not him that eateth not judge him that eateth: for God hath received him. Who art thou that judgest the servant of another? to his own lord he standeth or falleth. Yea, he shall be made to stand; for the Lord hath power to make him stand.* This weakness in faith consisted in doubts as to the propriety of eating meat, and not in the truth that Jesus is the Christ. Many Jewish Christians held that the law of Moses was still in force. They could not always be sure that the meat bought in the market was not from an animal which the law declared unclean, nor could they be sure that it had not been dedicated to an idol. They therefore ate herbs. Others had faith to eat any kind of meat. The sticklers for the law would brand the others as sinners, and themselves be condemned by the others as foolish. Neither would be willing to give the other full fellowship; each would question the other's scruples or lack of scruples. So long as one's faith in Christ is strong and unwavering, no one should condemn him for what he eats or does not eat; but no one should try to force others to comply with his notions about eating or not eating. No servant has a right to condemn another man's servant; his standing or falling is entirely between him and his lord. And so it is with our Lord and his servants. For one to condemn the Lord's servant does not change the Lord's attitude toward him. The Lord is able to make him stand, so long as his opinions do not interfere with his faith or obedience, or he does not try to force his opinions on others. Of course no one has a right to do anything that would lead another into sin.

Verses 5, 6: *One man esteemeth one day above another: another esteemeth every day alike. Let each man be fully assured in his own mind. He that regardeth the day, regardeth it unto the Lord: and he that eateth, eateth unto the Lord, for he giveth God thanks; and he that eateth not, unto the Lord he eateth not, and giveth God thanks.* The sabbath was not the only day set apart in the law of Moses for the children of Israel to observe. Many Jewish Christians still held that the law was binding and demanded that Gentile Christians also keep the law. The decrees of the apostles and elders in Jerusalem had no effect on some of them, as Paul's letters abundantly show. Such men would not only be contentious about eating meat, but would demand that Gentile Christians observe the days set apart in the law. In Paul's discussion of these matters of opinion, the Lord's appointments were not included. The Lord has set apart the Lord's day for worship; its observance is therefore not a matter of opinion or indifference. "Let each man be fully assured in his own mind" as to whether he will or will not devote any other day to study, meditation, and prayer. Concerning this the Lord has bound no one, and concerning such matters no one should seek to bind his notions on others. It is therefore evident that the leaders of a church could not adopt these Jewish holidays and demand that all the members observe them. The Judaizing teachers had got in their work among the churches of Galatia, which led Paul to say, "Ye observe days, and months, and seasons, and years. I am afraid of you, lest by any means I have bestowed labor upon you in vain" (Gal. 4:10, 11). If the leaders should set any such days to be observed by the church, the members should not submit to such an arrangement. "Let no man judge you in meat, or in drink, or in respect of a feast day or a new moon or a sabbath day" (Col. 2:16).

Verses 7-9: *For none of us liveth to himself, and none dieth to himself. For whether we live, we live unto the Lord; or whether we die, we die unto the Lord: whether we live therefore, or die we are the Lord's. For to this end Christ died and lived again, that he might be Lord of both the dead and the living.* The point in verse 7 is generally missed by assuming that Paul was speaking of our relations one with another. It is true that we cannot cut ourselves off from all relations with our fellow men, but that is not the lesson Paul is teaching. He was speaking of our relations to the Lord. The connection shows this plainly. Verse 8 really explains verse 7. None of us lives to himself, "for whether we live, we live unto the Lord; . . ." No one lives to himself, but to the Lord, for he is the Lord's servant. Paul was speaking of Christians. The Christian cannot cut himself off from any connection with the Lord, and live his own life as he pleases. Even in death the Christian is the Lord's. "Whether we live therefore, or die, we are the Lord's." Christ died and lived again, that this very relationship might be established—"that he might be Lord of both the dead and the living." So far as the Greek is concerned we might as well have "for" in verses 7 and 8 as "to" and "unto." "No one lives for himself, and no one dies for himself. For whether we live, we live for the Lord; or whether we die, we die for the Lord." In life and in death we are his.

Verses 10-13: *But thou, why dost thou judge thy brother? or thou, again, why dost thou set at nought thy brother? for we shall all stand before the judgment-seat of God. For it is written, As I live, saith the Lord, to me every knee shall bow, and every tongue shall confess to God. So then each one of us shall give account of himself to God. Let us not therefore judge one another any more; but judge ye this rather, that no man put a stumblingblock in his brother's way, or an occasion of falling.* To judge, as here used, is to condemn. Those who believed they should observe the days required in the law, and refused to eat meats prohibited by the law, would condemn as sinners those who did not do likewise; and those who ate meat and refused to observe certain days would count as foolish and unworthy of consideration those who did not eat meat and observed days. It was a bad situation. Such sentiments could not long prevail without serious consequences to the church. Hence, Paul's rebuke. God is the judge, and he will make final adjustment of all things when we all stand before his judgment-seat. If we do not voluntarily bow the knee to his authority here, we will have to do so when we stand before him; and then every tongue shall confess to him. Then every one shall give account of himself, and not of another; and then none of us shall judge another. "Let us therefore not judge one another." But it seems to me that this injunction against judging must be confined to such matters as Paul was discussing. How could any one beware of false prophets, unless we first judge them to be false prophets? (Matt. 7:15). And we must judge a man to be an evil worker, or we could not obey the command to "beware of the evil workers" (Phil. 3:2). Neither could we obey Paul's injunction in Rom. 16:17, 18 without judging which men belong to the class he mentions. And how could a church withdraw from the disorderly without first judging a man to be disorderly? And we must be very strict in judging our own actions and their possible results. "Judge ye this rather, that no man put a stumbling-block in his brother's way, or an occasion of falling." If a man's eating meat as food led some brother to think he was eating it in honor of an idol, and was thereby led to eat meat in honor of an idol, his eating the meat became a stumbling-block over which his brother stumbled and fell. A man should never insist on exercising his rights or liberties, if harm comes of his doing so.

Verse 14: *I know, and am persuaded in the Lord Jesus, that nothing is unclean of itself: save that to him who accounteth anything to be unclean, to him it is unclean.* By this emphatic statement Paul declared that the distinction the law made between clean and

unclean animals was no longer in force. The Gentiles
were right and the Jews were wrong in the matter of
eating meats. On this point it took a special revelation to Peter to convince him that such legal distinctions were no longer in force (Acts 10:9-16). And yet,
if a man thought the Lord prohibited the use of certain
animals for food, he should not so use them. A man
should not go against his convictions, and thus wound
his conscience. No thoughtful Christian will try to
cause any one to go against his convictions, however
foolish he may think his convictions are. Teach him
what is right, but do not try to induce him to do what
he thinks is wrong. Do not destroy his conscience.

Verses 15, 16: *For if because of meat thy brother is
grieved, thou walkest no longer in love. Destroy not
with thy meat him for whom Christ died. Let not then
your good be evil spoken of.* Verse 14 is parenthetical.
Verse 15 connects directly with verse 13. Read these
two verses, leaving out verse 14, and you will see the
connection. The connection shows clearly that the
warning against doing anything whereby a brother is
grieved means more than simply a warning against
doing anything to hurt his feelings; for the next sentence says, "Destroy not with thy meat him for whom
Christ died," that is, do not destroy him as a Christian.
You do not destroy a Christian by violating his preju-
dices or notions. "Is grieved"—is brought to grief.
No one should, by eating meat, bring his brother to
grief, that is, destroy him as a brother. He would do
this, if eating meat led a brother to eat it in honor
of an idol, under the impression that you were eating
in honor of an idol. A man's freedom in Christ should
not therefore be so used as to lead a brother into sin,

and thereby destroy one for whom Christ died. Such conduct would make one an enemy of both his brother and Christ. Hence a Christian may do a thing that is good within itself, and yet under certain circumstances evil may result from doing what within itself is good. If that should be the result, then his good would be evil spoken of. His influence as a Christian would be greatly injured.

Verses 17, 18: *For the kingdom of God is not eating and drinking, but righteousness and peace and joy in the Holy Spirit. For he that herein serveth Christ is well-pleasing to God, and approved of men.* The kingdom of God does not consist in distinctions about meats and drinks; but no man should conclude that freedom from the law in which such distinctions were made gives him the right to eat and drink as he pleases regardless of consequences. Righteousness has to do primarily with our treatment of others; it is doing right by others. You do not treat your fellow-Christian right, if in the exercise of your supposed freedom you lead him to do wrong. And peace in this connection refers to peace among members of the church. In a church where all members treat one another right, and are at peace among themselves, there is joy in the Holy Spirit. And the one who promotes such conditions in a church is well-pleasing to God, and is approved by all right thinking people.

Verses 19-21: *So then let us follow after things which make for peace, and things whereby we may edify one another. Overthrow not for meat's sake the work of God. All things indeed are clean; howbeit it is evil for that man who eateth with offense. It is good not to eat flesh, nor to drink wine, nor to do any-*

thing whereby thy brother stumbleth. No Christian should push his opinions and personal rights to the disturbance of the church. Peace is so delightful and helpful that no thoughtful Christian will needlessly cause confusion and strife, but will give "diligence to keep the unity of the Spirit in the bond of peace" (Eph. 4:3). Peace with one another is necessary to edifying one another. To edify is to build up—to build up in knowledge, faith, and right living. Confusion does not edify any one; it builds up nothing but strife and parties in the church. But if the truth of God is at stake, the good soldier of Jesus Christ will fight the good fight. He will contend earnestly for the faith, but not for traditions, opinions, and customs. If a professed Christian indulges in questionable practices, or in his determination to have his way about things of no importance, he may overthrow the faith of one whose faith is not very strong. A Christian is a work of God. The command, "Overthrow not for meat's sake the work of God," will apply to any matter of indifference or of personal rights. In overthrowing the faith of a Christian we destroy the work of God, and that is a serious matter. The statement that "all things are clean" applies to meats. The law declared certain animals unclean; that law was no longer binding. Legally no animal was now unclean, but it is evil to the man who eats with offense. And this has no reference to merely hurting the feelings of another. Here are some of the meanings of *offense* as given by Webster: *"An occasion of sin; a stumbling block. . . . A* breach of conduct; an infraction of law; crime; sin; transgression; misdeed." Thayer gives this definition and explanation of the Greek word: *"A stumbling-*

block, i.e. an obstacle in the way which if one strikes his foot against he necessarily stumbles or falls; trop., that over which the soul stumbles, i.e. by which it is impelled to sin." To eat with offense was to eat certain meat under circumstances that would lead a weaker person to eat against his convictions. A Christian stumbles, or sins, when he violates his convictions; and it is evil for any one to lead a person to go against his convictions, no matter how innocent the act within itself may be. Verse 21 shows clearly that to eat with offense is to eat under circumstances that causes a brother to stumble. There is no danger in this country that eating meat will cause any one to go against his convictions, nor to eat in honor of an idol, and thereby destroy him; but a person by moderate drinking may lead another to become a drunkard. A Christian should think of the possible influence of his actions before he engages in things that seem to him to be innocent. It is good to keep out of anything that might cause another to stumble.

Verse 22: *The faith which thou hast, have thou to thyself before God. Happy is he that judgeth not himself in that which he approveth.* The Christian is not charged to keep his faith in Christ and the gospel to himself; that faith must be spread abroad throughout the world. The Christian who was well taught knew that the legal distinction between clean and unclean animals had been done away; he would therefore likely believe that he could eat any meat he chose to eat. Verse 2: "One man hath faith to eat all things." But the whole chapter shows that such faith must not be exercised under circumstances that might lead others to sin against their convictions. He might eat the meat in his own home in the presence of God. Bloomfield has this: "Keep this persuasion to yourself, and your God; use it when you have no other witness." A man condemns himself in what he approves, if in holding to it and practicing it he causes others to stumble.

Verse 23: *But he that doubteth is condemned if he eat, because he eateth not of faith; and whatsoever is not of faith is sin.* Believing a thing is right does not make it right; but doing a wrong thing, believing it is right, shows honesty of purpose. Saul of Tarsus thought he was doing right in persecuting Christians; he was true to what he believed was right—that commended him to God. He was a sinner, but an honest sinner. The Jew who believed it wrong to eat certain meat, and yet ate the meat rather than to be called odd or foolish, sinned against himself and against God. If a man even has a doubt about the rightfulness of a certain thing, he should not engage in it. He is condemned if he does a doubtful thing. A man cannot go against his idea of right without great injury to his character. "He eateth not of faith," means that he did not fully believe that such eating was right. And that principle holds good concerning any practice about which we have doubts. "Whatsoever is not of faith is sin." This does not refer to faith in Christ or the gospel; but to faith in the righteousness of what we do. If a Christian does a thing without being fully persuaded that it is right, he sins. A man may sin believing he is doing right; but he sins in doing anything, if he doubts that it is right. If he doubts, the act is not of faith.

There is this truth about the whole matter of eating meat and observing days: If the Christian Jews had

had an undivided faith in Christ instead of dividing it between Moses and Christ, between the law and the gospel, they would have known that all things centered in Christ, and that the regulations about meats and days was no part of the gospel.

Chapter 15

15:1 Now we that are strong ought to bear the infirmities of the weak, and
not to please ourselves. 2 Let each one of us please his neighbor for that which
is good, unto edifying. 3 For Christ also pleased not himself; but, as it is written, The reproaches of them that reproached thee fell upon me. 4 For whatsoever things were written aforetime were written for our learning, that through
patience and through comfort of the scriptures we might have hope. 5 Now the
God of patience and of comfort grant you to be of the same mind one with another
according to Christ Jesus: 6 that with one accord ye may with one mouth glorify
the God and Father of our Lord Jesus Christ. 7 Wherefore receive ye one another, even as Christ also received you, to the glory of God. 8 For I say that
Christ hath been made a minister of the circumcision for the truth of God, that he
might confirm the promises *given* unto the fathers, 9 and that the Gentiles might
glorify God for his mercy; as it is written,
    Therefore will I give praise unto thee among the Gentiles,
    And sing unto thy name.
10   And again he saith,
    Rejoice, ye Gentiles, with his people.
11   And again.
    Praise the Lord, all ye Gentiles;
    And let all the peoples praise him.
12   And again, Isaiah saith,
    There shall be the root of Jesse,
    And he that ariseth to rule over the Gentiles;
    On him shall the Gentiles hope.
13 Now the God of hope fill you with all joy and peace in believing, that
ye may abound in hope, in the power of the Holy Spirit.
14 And I myself also am persuaded of you, my brethren, that ye yourselves
are full of goodness, filled with all knowledge, able also to admonish one another.
15 But I write the more boldly unto you in some measure, as putting you again
in remembrance, because of the grace that was given me of God. 16 that I should
be a minister of Christ Jesus unto the Gentiles, ministering the gospel of God,
that the offering up of the Gentiles might be made acceptable, being sanctified by
the Holy Spirit. 17 I have therefore my glorying in Christ Jesus in things pertaining to God. 18 For I will not dare to speak of any things save those which
Christ wrought through me, for the obedience of the Gentiles, by word and deed,
19 in the power of signs and wonders, in the power of the Holy Spirit: so that
from Jerusalem, and round about even unto Illyricum, I have fully preached the
gospel of Christ; 20 yea, making it my aim so to preach the gospel, not where
Christ was *already* named, that I might not build upon another man's foundation:
21 but, as it is written,
    They shall see, to whom no tidings of him came.
    And they who have not heard shall understand.
22 Wherefore also I was hindered these many times from coming to you: 23
but now, having no more any place in these regions, and having these many years
a longing to come unto you, 24 whensoever I go unto Spain (for I hope to see
you in my journey, and to be brought on my way thitherward by you, if first in
some measure I shall have been satisfied with your company)—25 but now, *I say*,
I go unto Jerusalem, ministering unto the saints. 26 For it hath been the good
pleasure of Macedonia and Achaia to make a certain contribution for the poor
among the saints that are at Jerusalem. 27 Yea, it hath been their good pleasure:
and their debtors they are. For if the Gentiles have been made partakers of their

spiritual things, they owe it *to them* also to minister unto them in carnal things. 28 When therefore I have accomplished this, and have sealed to them this fruit, I will go on by you unto Spain. 29 And I know that, when I come unto you, I shall come in the fulness of the blessing of Christ.

30 Now I beseech you, brethren, by our Lord Jesus Christ, and by the love of the Spirit, that ye strive together with me in your prayers to God for me: 31 that I may be delivered from them] that are disobedient in Judæa, and *that* my ministration which *I have* for Jerusalem may be acceptable to the saints; 32 that I may come unto you in joy through the will of God, and together with you find rest. 33 Now the God of peace be with you all. Amen.

Verses 1-3: *Now we that are strong ought to bear the infirmities of the weak, and not to please ourselves. Let each one of us please his neighbor for that which is good, unto edifying. For Christ pleased not himself; but, as it is written, the reproaches of them that reproached thee fell upon me.* Christ himself said, "I do always the things that are pleasing to him" (John 8:29). Concerning his teaching Jesus said, "For I spake not from myself; but the Father that sent me, he hath given me a commandment, what I should say, and what I should speak" (John 12:49). And so, in both word and deed Jesus did his Father's will. Therefore in fighting against Jesus the Jews were in reality fighting against the Father, but all their fury fell on Jesus. The devoted Christian will now suffer persecution, but the sin of it is against God.

Verse 4: *For whatsoever things were written aforetime were written for our learning, that through patience and through comfort of the scriptures we might have hope.* Paul had just quoted a statement from Psalm 69:9. Verse 4 therefore refers to the Old Testament scriptures. The Old Testament scriptures were therefore not written alone for the benefit of those who then lived, but for us also. Patience is steadfastness—the quality of holding on under trying conditions. It does not seem that such a quality can be affirmed of the scriptures. Besides, it seems that the repetition of the preposition "through" in each phrase indicates that the phrase "of the scriptures" modifies only the word comfort. Hence, by steadfastness and by the comfort of the scriptures the Christian can have, or maintain, hope. It is therefore important that the Christian study the Old Testament.

Verses 5-7: *Now the God of patience and of comfort grant you to be of the same mind one with another according to Christ Jesus: that with one accord ye may with one mouth glorify the God and Father of our Lord Jesus Christ. Wherefore receive ye one another, even as also Christ received you, to the glory of God.* Paul shifts the thought from the scriptures to God the author of the scriptures. Because he is the author of the scriptures, whatever is attributed to the scriptures is rightly attributed to him. Through the word of God the gospel which is God's power for salvation, God gives us hope and develops within us steadfastness of character. Paul prays that unity of thought and conduct prevail among them, "according to Christ Jesus." Jesus stirred up no confusion about such matters as Paul discussed in chapter 14; matters of no importance should never be allowed to disturb the fellowship of a church. Though Jewish converts were slow to give up their customs, they wanted Gentile Christians to adopt their customs. This caused friction. Such confusion was a great hindrance to unity and Christian growth. To be of the same mind one toward the other meant that no one was to feel that he had superior rights over another; neither Jew nor Greek should feel any superiority over the other. This oneness is necessary if we would "glorify the God and

Father of our Lord Jesus Christ." As Christ received us, so should we receive, or accept, one another, in spite of the fact that we do not all belong to the same race. The religion of Christ is designed to make peace between Jew and Gentile (Eph. 2:11-22). Let no one destroy God's purpose in this matter.

Verse 8: *For I say that Christ hath been made a minister of the circumcision for the truth of God, that he might confirm the promises given unto the fathers.* The fathers were Abraham, Isaac, and Jacob; the promises are found in Gen. 12:1-3; 22:15-18; 26:3, 4; 28:13, 14. The part of these promises that referred particularly to Christ is this: "In thy seed shall all nations of the earth be blessed." Paul makes this clear in Gal. 3:16: "Now to Abraham were the promises spoken, and to his seed. He saith not, And to seeds, as of many; but as of one, And to thy seed, which is Christ." In view of the scope of these passages, it seems to me that a number of commentators miss the point Paul had in mind when he said that Christ was a minister of circumcision for the truth of God (that is, that the truth of God might be established). Most commentators, it seems, take the meaning to be, that Christ's personal ministry was confined to the Jews, the circumcision; but I cannot see how confining his personal ministry to the Jews would confirm the promise that all nations would be blessed in him. Just how a ministry confined to one nation would confirm a promise to all nations is more than I can see. May not the phrase "a minister of the circumcision" indicate the source rather than object? We know that Jesus did come of the circumcision, and that he had to come of the circumcision in order to fulfill the promise made to the fathers. "For the truth of God" equals "on behalf of the truth of God," or, "in favor of the truth of God."

Verses 9-12: *"And that the Gentiles might glorify God for his mercy: as it is written,*

Therefore will I give praise unto thee among the Gentiles,

And sing unto thy name.

And again he saith,

Rejoice, ye Gentiles, with his people.

And again,

Praise the Lord, all ye Gentiles;

And let all the people praise him.

And again, Isaiah saith,

There shall be the root of Jesse,

And he that ariseth to rule over the Gentiles;

On him shall the Gentiles hope.

Christ became a minister of the seed of Abraham in behalf of the truth of God; and a part of the truth of the promise made to the fathers was, "that the Gentiles might glorify God for his mercy." The promised blessings were to be for all nations, with no difference between Jew and Gentile. Paul's use of the promise made to the fathers would not please the exclusive Jewish Christians; and so he quotes some Old Testament Scriptures to show that it had been God's plan all down the ages to include the Gentiles in the blessings of the promised seed. This would show both Jew and Gentile that neither had any right to feel superior to the other, and such feeling would promote better fellowship between them. The passages in the order quoted are Ps. 18:49 (or 2 Sam. 22:50); Deut. 32:43; Ps. 117:1; Isa. 11:10. The Gentiles as well as the Jews, would praise Jehovah for his mercy, and would also enjoy the blessings of his rule. Paul quotes the passages to show that they were then being fulfilled; and that, as both Jew and Gentile were enjoying the same blessings and both were under the rule of the Messiah, there should be peace between Jewish Christians and Gentile Christians. It is strange that some Jewish Christians never would see the plain teaching of the promises and prophecies, and by their stubborn blindness created much confusion in many churches and gave Paul no end of trouble by their contention that all Gentile Christians had to become subservient to all things Jewish, or they could not be saved. But it is even stranger that some professed Christians today hold to that Judaizing notion, and project the fulfillment of the promises and prophecies to some future time. There is less excuse today for such heretical teaching than there was in the early churches.

Verse 13: *Now the God of hope fill you with all joy and peace in believing, that ye may abound in hope, in the power of the Holy Spirit.* Concerning the Messiah Isaiah had said, "On him shall the Gentiles hope." And so to the Gentiles as well as to the Jews God was the God of hope—he made hope possible even to those who formerly had been without God and without hope (Eph. 2:12). Without this hope there could be no joy and no peace—no peace of mind and no peace with one another. But we are to be filled with joy and peace in believing, in continuous, active believing. And to be filled with joy and peace increases our hope. The power of the Holy Spirit made this hope and peace possible; for the Holy Spirit revealed all we know about God and Christ and the plan of salvation, and confirmed that revelation by signs and wonders. And the things the Holy Spirit revealed to us is the source of all our knowledge, joy, peace, and hope.

Verse 14: *And I myself also am persuaded of you, my brethren, that ye yourselves are full of goodness, filled with all knowledge, able also to admonish one another.* Here Paul takes up some personal matters. One or more brethren had made a report to Paul about conditions at Rome, and expressed confidence in the brethren there; otherwise why should he say, "And I myself also am persuaded of you. . . . " Paul felt assured that they, even with their differences about observing days and eating meats, were good people. It is likely that only a small minority were disturbed about these things. In his words of praise Paul must have had the greater part of the church in mind. "Filled with knowledge" could not have been well applied to those who were so disturbed about the matters discussed in chapter 14. Spiritually gifted men in that church would be able to teach and admonish the weak. Paul's words of commendation would be encouraging to these brethren. Paul never flattered, but he did commend brethren when he had grounds for doing so. A preacher who scolds and criticises all the time never brings out the best that is in men.

Verse 15: *But I write the more boldly unto you in some measure, as putting you again in remembrance, because of the grace that was given me of God.* Paul gave his reason for writing so boldly to them—"because of the grace that was given me of God." Paul speaks of his being made an apostle as grace bestowed upon him. On this point see also Rom. 12:3; 1 Cor. 3:10; 15:9; Gal. 2:9; Eph. 3:7. The phrase, "in some measure," is somewhat vague; but some authorities tell us that the Greek phrase means, *in part, or partly, or somewhat.* Part of his purpose in writing to them was to put them again in remembrance—to stir up their memories concerning things they had been taught, but he did not say this was his sole purpose in writing them. In fact, he had also discussed the great principles of God's dealing with men and nations in the development of his plans.

Verse 16: ... *that I should be a minister of Christ Jesus unto the Gentiles, ministering the gospel of God, that the offering up of the Gentiles might be made acceptable, being sanctified by the Holy Spirit.* Paul was chosen as an apostle to the Gentiles (Acts 9:15; Rom. 11:13; Gal. 1:16; Eph. 3:8; 1 Tim. 2:7). The word here translated minister is not *diakonos*, the usual word for minister, or servant, but *leitourgos*, a word that usually had an official significance, one who performs a public service. Of its use here the Cambridge Greek Testament says, "The classical meaning of a public service performed to the community still colors the word. S. Paul adds here the name of the authority who orders the performance, and the persons to whose benefit it is directed. As compared with diakonòs the public and representative character is emphasized. ... Here the context gives it the specially religious sense." Paul was not only an apostle to the Gentiles, but also an apostle of the Gentiles; he was their apostle. By ministering the gospel to the Gentiles he converted many of them to God. These converts were his offering to God, sanctified by the Holy Spirit. Jesus said, "Sanctify them in the truth: thy word is truth" (John 17:17). There is no conflict, for the words Paul used were the words of the Holy Spirit. Besides, the many signs Paul wrought in connection with his preaching to the Gentiles showed that God approved his work, and that all Gentile converts were as acceptable to God as were Jewish converts, no matter what Judaizing teachers said to the contrary. It was a decisive argument thrown in without seeming to have the Judaizers in mind at all.

Verse 17: *I have therefore my glorying in Christ Jesus in things pertaining to God.* The "therefore" connects this verse with what Paul had just said. His ministering the gospel in making Gentile converts as his offering to God was the work in which he gloried. He thus reminded the Judaizers and all who might be influenced by them that he did not glory in his Jewish blood nor in anything that pertained to Judaism, but only in Christ Jesus in things pertaining to God; "for we are the circumcision, who worship by the Spirit of God, and glory in Christ Jesus, and have no confidence in the flesh." That is, he had no confidence in his Jewish flesh—no confidence in the fact that he was a Jew. Christ Jesus was the center of all Paul's preaching; the purpose of his life was to do all things that were pleasing to him. "For I determined not to know anything among you, save Jesus Christ, and him crucified" (1 Cor. 2:2). "They desire to have you circumcised, that they may glory in your flesh. But be it far from me to glory, save in the cross of our Lord Jesus Christ" (Gal. 6:13, 14).

Verses 18, 19: *For I will not dare to speak of any things save those which Christ wrought through me, for the obedience of the Gentiles, by word and deed, in the power of signs and wonders, in the power of the*

Holy Spirit; so that from Jerusalem, and round about even unto Illyricum, I have fully preached the gospel of Christ. Many of Paul's Gentile converts were effective workers in the Lord's vineyard, and he might have claimed some credit for their successes; but he did not —he would speak only of the things which Christ wrought through him, "for the obedience of the Gentiles." His language does not fit in with the theory that human agency has no part in the conversion of sinners, but it does fit in with what the Lord said to him in giving him his commission, namely, "to open their eyes, that they may turn from darkness to light and from the power of Satan unto God, that they may receive remission of sins and an inheritance among them that are sanctified by faith in me" (Acts 26:18).

An authority works through its agents or ambassadors. There is nothing mysterious about that. Paul was Christ's agent for the purpose of bringing about obedience among the Gentiles; in that way Christ worked through him, "by word and deed"—by his preaching the gospel, and performing miracles to show that God was with him. The Holy Spirit enabled him to preach and to perform signs and wonders—signs to confirm his preaching, and wonders to amaze the people. "From Jerusalem, and round about even unto Illyricum," shows the wide scope of territory Paul covered in his preaching.

Verses 20, 21: *Yea, making it my aim so to preach the gospel, not where Christ was already named, that I might not build upon another man's foundation; but, as it is written, They shall see, to whom no tidings of him came, And they who have not heard shall understand.* Paul did not seek easy places, nor places that paid the most money. He preached where the gospel was most needed, and where there appeared to be an opportunity to reap a harvest. At least, he was sometimes divinely guided to a field. Every place needed the gospel, but not every place was ripe unto harvest. His whole aim was to preach where Christ had not been named. But this may be said: Paul had no family, no wife, to cause him to have a care for the material things of this world (1 Cor. 7:32, 33).

One who is not blinded by a theory can see how often Paul makes the point, that his preaching the gospel to Gentiles was a fulfillment of prophecies. But the Jew, in his feeling of superiority, interpreted these prophecies, as do some present-day theorists, to mean that Gentiles would be blessed only in subserviency to the Jews; but the Holy Spirit through Paul plainly contradicts such a theory. Till the gospel was preached to them, no tidings had come to Gentiles. Paul was sent to open the eyes of the Gentiles, to turn them from darkness to the light, that they might see (Acts 26:14-20). Hence, those who had never heard were made to understand.

Verses 22-24: *Wherefore also I was hindered these many times from coming to you: but now, having no more any place in these regions, and having these many years a longing to come unto you, whensoever I go unto Spain (for I hope to see you in my journey, and to be brought on my way thitherward by you, if first in some measure I shall have been satisfied with your company).* Paul's purposes and plans were not always inspired. Over a period of many years he had a longing to visit the brethren in Rome, but had been hindered from doing so. (See also Chapter 1:9-13). Every time he had planned to visit Rome other work pressed upon him; "but now, having no more any place in these regions," the regions about Corinth, or perhaps all of Greece, he turned his mind again toward Rome. But Paul would not have it appear that he would force himself on them; he would visit them on his way to Spain. And he hoped that they would assist him on his journey into Spain. Paul knew he had enemies, the Judaizers, in many churches; and it seems that he had some doubts as to whether his association with the Roman brethren would be fully satisfactory—certainly not, if there were in that church any of the Judaizers.

Verses 25-28: *But now, I say, I go unto Jerusalem, ministering unto the saints. For it hath been the good pleasure of Macedonia and Achaia to make a certain contribution for the poor among the saints that are at Jerusalem. Yea, it hath been their good pleasure; and their debtors they are. For if the Gentiles have been made partakers of their spiritual things, they owe it to them also to minister unto them in carnal things. When therefore I have accomplished this, and have sealed to them this fruit, I will go on by you unto Spain.* Before visiting them on his intended journey into Spain, he had a mission to fulfill in Jerusalem. For sometime he had been stirring up the churches of the Gentiles to make contributions for the poor saints in Judea. Many facts concerning this collection for the saints may be learned from 1 Cor. 16:1-4; 2 Cor. 8:1-7; 9:1-15. Through the instrumentality of the Jews, yet in spite of some Jews, the Gentiles had received the gospel. These Gentile Christians felt an obligation therefore to do what they could to supply the material needs of the poor saints in Judea. Paul now promises to visit Rome on his way to Spain, after he had completed the business of taking the contributions of the churches to Jerusalem. And he did go to Rome, but how he was to go had not been then revealed to him. If he ever reached Spain, we have no record of it.

Verse 29: *And I know that, when I come unto you, I shall come in the fulness of the blessing of Christ.* Before a church, or an individual, can receive the "fulness of the blessings of Christ," the heart must be open to receive such blessings. It seems that Paul felt sure that the brethren at Rome were ready in heart and mind to receive whatever additional blessings they needed. Perhaps this included additional spiritual gifts.

Verses 30-33: *Now I beseech you, brethren, by our Lord Jesus Christ, and by the love of the Spirit, that ye strive together with me in your prayers to God for me; that I may be delivered from them that are disobedient in Judea, and that my ministration which I have for Jerusalem may be acceptable to the saints; that I may come unto you in joy through the will of God, and together with you find rest. Now the God of peace be with you all. Amen.* Paul knew he had bitter enemies in Jerusalem, who would kill him if they got a chance. Even amongst the saints whose needs he was preparing to supply, there were bitter enemies of Paul. But he believed the prayers of others would be helpful, and so he begs the Roman brethren to strive together with him in praying that no harm befall him. People can sometimes be so antagonistic to others as to refuse all assistance from them. Paul feared the antagonism of the Jews to the Gentiles was so great his contributions from the Gentiles would not be accepted by the saints in Jerusalem. Therefore, he asked the saints at Rome to pray that his ministration would be accepted by the brethren at Jerusalem. This shows that the relations between Jewish churches and Gentile churches were much strained at the time. The theory has been advanced that one reason Paul was so anxious to collect much help for the poor saints in Judea was, to bring the Jewish churches to a better feeling toward Gentile churches. If the brethren of Judea would accept his gift, he could then go to Rome in joy through the will of God; that is, if it was God's will for him to go to Rome. And if the Judean saints did accept his collected contributions, one cause of great worry would be removed from his mind, and he could find rest at Rome. "Now the God of peace be with you all. Amen."

Chapter 16

16:1 I commend unto you Phœbe our sister, who is a servant of the church
that is at Cenchreæ: 2 that ye receive her in the Lord, worthily of the saints,
and that ye assist her in whatsoever matter she may have need of you: for she
herself also hath been a helper of many, and of mine own self.

3 Salute Prisca and Aquila my fellow-workers in Christ Jesus, 4 who for my
life laid down their own necks; unto whom not only I give thanks, but also all
the churches of the Gentiles: 5 and *salute* the church that is in their house. Salute
Epænetus my beloved, who is the firstfruits of Asia unto Christ. 6 Salute Mary, who
bestowed much labor on you. 7 Salute Andronicus and Junias, my kinsmen, and my
fellow-prisoners, who are of note among the apostles, who also have been in Christ
before me. 8 Salute Ampliatus my beloved in the Lord. 9 Salute Urbanus our
fellow-worker in Christ, and Stachys my beloved. 10 Salute Apelles the approved in
Christ. Salute them that are of the *household* of Aristobulus. 11 Salute Herodion
my kinsman. Salute them of the *household* of Narcissus, that are in the Lord. 12
Salute Tryphæna and Tryphosa, who labor in the Lord. Salute Persis the beloved,
who labored much in the Lord. 13 Salute Rufus the chosen in the Lord, and his
mother and mine. 14 Salute Asyncritus, Phlegon, Hermes, Patrobas, Hermas, and
the brethren that are with them. 15 Salute Philologus and Julia, Nereus and his
sister, and Olympas, and all the saints that are with them. 16 Salute one another
with a holy kiss. All the churches of Christ salute you.

17 Now I beseech you, brethren, mark them that are causing the divisions and
occasions of stumbling, contrary to the doctrine which ye learned: and turn away
from them. 18 For they that are such serve not our Lord Christ, but their own
belly; and by their smooth and fair speech they beguile the hearts of the innocent.
19 For your obedience is come abroad unto all men. I rejoice therefore over you:
but I would have you wise unto that which is good, and simple unto that which is
evil. 20 And the God of peace shall bruise Satan under your feet shortly.
The grace of our Lord Jesus Christ be with you.

21 Timothy my fellow-worker saluteth you; and Lucius and Jason and Sosipater, my kinsmen. 22 I Tertius, who write the epistle, salute you in the Lord.
23 Gaius my host, and of the whole church, saluteth you. Erastus the treasurer
of the city saluteth you, and Quartus the brother.

25 Now to him that is able to establish you according to my gospel and the
preaching of Jesus Christ, according to the revelation of the mystery which hath
been kept in silence through times eternal, 26 but now is manifested, and by the
scriptures of the prophets, according to the commandment of the eternal God, is
made known unto all the nations unto obedience of faith: 27 to the only wise
God, through Jesus Christ, to whom be the glory for ever. Amen.

Verses 1, 2: *I commend unto you Phoebe our sister,
who is a servant of the church that is at Cenchrea:
that ye receive her in the Lord, worthily of the saints,
and that ye assist her in whatsoever matter she may
have need of you: for she herself also hath been a helper of many, and of mine own self.* Cenchrea was the
home of Phoebe. It was the eastern seaport of Corinth,

a few miles across the Isthmus from Corinth. There
has been much said for and against the possibility that
Phoebe was an official deaconess of her home church.
But the use of the word *diakonos*, here translated servant, does not prove that she occupied an official position. In these letters to the churches the word is used
a number of times, but not in any official sense, unless
in this one place. We let our minds run to officialism
too much. On account of the social condition of women
of that age, aged women of experience, piety and ability
were needed to teach, encourage, and otherwise help
young women. On this point see 1 Tim. 5:3-16; Tit.
2:3-6. To select a person for a certain work does not
necessarily make him an officer in the common accepta-
tion of that term. To select a man to hold a series of
meetings does not make him an officer, and no one
thinks so. Selecting a song-leader does not make him
an officer. Selecting certain women to attend to certain duties does not make them deaconesses in any
official sense. *Diakonos* therefore had no official significance. It is thought by some that she was the bear-
er of Paul's letter to Rome, but that is not certain. She
evidently went to Rome on certain business, for Paul
urges the brethren to "assist her in whatever matter
she may have need." To receive her in the Lord was
to treat her as a worthy Christian should be treated;
"for she herself also hath been a helper of many, and
of mine own self." Those who help others always
commend themselves to the Lord.

Verses 3, 4: *Salute Prisca and Aquila my fellow-
workers in Christ Jesus, who for my life laid down
their own necks; unto whom not only I give thanks,
but also all the churches of the Gentiles.* Prisca is short

for Priscilla. This good woman and her husband first
joined in work with Paul at Corinth (Acts 18:1-3).
They next appear in active service to the Lord at
Ephesus (Acts 18:24-26). Just when they endangered
their own lives—"laid down their own necks"—for
the life of Paul we are not informed. Probably it was
during that uproar at Ephesus (Acts 19:33-41). Paul
and all the churches of the Gentiles gave thanks to them
for what they had done for him. The many that Paul
mentions by name were people he had worked with,
who had gone to Rome from points where Paul had
preached. One wonders how he had kept track of them
in that day of inconvenient communications.

Verses 5-16: *And salute the church that is in their
house. Salute Epaenetus my beloved, who is the first-
fruits of Asia unto Christ. Salute Mary, who bestowed
much labor on you. Salute Andronicus and Junias,
my kinsmen, and my fellow-prisoners, who are of note
among the apostles, who have also been in Christ before me. Salute Ampliatus my beloved in the Lord.
Salute Urbanus our fellow-worker in Christ and
Stachys my beloved. Salute Apelles the approved in
Christ. Salute them that are of the household of Aristobulus. Salute Herodion my kinsman. Salute them
of the household of Narcissus, that are in the Lord.
Salute Tryphaena and Tryphosa, who labor in the Lord.
Salute Persis the beloved, who labored much in the
Lord. Salute Rufus the chosen in the Lord, and his
mother and mine. Salute Asyncritus, Phlegon,
Hermes, Patrobas, Hermas, and the brethren that are
with them. Salute Philologus and Julia, Nereus and
his sister, and Olympas, and all the saints that are
with them. Salute one another with a holy kiss. All*

the churches of Christ salute you. "Salute the church
that is in their house." This evidently refers to a
group of Christians who met for worship in the house
of Priscilla and Aquila. In those days a large place
was not always available in which a large group of
Christians could meet. Several groups met in the
homes of various members. It will be noticed that
each group was called a church.

In these salutations the outstanding traits of some
of them are mentioned. Epaenetus, the first fruits of
Asia had endeared himself to Paul. Mary had been a
good worker in the church at Rome. Andronicus and
Junias, Paul's kinsmen, who had been converted to
Christ before Paul was, had rendered such devoted
service to the Lord as to become noted among the apostles. Ampliatus had made himself very dear to Paul.
At some place Urbanus had been a fellow-worker with
Paul, and may have been with him in some of his jour-
neys. And Apelles was an approved servant of
Christ. Tryphaena and Tryphosa were laborers in the
Lord; and Persis the beloved labored much in the Lord.
"Salute Rufus the chosen of the Lord, and his mother
and mine." The mother of Rufus had been a mother
to Paul at some place where he preached. The common method of salutation there was the kiss. Paul
demanded that the kiss be holy. From Paul's list we
learn that the church at Rome had in it many faithful
workers; likely there were many such whom Paul did
not know.

Verses 17, 18: *Now I beseech you, brethren, mark
them that are causing the divisions and occasions of
stumbling, contrary to the doctrine which ye learned:
and turn away from them. For they that are such*

*serve not our Lord Christ, but their own belly; and by
their smooth and fair speech they beguile the hearts
of the innocent.* Not all was smooth sailing in that
church. Some there were stirring up trouble—causing
divisions and occasions of stumbling—contrary to the
gospel. Judaizing teachers were the main trouble
makers in the territory of Paul's labors; they were determined to convince all Gentile Christians that they
had to be circumcised and keep the law, or they could
not be saved. They were professed Christians. Likely they had gained some Gentile Christians as helpers.
If these disturbers had not reached Rome, Paul knew
they *would* be there. Even today advocates of a modified form of this same theory of Jewish supremacy are
troubling churches all over the country. Said Paul,
"mark them"—eye them closely. Do not shut your eyes
to what they are doing, nor make excuses for them,
nor for any others who cause divisions and occasions
of stumbling contrary to the gospel, but turn away
from them. This means that the brethren should have
no fellowship with them. "Contrary to the doctrine
which ye learned" covers a wide field, such as mechan-
ical music in the worship, the organization of socie-
ties to do the work of the church, and various schemes
to raise money. The man who causes divisions in the
Lord's church by the introduction of things not taught
is an enemy of Christ, even though he may not think
so. His interest is in self, and not in Christ. "They
that are such serve not our Lord, but their own belly."
The more a man appears to be interested in people the
more he can deceive—"by their smooth and fair speech
they beguile the hearts of the simple"—the trusting
and unsuspecting are more easily deceived. The word

translated simple does not mean weakminded, but rather, unsuspicious. The deceiver knows how to get the unsuspicious to follow him. People seem never to learn that smooth and fair speech is "the stock in trade" of a deceiver. If he were to announce that he was a wolf in sheep's clothing and that he had come to destroy and not to feed, he would not deceive even the simple. "For even Satan fashioneth himself into an angel of light. It is no great thing therefore if his ministers also fashion themselves as ministers of righteousness" (2 Cor. 11:14, 15). Paul warned the Colossians against being deluded by "persuasiveness of speech" (Col. 2:4). "And in covetousness shall they with feigned words make merchandise of you" (2 Pet. 2:3). From all such we should turn away.

Verses 19, 20: *For your obedience is come abroad unto all men. I rejoice therefore over you: but I would have you wise unto that which is good, and simple unto that which is evil. And the God of peace shall bruise Satan under your feet shortly. The grace of our Lord Jesus Christ be with you.* The church at Rome was old enough and active enough for the report of its obedience to become widely circulated. This was a source of joy to Paul. He would have them to sustain that reputation by continued obedience. If they allowed false teachers to cause divisions and scandals, they would have a bad influence over churches that had cause to regard them so highly. He would have them to be wise to that which was good, so as to be able to distinguish between the good and the evil. People do not have to indulge in evil things in order to know what is evil—be "simple unto that which is evil." People who are wise unto the good know evil. Only the

person who knows what is good has a clear idea of what
is evil. The writer of Hebrews speaks of "those who
by reason of use have their senses exercised to discern
good and evil" (Heb. 5:14). Living in sin and ignorance so blinds a person that he can not see what is
good or evil. "Woe unto them that call evil good and
good evil; that put darkness for light, and light for
darkness; that put bitter for sweet, and sweet for bitter. Woe unto them that are wise in their own sight"
(Isa. 5:20, 21). Paul gives them the comforting assurance that, if they would turn away from evil and
be wise unto that which was good, they would soon
triumph over that which was evil—bruise Satan under
their feet. "Shortly"—that could not refer to things
yet future; they were to accomplish this while they
lived.

Verse 21: *Timothy my fellow-worker saluteth you;
and Lucius and Jason and Sosipater, my kinsmen.*
Timothy was with Paul at Corinth when this letter was
written, and joined in saluting the Roman brethren. He
was Paul's beloved son in the gospel and a fellow-worker with him in many hard places. It is possible, though
not certain, that Lucius was the Lucius of Acts 13:1.
And Jason may have been the Jason mentioned in Acts
17:7-9. And it is thought, that Sosipater was the
Sopater of Acts 20:4. Paul refers to others in these
salutations as his kinsmen. Some think he referred
to them as kinsmen just as he referred to all Jews as
kinsmen in Rom. 9:1-3; but there are Jews in these
salutations to whom he did not refer as his kinsmen.

Verses 22, 23: *I Tertius, who write the epistle salute
you in the Lord. Gaius my host, and of the whole
church, saluteth you. Erastus the treasurer of the city*

saluteth you, and Quartus the brother. It was not Paul's custom to write his epistles with his own hand; he had a secretary to write as he dictated. Tertius wrote this letter at Paul's dictation. He joins in saluting the saints in Rome. It is possible, as some think, that verse 23 are the words of Tertius. It is hardly possible that the whole church at Corinth met in the home of Gaius; rather, it seems that his doors were open to any saint that needed shelter. It is hardly possible that a large church could all use the house of Gaius as a place to meet for worship. This Gaius must have been the Gaius whom Paul baptized in the early days of his preaching at Corinth (1 Cor. 1:14). He was therefore a citizen of Corinth, and owned a home there. The Gaius mentioned in Acts 20:4 was a citizen of Derbe. And a Gaius of Macedonia, one of Paul's companions in travel, is mentioned in Acts 19:29. I cannot make all these passages refer to the same man. And the name Erastus occurs three times—Acts 19:22; Rom. 16:23; 2 Tim. 4:20. The Erastus mentioned in Acts and Second Timothy was one of Paul's fellow-travelers. It has been assumed, but not by all, that the three passages refer to the same man, and that therefore, while traveling so extensively, he could not have been the treasurer of the city government, but must therefore have been the treasurer of the church in Corinth. But would not his extensive traveling interfere as effectively with his being treasurer of the one as of the other? Paul's statement to Timothy that "Erastus remained at Corinth," was made several years after Paul wrote to the Romans. It is very likely that there were at least two men named Erastus. It does not seem that a man would be designated as the treasurer of a city, if he

were only the treasurer of the church in that city. Any
way we look at the matter there are some difficulties,
but it is usually safest to take a statement of fact at its
face value. Quartus is named only in this place.

Verses 25-27: *Now to him who is able to establish
you according to my gospel and the preaching of Jesus
Christ, according to the revelation of the mystery
which hath been kept in silence through times eternal,
but now is manifested, and by the scriptures of the
prophets, according to the commandment of the eternal
God, is made known unto all the nations unto obedience
of faith: to the only wise God, through Jesus Christ, to
whom be glory for ever. Amen.* These verses were
written with Paul's own hands. It was his custom to
write with his own hands the closing part of each letter as a means of showing the letter to be his. "The
salutation of me Paul with mine own hand" (Col.
4:18). "The salutation of me Paul with mine own
hand, which is the token in every epistle" (2 Thes.
3:17).

"My gospel" was the gospel which Paul preached,
and not the perverted gospel of the Judaizers; and "the
preaching of Jesus Christ" was the preaching Jesus
Christ commanded, and which had him as its center.
And that was the gospel of salvation for all men without distinction as to races. Paul would have all Christians established in the gospel he preached, and not in
the perverted gospel of the Judaizers. Paul had quoted
many prophecies to prove that Gentiles were to share
in the promise made to the fathers; but how either
Jews or Gentiles were to enjoy the blessings of the
Messiah had not been revealed by the prophets.

A mystery is a thing not understood. Neither Jew

nor Gentile had grasped the idea that Gentiles were to be fellow-citizens in the kingdom of the Messiah. It seems that this truth had been more fully revealed by Paul than by any other apostle or prophet (Eph. 3:1-8). Where this truth was clearly revealed, it could then be seen how this truth had been manifested in the scriptures of the prophets. It could also then be seen that it was all according to the commandment of God when the great commission was given. "Go ye therefore, and make disciples of all the nations, baptizing them into the name of the Father and of the Son and of the Holy Spirit" (Matt. 28:18; Mk. 16:15, 16). The prophets had foretold, and Jesus had commanded, "that repentance and remission of sins should be preached in his name unto all the nations (Luke 24:46, 47). But for quite a while the apostles did not grasp the significance of the command to preach to all nations. But these commands were made known to all nations that they might become obedient to the faith —obedient to the gospel. Notice how Paul begins and ends his commendation. "Now to him that is able to establish you according to my gospel—to the only wise God, through Jesus Christ, to whom be glory forever and ever. Amen."

Printed in the United States
70044LV00001B/7-24